D0775562

"Bell advocates for just war as an extraordinarily difficult set of practices grounded in particular Christian theological and ecclesiological presuppositions. In this sense, the book is a prophetic critique of some secular versions of the just war tradition. Even more so, it is a [...] and church leaders for our failure to form co[...] with the real challenges of just war. I commend t[...] clergy, and laity."

DATE DUE

—Tim W. Whitake[...]

"There are many books on the just war traditi[...] means of helping Christians judge the justice of [...] or worse, as a crutch for those who make decisi[...] book is different and better. He depicts the just war tradition as a demanding discipline of the church, and in doing so he shows that this tradition can be a mode of enemy-love—a more demanding mode than pacifism in some ways. I know of no other book like this; it is essential reading for Christians in our bloody and violence-ridden times."

—**Paul J. Griffiths**, Duke Divinity School

"Bell's thorough and convincing work is not for the faint of heart or the weak of spirit. With definitive research and critical interpretation, Bell leads readers through the history of Christian thought on war to the truth that Christians must leave behind 'self-absorption, apathy, fear, and indifference' to embrace the call and demand to live justly all aspects of life as followers of Christ. Bell asks, 'How much are we willing to risk to follow Christ in loving our enemies?' We cannot answer glibly, for our very lives will be the answer."

—**Brenda Lynn Kneece**, executive minister,
South Carolina Christian Action Council

"By engaging *Just War as Christian Discipleship*, readers can fully arm themselves for the discussion and debate that rages around just war theory. With laser-sharp precision, this tightly argued, historically aware, and carefully documented work offers a penetrating analysis of the ethical reasons for Christians to engage (or not engage) in violent conflict. A chief merit of this book is its critical comparison of nonreligious uses of just war theory with distinctively Christian approaches to armed combat based on a cruciform commitment

to theological concerns. Whether one agrees or disagrees with Bell, all who discuss just war theory should be informed by his trenchant study."

—Donald Musser, Stetson University

"In the midst of wars and rumors of wars, Bell provides a provocative and insightful look at the just war tradition, removing it from the arena of simple public policy and allowing Christians to wrestle with how to follow Jesus faithfully into the fray. Pastors, congregations, adult forums, and reading groups will certainly benefit from this book."

—Brian O. Bennett, pastor, St. Paul Lutheran Church,
Morgantown, West Virginia

Just War as Christian Discipleship

*Recentering the Tradition in the Church
rather than the State*

Daniel M. Bell Jr.

Foreword by
Chaplain Lt. Col. Scott A. Sterling

BrazosPress
a division of Baker Publishing Group
www.BrazosPress.com

© 2009 Daniel M. Bell Jr.

Published by Brazos Press
a division of Baker Publishing Group
P.O. Box 6287, Grand Rapids, MI 49516-6287
www.brazospress.com

Printed in the United States of America

Library of Congress Cataloging-in-Publication Data
Bell, Daniel M., 1966–
    Just war as Christian discipleship : recentering the tradition in the church rather than the state / Daniel M. Bell, Jr. ; foreword by Chaplain Lt. Col. Scott A. Sterling.
        p.   cm.
    Includes bibliographical references and index.
    ISBN 978-1-58743-225-5 (pbk.)
    1. Just war doctrine. 2. War—Religious aspects—Christianity. I. Title.
BT736.2B437 2009
241′.6242—dc22   2009021689

Scripture quotations are from the New Revised Standard Version of the Bible, copyright © 1989, by the Division of Christian Education of the National Council of the Churches of Christ in the United States of America. Used by permission. All rights reserved.

09   10   11   12   13   14   15   7   6   5   4   3   2   1

Contents

Foreword

We had just completed the evening "Battle Update Briefing," where we were once again assaulted by the numbers of casualties reported by the intelligence officer. "Mission Accomplished" had been declared by the president on an aircraft carrier in the gulf, but the insurgency was just getting started on the ground in Iraq. On a bench outside the tent that served as the command center of the battalion, I chatted with a career noncommissioned officer, a bright, no-nonsense female soldier. She was in the midst of some serious soul searching and brought me into her own internal conversation.

"Chaplain, is it right that we're here? Are we doing any good? And even if we are, should we have invaded this country in the first place?" Although my answers didn't completely satisfy her at that point, we enjoyed a spirited conversation, and I was impressed by her hunger to make moral sense out of our combat experience. In fact, during that eight-month deployment, and a subsequent deployment of fifteen months, I was continually impressed by soldiers who wanted to talk about and resolve the moral and ethical dimensions of the war we were fighting in Iraq. These soldiers were young and old, male and female, of all ranks and positions, and of various religious traditions— or none at all.

My fellow chaplains and I eagerly took up the challenge to address the ethical issues. And although we didn't all share the same conclusions, we all had a commitment to assist our soldiers in coming to terms with the moral implications of their unique and terrible jobs. As in every war, the soldiers' task was simple and horrifying: find and kill enemy warriors, which often resulted in the destruction of homes and infrastructure and taking the lives of innocents along with enemy soldiers. We considered the discussion of the moral dimensions of war to be a crucial aspect of our ministry to soldiers, right alongside honoring the dead with memorial ceremonies and caring for the wounded in hospitals. Part of that discussion usually included addressing the basic criteria of the just war tradition.

Dan Bell has written a book that I wish I'd had during my deployments. *Just War as Christian Discipleship* addresses the just war tradition in a way that not only adds to our knowledge of the historical roots of the tradition but also contributes to the Christian soldier's desire to embody the principles as lifestyle. Many books have been written on the criteria and history of the just war tradition, but none that I am aware of have developed the argument that Bell presents in this book. He asserts and unpacks the theme that the just war tradition, properly understood in its historical context, is not merely a checklist of criteria to be consulted before going to war (or while waging war) but rather must be seen as a body of spiritual principles that make up a virtuous lifestyle—for soldiers and for the church. This lifestyle can be, indeed *must* be, habituated by Christian soldiers and those who make decisions about war. In the heat of battle it is much too late to begin to think through what it means to be a just warrior. Instead, the virtuous life of the Christian just warrior is shown through courageous decisions based on a life of ongoing moral reflection.

There were moments while reading Bell's book that I felt like he had been with me "downrange," listening to the moral challenges my soldiers expressed and hearing their gut-wrenching and heartfelt questions. "Jesus tells us to love our enemies; how do we do that while trying to kill them?" "How do we maintain our moral standards and fight 'justly' when our enemies seem to have no moral scruples at all? Should we?" "How do we protect innocent noncombatants in villages when we have to find and kill the terrorists living there?" And so on. I was amazed as I read this book that Bell, who has not served in the military, was able to anticipate and respond to these types of questions as if he were a seasoned soldier.

There are some challenging responses in the book, to be sure. For example, the concept of war as an act of love, not as a "lesser of evils," may take some time to digest. But Bell doesn't pull this idea—or others like it—out of thin air; rather, he grounds his arguments in the writings of the church fathers and scholars and has done an amazing job of footnoting the references from these ancient sources. Christians from across the ethical spectrum—from pacifists to just warriors to realists to crusaders—are forced to reconsider their perspective based on Bell's impeccable research.

Because none of us are (or should be) isolated from the rest of the Christian community—even soldiers—Bell focuses in each chapter on what he calls "The

Challenge to the Church." He recognizes that it is not solely the responsibility of the individual soldier to learn, internalize, and live out the virtues that make up the character of the just warrior. He challenges the church to teach and embody these virtues in all areas of life. The principles of the just war tradition need not be relegated merely to that small segment of the population that actually fights a nation's wars. The church must understand principles such as *just cause*, *right intent*, *proper authority*, and *proportionality* as they relate to *all* of our relationships, not just international relationships that may deteriorate into combat. Soldiers understand this. That's why chapel services and Bible studies are consistently filled, even after a hard day of patrolling. That's why, even in the absence of a chaplain, soldiers will often find their own ways to gather and express their faith through homemade rituals and earthy prayers. And that's why chaplains in combat have soldiers coming to them throughout the day and night seeking the sanctity and security of that holy space, in order to express their moral anguish, confess their sins, and seek God's grace and mercy.

Even though I write this in my own voice and not as an official representative of any government agency or institution, I am confident that I speak for my brothers and sisters in the military when I assert our desire to sincerely wrestle with the ethical implications of war. As I write this, our new administration is facing a continued war in Iraq, an increased military presence in Afghanistan, an inflamed Israeli/Palestinian conflict, and humanitarian crises throughout the world. In most—if not all—of these, our military will be involved in some way, and our service men and women will continue to be forced to consider the moral and ethical implications of their presence and activities. If the Christian community will take seriously Bell's call for a discipleship that embraces the just war tradition, we can all feel more confident that our nation will strive to maintain the moral high ground in its military endeavors and beyond.

Scott A. Sterling
Chaplain, Lieutenant Colonel, United States Army

Acknowledgments

This book has benefited from the labor of many people, for which I am grateful. Over much of the last decade my thinking about just war and the Christian life has been enriched by countless conversations in a variety of settings, from adult Sunday school classes and public lectures at colleges and universities to meetings with ministerial groups and community activists to semesters spent discussing the tradition with seminarians.

Several persons merit particular recognition, although they do not necessarily agree with the directions I have taken. Surprising as it may be to some who know him for his outspoken commitment to nonviolence, Stanley Hauerwas has been particularly influential in the initiation of this project. Many years ago, when I first began to think seriously about just war, I found it difficult to swallow the commonplace suggestion that it be understood as a kind of lesser evil. Since when, I thought, were Christians called to do evil, even a lesser evil? Moreover, I was struck by how popular treatments and uses of just war bore no intrinsic relation to Christian convictions and practices. This is to say, Christian faith appeared largely irrelevant to the understanding and practice of just war. It was Hauerwas's insistence that just war be taken seriously and not simply dismissed that set me on this long road, looking for a more faithful account of just war, an account that rendered just war worthy of the church's embrace.

That road led me to the work of John Howard Yoder and Grady Scott Davis. These thinkers provided a glimpse of what I was looking for when they brought to my attention the changes effected in just war by the shift from the medieval Christian to the modern secular world. As will be made clear, this shift is crucial to the argument of this book.

Once the research and writing got underway, I was fortunate to have persons like Tobias Winright with whom to converse. Tobias, besides being a good friend for two decades, has been an unfailing source of wisdom and bibliographical advice. Chaplains Scott Sterling, John Connolly, Stephen Alsleben, and Larry Dabeck have been both an inspiration in their moral seriousness and a constant source of insight that is unique to soldiers who wrestle with following the call of discipleship in the midst of battle.

Over the years, a number of persons have been gracious enough to read and comment on my work and stay in the conversation even when I did not listen to them. These gracious souls include: Brian Bennett, John Berkman, Jason Byassee, Brent Laytham, Steve Long, Joel Shuman, Rob Waizenhofer, and Steven Zittergruen. Rodney Clapp was a source of both encouragement and insight from the beginning of this project; it is a better work because of his efforts and insights. There were several others who responded with charity to a stranger's inquiry regarding some aspect of moral theology and the just war tradition. Their kind assistance was much appreciated.

I would be remiss if I did not mention as well the generosity, good humor, and patience with which Jo Ellen White, Debbie Lineberger, and Leslie Walker assisted me in procuring various resources. Karen Schmidt deserves a word of thanks for compiling the index.

Finally, although it was unbidden and may go unnoticed, this work is dedicated to the bishops of The United Methodist Church. The church is a theologian's audience; our work is always dedicated to its mission. Hence I offer this modest effort in the hope that it might in some small way contribute to a conversation about the character of the church and its mission in times of war and peace.

Daniel M. Bell Jr.
Advent 2008

Introduction

Living Faithfully in a Time of War

In the Gospels Jesus encourages his disciples that when they hear of wars and rumors of wars they should not be alarmed (Matt. 24:6). Since the horrific terrorist attacks of September 11, 2001, the alarm has been sounded and we have been immersed in wars and rumors of wars. With these developments has arisen a flood of conversation and debate about the moral legitimacy and wisdom of various wars and possible wars. Much of the discussion has invoked the language of just war. On the editorial pages of local and national papers and publications, over the airways, in church statements, during meals, around the water cooler, in Sunday school classes and from pulpits we hear "just war" invoked either in support of or to discredit various wars and rumors of war. Was the invasion of Afghanistan just? The Iraq war? What about the global war against terror? Is a preventative war just? Would a war against North Korea or Iran be just? Should troops be sent into Sudan to stop the genocide in Darfur?

Why This Book?

Since that fateful September morning, I have been involved in a host of conversations regarding war, and specifically just war, in a variety of settings with a diverse range of persons—with Christians and non-Christians, laity and pastors, soldiers, chaplains, veterans and civilians, undergraduates, seminarians, and so forth. In the course of these conversations two realities have struck me with particular clarity.

First, by and large people do not know the just war tradition. For all the talk about just war—whether by supporters or critics of a particular war—the degree of actual engagement with the just war tradition is typically rather superficial. Just war spelled out in the space of a few column inches in a newspaper editorial or a paragraph or two in a church social statement is not succeeding in informing us, much less forming us, as a just war people. The unfortunate reality is that the *quantity* of just war talk frequently surpasses the *quality* of the discussion. While some of us might be able to identify bits and pieces of the tradition and what constitutes a just as opposed to an unjust war, we cannot fit the few pieces we manage to recall into a coherent whole. For example, try this test. Do you consider yourself an advocate of just war? Or perhaps you consider yourself a critic of modern wars on just war grounds? If you answered yes to either of these questions, then take a moment to write down the principles and criteria that constitute the just war tradition. What makes a war just? What makes a war unjust? If you are like the vast majority of people with whom I have been in conversation, you probably did not get very far in your list. It is rare to find people—be they pastors, politicians, laity, soldiers, or veterans—who can name more than a few of the criteria and rarer still to find persons who can articulate how the criteria hold together as a coherent vision of justice, war, and political life.

If the first thing that struck me was our unfamiliarity with the just war tradition, the second was that, by and large, folks want to know the just war tradition. There is a genuine interest in learning the tradition. People want to do the right thing in the midst of war. Perhaps because they recognize that so much is at stake in war, they want moral guidance, and at some level they realize that in spite of all the talk and maybe because of all the political posturing they are not getting it. Perhaps we realize that much of the talk about justice and war by pundits and politicians, ideologues and party spokespersons, rarely rises above the level of hollow entertainment, another volley in the "culture wars," or another cynical "spin" cycle that chases after the ubiquitous opinion polls. We sense that warfare and all that accompanies it is far too serious a moral matter, that too much is at stake in warfare, to be satisfied with anything less than substantive guidance and reflection on the morality of warfare.

Hence this book. It is written not primarily for specialists and scholars of just war, from whom I have learned, and continue to learn, much. Rather, it is written for nonspecialists, for ordinary folks as an introduction to the just war tradition. More specifically, it is written for Christians—laity, educators, pastors, seminarians, soldiers, and so on—who want help in thinking about justice in warfare as Christians, who want to know how just war relates to the Christian life and Christian discipleship. It is written for Christians who want to live faithfully in a time of war and rumors of war.

Of course, this particular focus is not meant to discourage persons who do not profess the Christian faith from engaging with this book. Not only might they learn something about both Christianity and the just war tradition, but they might also be better prepared to hold Christians accountable to their convictions regarding justice and war. And Christians should welcome this help.

Furthermore, in writing this primer I do not aspire to provide answers to all the questions of faith and justice with regard to war in general or even with regard to particular wars. This is the case for several reasons. First, in the course of speaking and teaching, I have found that offering even tentative judgments on contemporary or not-so-contemporary wars is more often than not a distraction rather than an aid to the central task of learning the tradition well. In today's contentious, ideologically charged, and highly polarized political environment, such judgments almost always lead to arguments, even before we have a firm grasp of the tools of the tradition to know what we should be arguing about. These arguments detract from the main focus of this book, which is learning the tradition well. Second and, as we shall see, more importantly, just war as Christian discipleship is not a matter of isolated individuals, even scholars and experts, offering their judgments and opinions. Rather, it is the practice of a community; it is a matter not of an individual's but of the community's reflection and discernment. The point of this book, then, is not to advance my judgments about any particular war but to contribute to and aid the church's ongoing reflection about the practice of justice in war.

This is not to deny the importance of making judgments, only to suggest that before we can make or hear judgments on faith and war, we need some clarity on the criteria that properly shape and form our judgments. In other words, by forgoing particular judgments about particular wars, I am trying to start a conversation and assist reflection, not bring it to an end.

This work is about interpreting the just war tradition in terms of concrete practices that might contribute to the church's ability to make faithful moral judgments regarding justice in war and then live out those judgments. Therefore, the practical impulse of this work revolves around challenging the church with questions like: What kind of people would we have to be to embody this tradition faithfully? How would our churches have to be organized that we might be formed into the kind of people who support only just wars? How does our worship, preaching and pastoring, teaching, youth leadership, outreach, daily and weekly interaction, and so on, contribute to making us the kind of people who can abide by the just war discipline? What virtues—what habits and practices—are necessary if we are to be a people who support and wage wars in a manner disciplined by the just war tradition?

To this practical end, each chapter concludes with extended reflection on the kinds of challenges that a particular dimension of the just war tradition puts to the church and on the practices and disciplines that might aid Christians in meeting those challenges. Again, because my hope is not to end a conversation but to start one, these practical reflections are meant to be suggestive and evocative rather than comprehensive and definitive. It remains for the church to develop and strengthen this modest proposal.

The Importance of Disciplined Reflection

If this book is a response to the desire expressed by many to learn and live up to the claim to be a just war people, it is also an effort to avoid what happens when we do not know and live the tradition well. Consider the alternative to learning and living the tradition. Consider the consequences of ignorance regarding just war. I was once discussing the moral life with Christian young people, and a consensus emerged that the Ten Commandments were a good summary of the moral life. Only afterward did I discover that the group could name only two of those commandments. Similarly, if we claim to be a just war people and yet do not know what a just war is, there is something wrong. At best we are exposed as hypocrites; at worst, we are susceptible to being manipulated and misled into endorsing forms of war and fighting that we ought not, perhaps simply because just war language is invoked by those doing the manipulating. Indeed, one would have to search long and hard to find a war whose supporters did not claim their cause was just. Few set off to war while declaring that they are unjust in doing so. If, as the early church theologian and bishop Augustine said, everyone desires peace, so everyone who wages war insists that they are just in doing so. Thus, in the absence of serious engagement with the just war tradition, the language of justice and just war is continually at risk of becoming a thin veneer of righteousness spread over forms of warfare that otherwise find little justification or sanction in Christianity.

In this regard, consider the stories of two young men. Both are set on the eve of the Second World War, and both are true stories.

> Martin is a good Lutheran, the son of a Lutheran pastor, who had been taught that a good Christian is a good citizen and a good soldier. A decorated subma-

rine commander in World War I, he had fought valiantly against tyranny and oppression. After the war, he was married, had two kids, and himself became a Lutheran pastor. As the storm clouds of World War II began to gather, he felt called to defend freedom and so began to speak to his congregation of the hope for a meeting between the church and the nation and the nation and God. He began to preach that "When this great nation was formed, God gave it Christianity as its soul, and it is from these Christian roots that it has grown and developed." For its part, the government held up the standard of positive Christianity, of the importance of the churches in the moral and ethical renewal of the nation, and the president spoke openly of the blessings of the Almighty, of the strength he drew from the Word of God in order to defend freedom and face tyranny and oppression. In the face of those who opposed the preparation for war (pacifists), the church and several prominent theologians appealed to Luther, Romans 13, and so forth, in defense of the gathering effort. When the war breaks out, Martin's two sons join the army and he himself offers to serve in the navy.[1]

Frank was not much of a Christian—a nominal Catholic at best—whose father had been killed in World War I. He grew up in a rural community and had a reputation for being rather wild. This changed when he was married. His marriage and the subsequent birth of his children sparked a spiritual awakening in him. As a part of this religious awakening, he became convinced that war was intrinsically unjust, incompatible with his theological beliefs, and that he could not serve in the military. Eventually he received induction orders and consulted his pastor, who reminded him of his responsibilities to the civil authorities and to his family and encouraged him to report for service as ordered. His mother, the mayor, and even his wife pleaded with him to serve. Nevertheless, he refused to fight and as a result was imprisoned (conscientious objection was not legally recognized at that time).[2]

What are we to make of the decisions of these two young men? From the perspective of persons inclined toward just war, we might be sympathetic to the sincerity of the second young man's convictions but find ourselves drawn toward the moral judgments of the first young man. The problem is that these examples are taken from the lives of Martin Niemöller and Franz Jägerstätter, and the army in question was the Nazi army. Martin volunteered to serve in the German army while Franz refused on just war grounds.

The point here is to highlight the importance of disciplined reflection on just war. Too often Christian thinking, teaching, and preaching about war is shallow and undisciplined, uninformed by the tradition. As a result, what we say about war too easily ends up providing legitimation for anything, for forms of war that do not in fact merit the label "just." Hence, we end up supporting kinds of warfare that are at odds with the just war tradition, even as we think we are a just war people, simply because we do not know the just war tradition well enough to know when we are being misled.

For example, at times Christians have thought we were about the business of just war when our support for war has amounted to little more than a "blank check" handed to the ruling powers, whereby we have simply thrown our support behind whatever war the governing authorities have set before us.[3] At other times, we have approached warfare in terms of what has been called an "aggressor/defender" model.[4] According to this way of thinking about war, we steadfastly refuse to shoot first. That is, we will not be the aggressor. But once we are attacked, look out, because anything goes. We are peaceable when left alone, but when provoked, we will respond to aggression with little restraint, with any and all means necessary to address the injustice and turn back aggression. Finally, another approach to war that Christians have historically adopted is that of the crusade. Today many rightly argue that a crusade approach to war is contrary to just war, but as it initially developed in the Middle Ages, the crusade was a subset of just war.[5] More specifically, it was a just war waged against non-Christians and others who were not thought to merit the usual protections and restraints that accompanied just war. The crusade mentality tends to cast war in terms of pure good and pure evil. A crusade is a war of pure good on one side waged against pure evil on the other side. It follows from this that the enemy tends to be demonized and stripped of all rights, and the war against them is waged without limits or restraint, often for unconditional surrender. Furthermore, because one is fighting for pure good against pure evil, going to war need not be a last resort. Additionally, because one fights "on principle," one fights even if the war is unwinnable.

So we arrive at the first challenge to the church presented by the just war tradition: that of learning the tradition, teaching it, and living it so that Christians might avoid the hypocrisy of claiming to be a just war people when we do not really know what that means. If we claim to be just warriors then we should learn and teach the tradition, we should foster the discipline and virtues it entails, and we should hold one another accountable to it. Only then might we avoid the twin errors of either failing to act when we should or acting improperly (unjustly) even as we call ourselves just. Only then do we stand a chance of resisting the lure of other, less-than-faithful forms of fighting. Only then can we make the case that Christian fighting can be a form of faithful discipleship.

This book, then, is not merely an effort to satisfy curiosity about what constitutes just war; rather, it is born of the desire to contribute to how Christians witness to the love and justice of God even in the midst of war.

Just War as Christian Discipleship

In this book I introduce the just war tradition and suggest how that tradition might be lived out as a form of Christian discipleship. This is a concern that should have broad appeal insofar as most churches would identify in some way with the just war tradition. Even those that do not, inclining instead toward pacifism, ought to have an interest in aiding their just war sisters and brothers in avoiding other, unjust forms of warfare. I do not argue for the just war tradition against those Christians who are persuaded that faithful discipleship is a matter of nonviolence or pacifism. There are many other books and authors who take up that important debate. Instead, I argue against those pressures and forces that tempt us to wage war unjustly. In other words, the focus of this book is not "just war versus pacifism" but "just war versus unjust war." Actually, the focus is even more specific. As I have already hinted, this work is geared particularly toward the Christian faith. At its starting point are the convictions and confessions that constitute the Christian faith, and the overarching question is, how does just war mesh with the Christian life? The focus, then, is not simply just war but just war as a form of faithful Christian discipleship. This requires some explanation.

As already noted, war and just war are popular topics these days. The notion of just war has experienced something of a revival over the past forty years or so and has been constantly before us since September 2001, as witnessed by the proliferation of books, articles, editorials, talk shows, church statements, and so forth. Most of the conversations and debates surrounding war and just war can be characterized in one of two ways (or both). Much of the talk about just war is little more than a contribution to the culture wars and political polarization of contemporary society. In these instances, just war is not so much explained or unpacked as invoked to pummel a position or person one disagrees with. So, for example, we invoke just war to beat up the liberal elites opposed to a particular military plan, or we wrap ourselves in the banner of just war as we denounce the imperial ambitions of the neocons. In both of these cases, just war is not so much engaged as it is appealed to for the sake of discrediting one's opponent. One walks away from these kinds of treatments not really knowing anything more about the discipline of just war but quite sure that one's political or ideological opponents are dead wrong and perhaps maliciously so.

The other common way of dealing with just war is to frame it in terms of public policy. The just war tradition is treated as if it were first and foremost a tool for those who shape and enact public policy. Just war is equated with a list of criteria to be checked off in evaluating the propriety of a particular military plan or action. In its most extreme form, this approach suggests that the just war criteria are *only* for the political leaders of a society and that the general public has no real standing to debate or pass judgment on the justice or injustice of a given war. This public policy approach is by far the most common way of dealing with the just war tradition today. Indeed, even the more ideological invocations of just war mentioned above tend to share this public policy framework. Just war is a list of criteria meant to guide public policy with regard to war.

In contrast to these two commonplace uses of just war, this book engages the just war tradition in the hope of strengthening the church's practice of discipleship. Although it will certainly contribute to evaluating various positions and agendas and will certainly have implications for public policy, this treatment of the just war begins from the assumption that the first and overriding concern with regard to matters of war is the church's faithful following of Jesus Christ. Our first concern as Christians is not how to bolster our party or platform while discrediting the other side, nor is it steering politicians and public policy in the right direction. Our first concern when it comes to war should be how we might wage war (or not) in a manner that points to the One who came that all might have life and have it abundantly. How can we live as faithful disciples of Jesus Christ in the midst of wars and rumors of war? How do we follow Christ by loving and seeking justice for our neighbors in war?

A word of caution is in order because these questions are potentially misleading. As we will discover, loving and seeking justice for our neighbors in times of war is inextricably connected to how we love and seek justice for our neighbors in our everyday lives in times of peace. And this is as it should be, for discipleship is not just about what happens at church or on Sundays. Rather, discipleship is the sum total of our life as Christians. It is every time and every place—at home, in the factory or office, at the park, on the battlefield. Hence the justice (or injustice) of Christian war fighting is unavoidably connected to the justice (or injustice) of our ordinary lives apart from war.

Overview

The first and second chapters offer a brief historical overview of the emergence and development of the just war tradition with a moral twist. Key figures, developments, and ideas are introduced that help make sense of the criteria treated in the later chapters. The moral twist in each chapter concerns an important moral question that confronts the just war tradition as a whole. Chapter 1 raises the question of the nature of the moral life in the context of the emergence of the just war tradition in Christianity, primarily with St. Augustine. Specifically, it asks whether just war is a regrettable but necessary evil or a positive good. The answer to this question makes a significant difference for how just war is understood to relate to Christian discipleship. Chapter 2 uses the historical development of the tradition after Augustine as a foil for reflecting on the not uncommon questions regarding whether there ever has been or could be a just war.

The answers to these questions are crucial for the continuing discussion in chapter 3, where I outline two different ways of thinking about and living out just war. The two approaches are what I call "Just War as Public Policy Checklist" and "Just War as Christian Discipleship." At the heart of this book is the claim that just war lived out as a form of faithful Christian discipleship may be substantially different from the way just war is understood and used in the public policy approach that is so popular today. This chapter introduces this difference, which will be explored in more detail in the remainder of the book. After introducing these two approaches, the chapter takes up a common debate over whether Christianity and just war are rightly said to embody a presumption against war and violence as an opportunity to further articulate the difference between the two approaches. Finally, the chapter considers several ways in which the just war tradition can be misused before concluding with challenges for the church.

Chapters 4 through 8 are the heart of the book. They take up the traditional just war criteria, which address matters such as who is in charge of waging war and making judgments about war, and why, when, and how we are to fight if we would fight justly. Each chapter proceeds by comparing and contrasting just war as public policy checklist and just war as Christian discipleship. Each concludes with practical challenges for the church.

The conclusion functions as a kind of theological capstone for the book, bringing front and center what has been an undercurrent through the previous chapters. The distinction between just war as public policy checklist and just war as Christian discipleship is finally a matter of spirituality, of convictions and practices regarding God's ways in the world today. In the appendix, I provide a chart that summarizes the contours of the two approaches.

1

Love and Evil in the Christian Life

The Emergence of Just War

This chapter and the next offer a brief historical survey of the development of the just war tradition, focusing on key figures, events, and concepts that are important for understanding the just war criteria in the chapters that follow. More than a mere historical survey, however, these chapters use the history of just war's development as an opportunity to engage fundamental issues or challenges that just war sets before the church. In this chapter, the central issue is the nature of the moral life. Specifically, how good can we be? Or, more pointedly, can we even be good or is the best we can do a kind of regrettable, if necessary, lesser evil? How we answer this question has a great deal to do with how we understand just war and the possibilities for embodying it as a faithful form of Christian discipleship. The context and foil for these and related questions is the emergence of just war as part of the Christian tradition in the fourth century through the work of the bishop-theologians Ambrose and Augustine, who adopted and adapted that tradition from ancient Rome.

The Early Church and War

At first glance, beginning an overview of the just war by examining the early church may seem a bit odd because it is widely recognized that the early church was opposed to Christian participation in warfare. Almost everyone thinks

Jesus renounced violence (at least Jesus in the Gospels), and most recognize that the early church did the same.

So why begin here instead of with the emergence of just war in the likes of Ambrose and Augustine a few centuries later? Because how we understand the transition from the church's earliest rejection of military service to its acceptance of a just war has everything to do with how or even whether we can begin to describe just war as a faithful form of Christian discipleship. The crux of the matter is this: does the movement from the rejection of war to just war stand as a fundamental break or rupture in the Christian tradition, or is it an organic development that is a change but not a departure from the fundamental tenets of the faith? This is to say, does just war mark a fall from an original righteousness? Is it a compromise with the world that was made necessary as the church moved from being a persecuted minority to attaining a significant amount of political power and influence and thus shouldering new responsibilities? Is just war a form of faithfulness, or is it a concession that the best we can do in this world is the lesser evil, that, try as we might, we cannot avoid sin and dirty hands?

The early church rejected military service and warfare. As the theologian Tertullian, reflecting on Jesus's actions in the Garden of Gethsemane, wrote, Christ, "in disarming Peter, unbelted every soldier."[1] The reasons for the early church's rejection of military service and warfare are a matter of debate. There are two reasons typically given. The first is, as Tertullian suggests, that they followed the teaching and example of Jesus and were opposed to bloodshed and violence. Although some scholars debate this, several of the leading just war thinkers of the church, such as Augustine, themselves acknowledged the early church's rejection of violence.[2] (We will look at them later.) The second reason for the early church's rejection of military service and warfare was that military service in the Roman Empire was deeply entangled in the cult or worship of the emperor. Military officers were expected to make sacrifices to the emperor, and soldiers were expected to participate in that worship. Related to this was the difficulty created when those who in baptism had taken an oath of allegiance to their Lord Jesus Christ were confronted by the expectation of the Roman military that a soldier take an oath of allegiance and devotion to the emperor. Thus, military service carried with it the risk either of idolatry for worshiping the emperor or of martyrdom for refusing to do so.

There are no records of Christians serving in the military forces of the Roman Empire until the end of the second century. Beginning around the years 170–80 CE, alongside the continued condemnation of military service in many early church sources, references appear to Christians in military service. Most likely these were pagans who had been converted to Christianity while in the military, a military that incidentally did not offer many options for quitting the service. Around this time we also find church leaders and theologians who sanction Christian military service. But this approval of military service is not universal and unconditional. On the contrary, the nature of this legitimation of military service is rather limited and particular. What we find are references to Christian soldiers and military service being sanctioned on the condition that such service does not involve one in killing and warfare.

At first glance such a condition may strike modern ears as rather bizarre. After all, as a popular military tattoo reminds us, the business of armies is killing. This was not always the case. In fact, much of Roman military service consisted of what might be called police and civil service functions—fire fighting, mail delivery, accounting, messenger services, general administration, custody of prisoners, public transport and road maintenance, and so forth.[3]

The space permitted for Christian military service continued to expand slowly in fits and starts over the next several centuries. Although the reign of Emperor Constantine—whose Edict of Milan (313 CE) formally tolerated Christianity—is a convenient marker for the shift in Christian thinking about the permissibility of killing in war, it would be a mistake to attribute to Constantine a sudden and wholesale shift in the church's moral evaluation of warfare. Voices sanctioning killing in war appeared before Constantine, and voices opposed to Christian participation in the violence of warfare continued to be heard after Constantine. In other words, it was a slow process that cannot be attributed fairly to one person's virtue or vice.

Again, the question is, what are we to make of this shift? Was it a fall from purity made necessary by Christianity's newfound influence in the empire, an influence that could only be maintained by risking dirty hands and embracing lesser evils, or was it understood as a continuation of the way of discipleship?

The Classic Roots of the Just War Tradition

The just war tradition did not begin with Christianity. Rather, Christianity adopted it from ancient Greek and Roman cultures and then developed it.[4] Perhaps as long as peoples have fought, there have been guidelines and limitations on how war was to be waged. The ancient Greek philosopher Aristotle (384–322 BCE) was the first person to use the phrase "just war," by which he meant that war and the martial virtues should not be an end in themselves, as might have been the case in some militaristic or warrior cultures like the ancient Spartans. Instead, he held that war was to be waged for higher goals and greater goods like peace and prosperity.[5] There is also evidence that, within the Greek culture, civilians and prisoners of war were accorded protections.[6] Not much should be made of this early vision of just war, however, for even as Greek culture developed certain restraints that might limit the destructiveness of war, it also marked a shift from older, primitive forms of fighting—where the point often was not to kill the enemy but to capture them or maneuver into an advantageous position such that the enemy could be talked down or paid off—toward face-to-face battles to the death.[7] Thus what was called a just war was not incompatible with warfare that was in fact *more* destructive than what preceded it.

The ancient Romans developed the notion of just war further, contributing in particular a more substantial account of what constitutes a just cause for going to war. The best-known Roman author on just war is Cicero (106–43 BCE). Cicero argued that the universe is governed by a moral law, called natural law. According to this natural law, unprovoked wars are unjust. A just war then, Cicero wrote, is a war that is fought for the sake of defense or to right wrongs that have been done. Furthermore, a just war must be declared and must be a matter of last resort, undertaken only after the enemy has been given the opportunity to make amends and correct the injustice. In addition, only soldiers may fight, and the intent in fighting should not be the enemy's destruction but the renewal of peaceful relations and community. Cicero was adamant that war be fought and won only by virtue and courage and that base or treacherous means be avoided. Thus Cicero urged that victors be merciful to the vanquished.[8]

The Roman vision of just war was a significant development over the Greek vision, although it was still only a shadow of what the tradition would become as it moved into the Christian world and eventually the realm of international law. Not only did wars continue to be waged in less restrained ways but even what passed for a just war left much to be desired. For example, Roman law did not adopt all of Cicero's advice and once there was just cause and war was declared, Roman law did not recognize any rights belonging to the enemy. Thus the capture of noncombatants, the destruction of land, and the plundering of cities were all permitted. No wonder the Roman historian Tacitus penned his famous critique of Rome's wars: "Where they make a wasteland, they call it peace." Others decried the solemn and legal wars of Rome by which it appropriated others' goods and took possession of the whole world for themselves.[9] Moreover, what just war restraints did exist did not apply to everyone. For example, pirates were not accorded the protections of just war and frequently neither were barbarians—the name given to any people with whom Rome did not have a formal legal relation.[10]

The Emergence of Just War in Christianity

Ambrose

Such was the state of just war when it was adopted and adapted for Christianity by two fourth-century bishops of the church. The first, Ambrose (340–97 CE), was a Roman governor in northern Italy before becoming a Christian and bishop of the church, so he was familiar with the Roman legal tradition and the work of Cicero. Indeed, Ambrose's few comments on just war come in an essay he writes that is consciously imitating Cicero. In that work Ambrose, like Cicero, speaks of the moral life in terms of virtues like prudence, justice, courage, and temperance. He asserts that justice must be preserved in war; that we are not to wage war unless driven to it; that we should forgo advantage in war, including even life itself, if that advantage or the preservation of life come at the cost of virtue and honor; and that we should be merciful toward the enemy. Moreover, it is worth noting for the sake of future developments that for Ambrose just war was a deeply religious undertaking. This is to say, just war was undertaken for reasons of faith, including defending the faith against pagans as well as the spread of heresy, and the outcome of such wars was determined not by the strength of arms and guile of humans but by the Lord.

Finally, it should be observed that even as Ambrose sanctioned just wars, he acknowledged the nonviolent call of Christ on his disciples. Specifically, even as he sanctioned just wars, Ambrose refused to recognize any right to lethal self-defense. Pointing to the example of Christ, he wrote: "I do not think that a Christian, a just and wise man, ought to save his own life by the death of another; just as when he meets an armed robber he cannot return his blows, lest in defending his life he should stain his love toward his neighbor. The verdict on this is plain and clear in the Gospels. 'Put up thy sword, for every one that taketh the sword shall perish with the sword.'"[11]

Augustine

Augustine (354–430 CE) was also a Roman government official before being converted to Christianity through the preaching of Ambrose. Like Ambrose, he was made a bishop. With regard to just war, however, his contribution was much more significant and lasting than that of Ambrose. Augustine is one of the greatest theologians of the church; his formative influence on the way Christians think about their life and faith, particularly in the West, is arguably second only to that of St. Paul. With regard to just war, he is generally considered the father of the just war tradition in Christianity. Even so, one looks in vain in his work for a full-fledged account of just war. Instead, we find bits and pieces of commentary on just war in the midst of his writings on a host of other matters and issues that kept the life of a Christian pastor and bishop more than busy.

Like Ambrose before him, Augustine assumes as the starting point for his comments on war the Roman conception of just war, particularly as it was spelled out by Cicero. Thus echoing Cicero, Augustine writes, "just wars are usually defined as those that avenge injuries," which he further explains in terms of "when a people or a city neglected either to punish wrongs done by its members or to restore what it had wrongly seized."[12] Augustine also follows Cicero in relating his understanding of justice and war to a universal moral order. Human society, he says, like a healthy body, should be well ordered for the sake of the harmony and happiness of the whole. Unlike Cicero, however, Augustine associates this universal moral order with the will of the blessed Trinity in creating humanity. God created humanity to live in a just and peaceable community, and just wars are sometimes appropriate means of restoring and maintaining the tranquility of that order. In this regard, Augustine writes, "A great deal depends on the causes for which men undertake wars, and on the authority they have for doing so; for the natural order which seeks the peace of [humankind], ordains that the monarch should have the power of undertaking war if he thinks it advisable, and that the soldiers should perform their military duties in behalf of the peace and safety of the community."[13]

How does Augustine deal with the nonviolent witness of the early church and Scriptures such as the Sermon on the Mount or Jesus's disarming Peter? His first response is to acknowledge that witness. But then he goes on to recognize as well that "times change" and that what was appropriate at one time may not be so at another.[14] By this he most definitely does not mean that God's norm or standard changes; rather, he means something like, even though the seasons change, the order of seasons remains fixed. Thus, whereas the prophets were permitted to wage war, the apostles were not.[15] Specifically, Augustine sees the change with regard to the church's endorsement of violence in terms of the fulfillment of prophecy. It was inappropriate to sanction the use of force until the prophecies regarding the kings and nations coming to the faith had been fulfilled.[16] In other words, he argues to the effect that pacifism was appropriate until prophecies about the gospel gaining a hearing among the nations and the church being in a position to influence kings and rulers were fulfilled. He also points to the presence of soldiers in the Gospels and argues that because neither Jesus, John the Baptist, nor Peter reprimanded soldiers for their service and immediately demanded that they quit, war fighting is permissible.[17]

With regard to the Sermon on the Mount and other passages of Scripture that encourage Christians in nonviolence, Augustine argues that such injunctions do not pertain to outward actions but rather to the inward disposition of the heart.[18] His principal example here is Christ, who when struck in John 18 did not turn the other cheek but instead rebuked his assailant, even as he was internally willing to be struck and even to die on the cross for the sake of the people who were persecuting him.[19]

How Augustine deals with Matthew 26 and Jesus's rebuke of Peter for taking up the sword in his defense—"all who take the sword will perish by the sword"—is of particular importance for the development of the just war tradition in Christianity in the centuries that follow. One response to this incident is already at hand. What was appropriate in the time of the apostles is not appropriate in a day and age when kings and nations have succumbed to the gospel. Augustine, however, does not pursue this line of argument. Instead, he takes up the important theological question of sovereignty over life and death and who has legitimate authority to take life. Discussing the commandment "thou shall not kill," Augustine argues that God is sovereign over life and death; God alone has final authority over life and death. The reason that the people of God are not to kill is not because life is sacred but because we do not have the authority to kill. Yet, Augustine argues, God shares that authority with human beings in two cases.[20] First, God delegates or shares authority over life and death with those who have the responsibility of governing. Therefore, when these persons wage just wars or put to death wicked persons, they are not violating the commandment. The second case where God shares authority over life and death with human beings is in those instances where God explicitly commands someone to kill. Augustine has in mind here various instances in the Old Testament, drawing from the experiences of Moses, Abraham, Jephthah, or Samson, where God commands persons to wage war or kill in ways that do not immediately and self-evidently correspond to what is commonly recognized as just.[21] Augustine's reasoning is simple. If God explicitly commands one to kill, then the killing is just, even if we do not understand it, because God is just and could not or would not command otherwise.

This reasoning informs how Augustine interprets Christ's prohibition of "taking the sword." What is at issue in this prohibition is the authority to take life. And as Augustine interprets it, "taking the sword" is a matter of killing without the authority to do so.[22] The authority to kill is granted either by the explicit command of God or by means of the authority God delegates to the governing body. Hence, when one kills with the proper authority, one is not "taking the sword." Rather, one has, in a sense, been *given* the sword by

God, either directly as an explicit command or indirectly through the power granted to governing authorities.

What is remarkable about this theological justification of killing and war is what it does not say, what it does not permit. Killing is deemed not to be murder when that killing is done under the auspices of the governing authority. Notice what this omits—killing in self-defense. On this point, Augustine writes: "As to killing others in order to defend one's own life, I do not approve of this, unless one happen to be a soldier or public functionary acting, not for himself, but in defence of others, or of the city in which he resides, if he acts according to the commission lawfully given him, and in the manner becoming his office."[23] Thus Augustine, even as he leads the way in establishing the legitimacy of just war in the Christian tradition, like Ambrose before him does not permit lethal self-defense. Augustine makes this point in a rather striking manner in the midst of a discussion with a secular ruler about the propriety of capital punishment. Specifically, Augustine is discussing how persons who have persecuted and even killed members of his congregation ought to be treated by the secular courts once they have been apprehended. He argues that it would be better that the murderers be released from custody, even if such a move put the members of his congregation at risk, than that the murderers be executed, for, he observes, Christians would rather be killed than kill.[24]

This prompts us to ask what is driving Augustine's vision of just war. Already we have seen that part of the rationale for just war is the political good of maintaining a certain peaceable order so that human life and community may flourish. But Augustine's reservations with regard to Christian lethal self-defense suggest that something else is also at work. After all, clearly just war as Augustine understood it was not simply a matter of protecting the innocent, since there are times when innocent Christians would prefer not to be protected with lethal force but instead face unjust death. What is the point of a just war according to Augustine if it is not self-defense? On what grounds is he not a pacifist?

Augustine was once pressed on this point by a secular magistrate, who on learning about the Christian faith concluded that Christians were pacifists and so could not participate in the defense of the city.[25] Augustine responded by arguing that the Christian refusal of vengeance and their willingness to suffer and even die at the hands of their enemies was born of the hope that evil persons might learn from the example of Christians what is to be valued truly and that through the patient goodwill of Christians they might be prompted to repent, reform, and restore the peace. As he said, "we do not ask for vengeance on our enemies on this earth. Our sufferings ought not constrict our spirits so narrowly that we forget the commandments given to us. . . . We love our enemies and we pray for them. That is why we desire their reform and not their deaths."[26] And, he points out, such a course of action (reformation and reconciliation via prayer) would certainly serve the welfare of the city far more than the miseries that inevitably accompany the violence of even just wars.[27]

Yet, as we know, this does not preclude Christian participation in just wars. Rather, it changes the point or intent of Christians going to war. As Augustine suggested in the passage just quoted, Christians are to love their enemies, and just war creates no exception to this. It is not as if Christians are called to love their neighbors, except when going to war against them. To the contrary, the commandment to love our enemies holds even in the midst of war. While it is perhaps not difficult to discern how waging a just war could be a form of love as one goes to the aid of an unjustly attacked, innocent party, it is more difficult to see how just war could be a form of loving one's enemy neighbor. But according to Augustine, it is. Indeed, Augustine writes that the failure to love destroys the justice of one's otherwise just actions in confronting a wrongdoer.[28]

In Augustine's view, just war is a form of love insofar as it is a sort of "kind harshness."[29] It is a kind harshness in the sense that the intent in waging a just war is the same as when Christians forgo self-defense: love of enemy for the sake of the enemy's repentance and reformation. It is harsh because it is an effort to help one's enemies against their will by punishment. But it is nevertheless a kindness because this punishment is a service to the defeated in the form of restoring justice and peace and depriving persons of the license to act wickedly. Thus a just war is one waged with mercy as it aims at taming disordered passions and vices.[30] It is in this vein that Augustine exhorts the just warrior to "be a peacemaker, even in war so that by conquering them you bring the benefit of peace even to those you defeat."[31]

But what about the deaths that inevitably occur in the midst of war? Does Augustine's rosy picture of just war as a kind of benevolent punishment or tough love gloss over the reality of killing and death in war? Augustine is well aware of the death and destruction that happens even in the midst of a just war; although, we twenty-first-century people would do well to note that wars were not always as deadly and bloody as they tend to be today. Augustine recognizes the real possibility of killing and death, but he insists "it ought to be necessity, and not your will, that destroys an enemy who is fighting you."[32] In other words, killing and death are possibilities, but they are not what a just war aims at. Rather, the aim of a just war is that the unjust enemy will turn from their wicked ways, make amends, and rejoin the community of peace and justice.

Moreover, Augustine notes, it is not the death of an enemy so that others may live in peace that is finally the great evil in war; rather, "the real evils in war are love of violence, revengeful cruelty, fierce and implacable enmity, wild resistance, and the lust of power."[33] Indeed, he goes on to argue, it is possible that a wicked person's loss of their mortal life may result in their eternal welfare.[34] Hence, the temporal judgment and punishment that a just war enacts may serve an eternal benefit as it forestalls eternal judgment and punishment.

Just War as a Lesser Evil?

Such is the vision that formed the starting point for the development of just war over the next sixteen hundred years. Before continuing with the overview of those developments in the next chapter, it is worthwhile to take some time to revisit the question raised earlier with regard to the emergence of just war in Christianity: whether just war represents a kind of fall from righteousness, a compromise with the world that is the cost and consequence of the church's increased influence and responsibility in the affairs of government.

A great many Christians, particularly modern Christians, answer yes, just war is a compromise of sorts; it is something less than following Jesus. After all, many argue, Jesus preached an ideal of love and peace, but in this world of sin it is not possible to live according to that ideal.[35] Maybe we can get close to it in our personal lives, in one-on-one relations, but certainly not in the public relations of communities and nations. Persons who make this argument might even appeal to Augustine's warning against the danger of thinking that we could live as if we were surrounded only by the holy and just.[36] Especially when we have the opportunity and responsibility to come to the aid of others who are suffering and afflicted by injustice and evil, we cannot self-righteously cling to the moral high ground that insists we keep our hands clean and that refuses to engage the world realistically, as it is instead of as we wish it were, which means getting our hands dirty and using the violence of just war.

When the moral life is understood this way, just war is cast as a lesser evil. It is a fall from the moral purity of the early church made necessary by the church's growing influence and responsibility. Of course, this line of reasoning goes, following Jesus in nonviolence and love makes sense when you have no responsibilities for the wider society. But once you can exert an influence on the direction of the ship of state, such moral purity is a luxury that can no longer be afforded. Granted, simply following Jesus would be good, but in this world, confronted by both our responsibility to care for others and the persistence of sin and evil, that is simply not possible. Put a little differently, if Jesus is the ideal that orients our moral lives, our lives are also determined by the reality and persistence of sin—both our own sin and the sin of others. Caught between these two poles, the ideal of the call of Jesus and the hard reality of sin, we cannot in any simple or straightforward manner follow Jesus. Instead, we do the best we can; we strive for the lesser evil. Thus we resort to the violence of just war as a lesser evil in the sincere hope of warding off greater evils like unchecked tyranny and longstanding oppression. Just war is a lesser evil for the sake of preventing a greater evil. And God's grace forgives us for falling short of the genuinely good.

According to this vision, what God does in this world is motivate Christians to go out there and get their hands dirty, secure in the knowledge that God will forgive them for the lesser evils they must do. What God does *not* do is cleanse or heal us from sin as we are washed in the waters of baptism, as we partake of the means of grace in the sacraments of the church and the disciplines of the Christian life, like prayer and fasting and the study of Scripture. Instead, salvation or redemption in this moral life here and now means only justification, pardon, forgiveness of sin. God might inspire or motivate us through the teaching and example of Jesus, but God does not sanctify, make holy, raise up saints here and now. For the time being, we are stuck in our sin; for the time being God is not redeeming us *from* sin, only inspiring us to go out there and do the lesser evil because the good that Christ proclaimed and embodied and to which he called others simply is not realistic right now.

For all its popularity, however, the claim that just war is a lesser evil and that the lesser evil is the best we can do is problematic for a number of reasons. Among those reasons is that the claim does not fit with what we have learned about the development of the just war tradition in Augustine. As Augustine made clear, going to war does not excuse one from the command to love. As he unpacks it, just war was a form of love and as such, it was to be rightly understood not as a departure from the moral vision of Jesus and the early church but as an extension of that vision in different times and under changed circumstances. Granted, just war was a harsh form of love—which some have since labeled an "alien act" of love or charity[37]—but it is nevertheless a form of loving our enemy neighbor. Thus Augustine insisted that the only just intention in war was loving. The intention of just war was the charitable one of the reformation of our enemy so that both they and their victims would be able to enjoy the fruits of peaceful community. This held even if the enemy was, of sad necessity, killed in the midst of a just war. Then it was hoped that such a temporal punishment might prepare the way for eternal communion. As such, in Augustine's eyes as well as the eyes of those who came after him for over a millennium, just war was not something less than faithfulness. Rather, just war was a faithful form of Christian discipleship. It was not a compromise of the high calling of the Christian life.

In addition to the historical difficulty with the claim that just war is a lesser evil, there is the practical problem that the logic of the lesser evil actually undercuts the moral force of the just war tradition. This is to say, the very logic of the lesser evil can be used against the just war tradition itself. After all, one could argue that the just war tradition itself represents an impossible ideal that at any given moment must be discarded for the sake of warding off a greater evil. For example, the same way that the lesser evil logic dismisses Jesus as an impossible ideal in this life, the just war criterion that prohibits directly killing civilians could be dismissed as an ideal that one has to violate as a lesser evil in order to ward off the greater evil of, say, a tyrant's victory. Likewise, in the name of the lesser evil one could dismiss the just war criterion of right intent, which expects soldiers to love instead of hate their enemy, as unrealistic. Indeed, there are many people who argue exactly along these lines today. They say that the just war discipline is too idealistic—akin to fighting with one hand tied behind one's back—and that we cannot afford to slavishly follow its guidelines, that we must get our hands dirty with lesser evils if we are to keep great evils at bay.

The Challenge for the Church: The Nature of the Christian Moral Life

The fundamental challenge put to the church by the adoption of the just war tradition has already been named. What is the nature of the Christian moral life? How good can those who are joined to Christ be expected to be? Is the Christian moral life at its heart about embracing lesser evils, or are Christians called to the good?

Those who adhere to the moral vision of the lesser evil suggest that while in our personal or private lives we may be able to get closer to the moral ideal, in our public and communal lives the best we can hope for is the lesser evil. This is a striking claim both for its running against the grain of much of Christian history and for what it says about God and the gift of salvation that is ours in Christ. To put the matter bluntly, only modern Christians have dared to argue that it is right to do an evil, even only a lesser evil, for the sake of a good end or result. While this kind of consequentialist thinking—that the ends justify the means, especially when the end is a greater good—may be rather commonplace today, especially in our political and economic life, it is alien to the majority of the Christian tradition. Indeed, it is the logic of those who crucified Christ (John 11:50; 18:14) and a logic that St. Paul spares no words in denouncing when he says of those who endorse evils for the sake of a good, "Their condemnation is deserved!" (Rom. 3:8).

The Christian tradition at its best has known and proclaimed the good news that Christ came to set us free from the power of sin and that through the sanctifying power of the Spirit manifest in the various means of grace that are available to the church, we are empowered not to settle for lesser evils but to inhabit the good. The good news is not simply that Jesus justifies sinners by pardoning or forgiving them of their sin. Although this is certainly true, it is not the whole of the gospel or the good news of salvation. The good news is that God offers us even more. The salvation that is ours in Christ not only pardons and forgives but also sanctifies and makes holy. Salvation is not simply about being let off the hook for sin, even as we are left in the misery of our sin. The good news is not that we are fallen and then Jesus comes along and says, "Don't worry about it, I will not hold it against you," but then does not actually lift us out of the gutter of sin. Rather, salvation is about both being let off the hook and our sin-sick souls being healed. In Christ, through the various means of grace and disciplines of discipleship, we are actually being picked up out of the ditch of sin and restored to the holiness for which we were created.

Prior to the advent of modern Christianity, no one thought that we *had* to commit actual sin, that the lesser evil was the best we could do. Such a claim would have struck our mothers and fathers in the faith as tantamount to denying the redemptive, sanctifying power of Christ. This is why the question of whether just war is a lesser evil or an (alien) act of love is finally a question about what God is doing now to redeem all of God's people from the bondage of sin. Whereas the lesser evil approach answers that God is not doing much now, and that is why we have to resign ourselves to the dirty business of war, Augustine's vision of just war was erected on a faith that trusted God was indeed active even now to redeem and set us free from sin. This is why Augustine can insist with a straight face that just warriors love their enemies. He could make what appears to be such a preposterous claim not because he was an unrealistic idealist but because he knew that Christians were not left to their own devices in this world, even in the midst of war. He knew that even now God was graciously renewing fallen humanity and empowering us to be better than we otherwise would or could be. He knew that in Christ, and more specifically in Christ's body the church, we have access to the means of grace, the spiritual disciplines and practices, that could actually make it possible for us (even the soldiers among us) to love our enemies even as we face them in battle. In Christ we have access to the means of grace that make possible what would otherwise appear impossible!

This is not to deny the persistence of sin in the life of Christians. Although it would take us too far afield to delve into the details of how the church before modernity thought about the persistence of sin and the moral life, suffice it to say that even as most of the tradition acknowledged that we necessarily continue to wrestle with the remains of sin even after being joined to Christ and made part of his body the church, that provided no excuse or rationale for embracing a "lesser evil." To the extent that we continue to wrestle with sin, that is something properly confessed and resisted, not sanctioned, justified, approved, encouraged, or blessed. At least this is how the pillars of the faith, like Augustine, would have understood things.

With regard to just war, if in the last analysis just war is a compromise between Jesus's nonviolent ideal and the demands of a violent reality, if it is something other than following Jesus, then it cannot be a faithful form of discipleship. Insofar as discipleship is a matter of following Jesus (after all, those who followed Jesus were called his disciples), then an ethic that makes of Jesus an unrealistic ideal and settles for something less than following in Jesus's footsteps is not a form of faithful discipleship. An ethic that embraces "the lesser evil," that insists that our life here and now is determined as much by sin as it is by grace, is not finally an ethic of discipleship. Although some have tried to argue that not following Jesus in this regard is the same thing as "following Jesus at a distance," such a claim merely displays a confusion regarding the difference between those who are properly called followers of Jesus and those who are best described as admirers.[38]

As we have seen in this chapter, Augustine certainly believed that just war was a faithful form of following Jesus and not simply a compromise forced on us by the realities of our responsibilities in a sinful and fallen world. And because it was a form of following Jesus, Augustine knew that a just warrior people could rely on—indeed must rely—on the sanctifying grace of God in order to wage war justly as an act of love not only for the unjustly attacked neighbor but for the enemy neighbor as well.

The emergence of just war as a form of faithful discipleship and not simply as a compromise with or resignation to sin sets before the church a multitude of challenges and opportunities. Some of these will be named here, some will be named later, and some will be named here and recur throughout the book. Furthermore, many of these challenges are necessarily open-ended, which is to say that I cannot simply provide "the answer" for how the church ought to address them. Instead, these challenges cry out for the church, in its many locations and forms, to be about the task of discerning how to love our enemy neighbors in warfare.

Among the challenges before the church presented by the debate over just war as a form of love or as a lesser evil are two that bear highlighting at this point. The first challenge is that of reflecting on the nature of the salvation that is ours in Christ. What is the character of the salvation that God gives in Christ? What does God give here and now and not just in the future, after death? Part of this conversation entails examining what justification and sanctification mean, how they are related to one another, and what difference they make in our life here and now. As I have suggested, the "lesser evil" approach tends to distinguish between them sharply and then displace the healing transformation of sanctification to some distant future. But does such a claim stand up to Scripture and tradition—to what we confess, sing, pray, and say and do in worship—and to what we see God doing in our own lives and in the lives of the saints?

Raising such questions and beginning such conversations leads naturally to consideration of the means of grace. In what ways does God make sanctifying grace available to us? How is the Holy Spirit at work transforming us from sinners to saints here and now? Granted, not all Christian communities identify the means of grace in the same way. Some emphasize Scripture and prayer and/or meditative stillness. Others may place more emphasis on liturgy, sacraments, or works of mercy. Still others tend to focus on a different mix of spiritual disciplines and practices. But all recognize that integral to the Christian life are various practices and spiritual disciplines of the community of faith whereby God graciously makes us better than we otherwise would be.

If just war is to be lived out as a form of faithful discipleship, as a form of love, then it is important to reflect on the ways, disciplines, and opportunities God presents to us for growth in holiness. How does God empower us? What disciplines and practices does God offer that can both support us and hold us accountable as we seek to faithfully love even our enemy neighbor? Can we name the means of grace that God graciously makes available to us in our immediate and concrete context?

In the Gospel of Mark, the story is told of Jesus's encounter with a blind man at Bethsaida. Jesus touches the man's eyes and as a result the man can see. But his sight is not fully recovered. He can see people, but they look like walking trees. So Jesus lays hands on him a second time and the man is able to see clearly (Mark 8:22–25). As we reflect on the nature of the Christian moral life and the means of grace, we may be like that blind man who can see but only in part. The gifts of God—the means of grace—are set before us. God has not held back; we do not need something in addition to or more than what we have been given in Jesus Christ and his body, the church. God has given us everything we need in Christ to be faithful disciples. Yet we cannot see these gifts. Or we see them, but like the blind man to whom people appear as walking trees, we fail to clearly discern what God has given us. Or we see only one dimension of God's good gifts. In a therapeutic age that often appears more focused on absolution and consolation than the redemption that would make absolution and consolation unnecessary, in an age more concerned with self-actualization and a pseudo-authenticity than with renewal and conformity to Christ (Rom. 12:1; Phil. 2:5), it may be difficult to discern that the means of grace that are set before us are indeed means not only of pardon but also of regeneration and sanctification.

But just such discernment is necessary if we are to live out just war as a form of Christian discipleship. Only if God sanctifies, and only if we recognize and receive the gifts that sanctify, can we hope to be a just war people who wage war as a form of love not only for the innocent neighbor but also for the enemy neighbor.

In the absence of such discernment and reception, then the best we can hope for may be the lesser evil. And if this is the case, then not only is just war not a form of faithful discipleship (for the reasons mentioned above), but it may not even be possible at all. For who apart from the power and promises of God could love their enemies or abide by the just war discipline even and especially when doing so meant risking defeat and perhaps even death?

The answer to this question will become evident as we proceed. For now, let us continue with the brief overview of just war and its development in the centuries after Augustine, which is the subject of the next chapter.

2

Can War Be Just?

A Brief History of Just War

Before continuing the overview of the development of just war in Christianity, let me linger for a moment over the unstated presupposition of the just war tradition, namely, that war can in fact be just. It is worth reflecting on this for a moment because it is not obviously true. The very notion of a just war—that war can and ought to be disciplined by the just war criteria—is one that is contested by persons of a variety of political and moral persuasions. On one hand, there are those who believe all warfare to be intrinsically unjust. For such pacifistically-inclined persons, just war is in the final analysis an oxymoron. War by definition cannot be just. Furthermore, the effort to articulate just war only serves to provide a kind of moral cover or legitimacy for what should be unequivocally and forthrightly rejected. On the other hand, there are those who think that the efforts to wage war within the parameters of just war are naive and unrealistic. War, by its very nature, defies any and every attempt at moral limitation. Furthermore, such efforts at limitation are counterproductive and hamper nations, leaders, and soldiers from doing what needs to be done. Just war, in other words, is equivalent to fighting with one hand tied behind one's back. For these realist types, such limitations and restraints are a recipe for failure and cannot really be an instrument of justice.

Although these critics of just war might inhabit different ends of the political spectrum, their criticisms reflect a common ground. Both sets of critics, for different reasons and to different ends, repeat in so many words the saying made famous by William Tecumseh Sherman regarding the US Civil War,

"War is hell." For these folks, war is akin to a natural disaster. It is something that happens to humanity, and try as we might, we cannot alter or change the nature of war. This is not to excuse humans from the role they play and the culpability they share in making war what it is. Rather, it is to acknowledge that humanity is not capable of waging war successfully in a manner that could be called just. Either a war is successful and therefore not just or war is restrained by the just war criteria and much less likely to be successful.

Obviously advocates of just war disagree with these critics, and this chapter offers a defense of just war as a genuine possibility. This defense proceeds by means of a continuation of the overview begun in the preceding chapter. Considering the historical record—and setting aside the imaginary and fantastic portraits of war painted by Hollywood—suggests that war has not always been, and therefore need not be now, "hell." Instead, the history of war reveals war to be a quintessentially human activity that is subject, like all other human activities, to moral guidelines and limitations. Indeed, as any military historian or informed soldier will tell us, warfare is not a chaotic, "anything goes" encounter analogous to a spontaneous, drunken barroom brawl. On the contrary, although there are certainly moments and even periods of chaos in the midst of war—what is commonly referred to as the "fog of war"—warfare is a rule-governed practice that is deeply shaped by the politics and cultures and institutions that form the people involved. Indeed, even the periods of chaos in war are not as chaotic as they appear, insofar as the actions of well-formed and well-trained soldiers in the midst of a chaotic situation will accord almost as a second nature with their formation and training.[1]

Therefore, when Sherman declared that war was hell, whatever he may have thought he was doing, he was not in fact making an accurate observation about the eternal and unchanging nature of war. He was not simply describing the way war must be, the way it always has been and always will be. Rather, he was, perhaps unwittingly, revealing much about his own moral, cultural, political, and military formation in a novel kind of warfare that was less restrained, more total, and less honorable than what preceded it.[2] In other words, it is not that Sherman and others like him discovered that war was hell; rather, they made it so. As Paul Ramsey puts it, "War first became total in the minds of men."[3] War is a human practice that is as amenable to moral deformation and corruption as it is to moral guidance and limitation. In what follows, we look at how the church and modern nation-states have worked to morally limit war. As the chapter draws to a close, we will revisit the question, can war be just? in light of the historical record and reframe the question in terms of the challenge that just war presents to the church.

Medieval Developments: Gratian

Augustine's death in 430 CE marks the beginning of a period during which the church continued to reflect on justice and war but contributed little that endured in the tradition. This situation changed, however, around the year 1148 CE when a monk named Gratian collected the official legal pronouncements and rulings of various church authorities that had been issued down through the centuries. Gratian took this material, which was officially called "canon law," and published it with his commentary. Gratian's *Decretum* became the most widely used and authoritative collection of the era, shaping the church's thought and practice throughout the remainder of the Middle Ages. Several things are noteworthy about this collection with regard to the ongoing development of just war. First, Gratian's collection highlights Augustine's teaching on just war. Thus, Gratian ensures that Augustine's thought will serve as one of the cornerstones of the church's thought on just war for the next thousand years. Second, even as it highlights the contribution of Augustine, Gratian's work reflects a development of Augustine in several ways.

Building on Augustine

Gratian's treatment of just war begins with the question, "Is military service a sin?"[4] Repeating Augustine's arguments on how to read various Scriptures, he concludes that the answer is no and then goes on to repeat Augustine's claim that a just war was meant as a benevolent punishment of the evildoer. In this way we see that Augustine's firm belief that just war was an act of love toward the enemy remains intact and at the foundation of medieval Christian thought about just war. Gratian then turns to the issues of just cause for war and the authority to wage war. With regard to just cause, he parses it in terms of three causes: to repel an unjust attack underway, to recover that which has been unjustly taken, and to avenge prior injuries. Although to modern ears this last cause, which could also be interpreted more bluntly as "punishment," may sound like a blessing of vindictiveness or cruelty, it is not. The language of avenging or punishing might share such connotations today, but in an earlier time they did not. Recall that for Augustine punishment was a matter of a harsh kindness that, it was hoped, would encourage repentance and reform of life. In other words, punishment was actually a means of restoration of the moral order and of the offender's proper role in that order. Gratian also followed certain trajectories in Augustine's thought to argue that defense of the faith from heretics and pagans fell under the heading of a just cause for war as well.

Questions of Authority

The second major focus of Gratian's work on just war is the question of who has the authority to wage a just war. Here again he follows Augustine, stating that just wars may only be waged by the explicit command of God or by God's delegates—that is, public authorities. Echoing Augustine, he argued that serving as a soldier at the behest of the public authority shielded one from Jesus's condemnation of those who take the sword. Furthermore, and still following Augustine, Gratian argued that serving under the public authority largely absolved one of responsibility for fighting in an unjust war. What this means, according to Gratian and Augustine, is that a soldier can serve and fight in good conscience so long as the injustice of the cause is not readily apparent to him. This is to say, while a soldier is not simply to be a robot who goes to war without question and without reflecting on the justice of the cause, he does owe the prince the benefit of the doubt.[5]

In the era of Christendom, when the church was fully established as the central institution of society, one of the major facets of the question of legitimate authority was that of the proper role of the church with regard to just war. Could the church instigate wars and could clergy fight in them? Given his inclusion of the defense of the faith under just cause, Gratian unsurprisingly approves of the church instigating persecution of heretics and wars for the defense of the church and her prerogatives—although he does not mention the Crusades, which were already underway. Following Ambrose and Augustine, however, he prohibits clergy from actually fighting and killing.

Reflecting a development of Augustine, Gratian also adds to just war the requirement that it be declared by a legitimate authority. The need for a declaration was a carryover from Roman practice, where war was preceded by the delivery to the enemy of a formal document stating the wrongs done and the correctives necessary to address those wrongs.[6]

The Conduct of War

With regard to the actual conduct of war, Gratian says very little, with the exception of repeating the exemption from harm of religious pilgrims, clerics, monks, women, and unarmed peasants that was found in various church authorities. Augustine displays a similar relative silence. Why is this? Perhaps the first thing to remember is that wars have not always endangered noncombatants to the extent that modern wars tend to do. Recall, for example, the stories of civilians coming to watch, as though it were a neatly contained spectator sport, early battles of the US Civil War. The point is that ancient and medieval wars were not normally "total war" that regularly entailed tremendous devastation heaped on noncombatants. Whether it was due to a particular moral ethos or the limitations of weapons and tactics imposed by technology and economic realities, the harshest effects of war were generally limited to combatants. There were exceptions, of course, throughout this period. But even when warfare threatened to impact noncombatants directly—such as the siege of a city—there were often mitigating factors that diffused the threat to noncombatants.

As we will see, as noncombatants are drawn into conflict and face more risk, the church does devote more energy to such issues. The relative silence by the likes of Augustine and Gratian is not a matter of their simply ignoring these issues so much as it is a reflection of what is felt to be most pressing in the given historical context. Gratian, especially, lived in a time when noncombatants were increasingly facing risk from both unemployed soldiers and changes in tactics regarding the siege of cities. Gratian's particular task, however, was not that of addressing contemporary concerns but of compiling and commenting on what authorities had said in the past. For the ongoing development of the tradition, we turn to those who used Gratian as the springboard for their reflections on just war in their day and context.

Gratian's work stimulated an outpouring of commentaries on existing canon law, as well as the enactment of new church laws and decrees as it became clear from his collection that certain important issues related to war had yet to be addressed. These commentaries and laws clarified and reinforced such matters as just cause (with some commentators offering a typology of seven different kinds of wars). They debated the extent and form of clerical participation in war, the extent to which violence is or is not permitted in self-defense, and so forth.

Medieval Developments: The Canonical Tradition

Authority Revisited

Among the matters debated and developed among canon lawyers, there are several that bear highlighting. The issue of legitimate authority to wage war remained a hot—and hotly contested—topic through the conclusion of the Middle Ages. Throughout this period, the centuries-long struggle between the various princes and the church to define the lines and spheres of authority with regard to both secular and churchly affairs, with both parties typically claiming complete sovereignty and authority over the other, came to a head. Furthermore, ever since the collapse of the relatively stable and centralized political structure of the Roman Empire, the lines of social and political authority had been muddled. In the years since, no centralized political structure with clear lines of authority had succeeded in establishing itself for very long. With the emergence in the tenth century of feudalism, in which the lines of authority were decentralized and overlapping, the question of authority became even more vexing.

Who constituted a legitimate authority in a situation where there was not any single authority with a monopoly on armies and weapons? Was it the emperor? The pope? A prince or king? Or might any feudal lord who could summon an army of knights be considered a legitimate authority for the purposes of undertaking a just war? The majority of those who dealt with canon law argued that the authority to wage a just war resided not only with the emperor or pope but reached down to the kings and princes as well.

But what of the church's authority with regard to just wars and what about wars for religious purposes? What did the canon lawyers say about these? On the whole, they upheld the church's legitimate authority to call for and evaluate the justice of a war, which the church exercised through episcopal intervention and mediation between the various princes and lords and through the threat of excommunication. At the same time, the canonists continued to insist that clergy could not directly participate in the fighting of a just war.

Crusades

Of particular interest is the way these reflections on the church's authority over war led to the legitimation of Crusades. Specifically, Crusades were classified as just wars initiated by the pope for the sake of defense of the faith against the enemies of the church. There were long debates regarding the grounds on which an enemy of the faith merited attack. Was unbelief sufficient or did pagans have to commit a crime against Christians (or the natural moral law) to be subject to just attack? In the end, the argument that carried the day was that peaceful pagans were not subject to just attack merely for being pagan. Instead, they had to be guilty of some offense against Christians or the natural moral law, like refusing to permit the free passage of missionaries through their land. Heretics, on the other hand, were another matter. Simply by being heretics, they were lawfully subject to coercion, and at least one Crusade was led against a heretical community.

Penance

Another aspect of canonical reflection on just war that bears mentioning is that of the requirement that even soldiers in a just war do penance.

Penance was an ancient practice of the church that, at its best, was meant as a gracious aid to sinners to help them unlearn the habits of sin and vice and internalize the habits of virtue. In the early Middle Ages, a host of canons enjoined penance on soldiers, even those who fought in just wars.[7] This expectation slowly receded as the Middle Ages waned, although it did not disappear entirely. This expectation has led some to conclude that even in the Middle Ages, just war was not understood as a form of faithful discipleship but rather was a lesser evil. Given Augustine's clear founding of the just war in charity or love, however, as well as the contradiction that the "lesser evil" position would establish in the church's moral vision (recall the discussion in the previous chapter), it is more likely that, among other reasons, an overriding concern was with the difficulty of a soldier's maintaining a disposition of love toward the enemy as well as with avoiding the various other temptations that often attend warfare and fighting.[8] In other words, it is likely that the expectation of penance was born of the recognition that the moral life is difficult. It would be even more so in the midst of battle, and thus it is probable that even a just warrior may be guilty of some vice that ought to be confessed and healed.

Conduct of War

The last aspect of the medieval canonical tradition that I wish to lift up concerns developments regarding how war is justly fought. Thus far, there has not been much attention given to the specifics of how a just war is to be waged, beyond that it should be carried out with love and mercy. Gratian did list categories of persons who were to be considered noncombatants, and in the years after him, this list was clarified and emphasized. Part of the impulse for this concern came from the changing nature of warfare—improvements in siege engines and tactics made the siege of cities a more significant part of late medieval warfare, thus endangering noncombatants. Part of it came from the code of chivalry that guided knights, a code that cast knights in the role of the defenders of the helpless and that deemed it dishonorable for a knight to fight, much less slay, persons who were beneath his station and standing. And part of the impulse for more attention to the protection of noncombatants came from the danger that ordinary folk were facing from roving bands of men-at-arms and, eventually, unemployed mercenaries. In this regard, the church developed what is known as "The Peace of God." This rule designated persons and places, such as clergy and merchants and peasant farmers, as well as their land and property, as protected from the violence of roving soldiers and family feuds and eventually from the effects of war as well.[9] (A similar effort, called the Truce of God, which attempted to declare certain days—typically Sundays and other holy days—off limits to warring never really took hold.)

This time period also saw the first efforts to ban particular weapons or tactics as unjust. The Lateran Council of 1139, for example, banned archers and crossbowmen from using their weapons against Christians. Although the exact reason for the ban is debated, it is important as a marker of the growing attention given to issues of just fighting, and it incidentally sheds light on how at this point in time, the norms of a just war could vary according to who one's opponents were. Thus, for example, Crusades, even though they were thought to be a form of just war, often did not operate according to the same rules that applied to just wars waged against Christians.

Medieval Developments: The Theologians

The last medieval contribution to just war to be considered here is that of the theologians. On the whole, the theologians of the age said relatively little regarding just war. What they did say was firmly rooted in the Augustinian vision that was handed down through Gratian and the canonists. There are two theologians, however, who merit attention for the ways their work stands as a synopsis of developments in the tradition at their respective historical moments and for the influence their work had on future developments.

Thomas Aquinas

The first of these theologians is Thomas Aquinas (1225–74 CE). Aquinas is important for two reasons. First, his work represents a succinct statement of the general consensus on just war in the thirteenth century. In this regard, Aquinas identifies three criteria of a just war: legitimate authority, just cause, and right intention. He unpacks each of these in a rather Augustinian manner in accord with the general trajectory of the medieval canonists that we have already mentioned. Second, Aquinas is significant for the influence his work will have on the tradition in the centuries that follow. Although Aquinas's conclusions regarding just war were not particularly novel, in the centuries after his death his work attained a stature and authority that rivaled that of Augustine. Aquinas's work in many ways becomes the cornerstone of the church's reflection for at least the next five hundred years. In this regard, there are two particular nuances that Aquinas gives to his Augustinian heritage that are worth noting.

First, recall that Augustine's account of just war rested on the conviction that the intention of just war be benevolent. That is, the goal was to bring the benefits of peace to the enemy by means of a harsh kindness or punishment that would hopefully lead to repentance and reform. Furthermore, according to Augustine the lack of this intent undercut the moral legitimacy of what was otherwise a just war. Aquinas certainly shared this understanding of the intent of a just war as well as the importance of right intent in waging a war justly. But to this he added a notion of the common good. He developed an aspect of intent that was present in Augustine but not as prominent—the tranquility of order. Under the influence of the ancient philosopher Aristotle, Aquinas argued that the intent in waging a just war was not only that of correcting the sinner by punishing sin but was also a matter of defending the common good. Aquinas presents just war as a matter of undoing the damage sinners do to themselves by sinning against their neighbor and justice and undoing the damage that the sinner does to the common good of the larger community. (Aquinas used the memorable image of a surgeon excising a decayed or infectious member from the body.)[10] This is not to suggest that the sense of preserving and restoring the social order was absent from earlier reflection on just war, only that it tended to be overshadowed by the stronger emphasis in Augustine's account on just war as a benevolent punishment of the sinner. In the centuries ahead, particularly as we move into the modern era, this emphasis on defense of the common good will become even more prominent.

The second feature of Aquinas's work that had a significant impact on the future shape of just war actually derives not from his treatment of war per se but from his treatment of murder, and more specifically of killing and self-defense. Even as killing in just war was sanctioned by the church, the likes of Ambrose and Augustine continued to prohibit lethal self-defense, lest, in the memorable words of Ambrose, we stain our love toward our neighbor. Aquinas, in his reflection on self-defense, offers a slight nuance on this prohibition. Discussing the question of whether it is lawful to kill someone in self-defense, Aquinas argued, in accord with the spirit of Augustine, that a private individual (that is, one who has not been given the sword by a legitimate public authority) may not *intend* to kill an assailant. But he goes on to point out that one action may have two effects, one of which is intended and the other of which is not. What he has in mind here is private individuals acting to defend themselves against an aggressor and in the course of that defense, while not intending to do so, inadvertently killing the attacker. Such individuals, says Aquinas, are not guilty of any crime or sin, so long as they did not use more force in their defense than was necessary.[11] Aquinas's argument gives rise to what has come to be known as the "principle of double effect," named for the fact that an act can have both intentional and unintentional effects. As we will see, this principle comes to play a significant role in how the church understands the protections that are due noncombatants in the midst of just wars.

Francisco de Vitoria

The second theologian to be mentioned is Francisco de Vitoria (1485–1546 CE). Like Aquinas, Vitoria is noteworthy in part for the way he managed to pull together the various strands of the tradition into a coherent whole, even as he added some novel twists, and also for the way his work impacted future developments of just war. In the latter case, if Aquinas served as the starting point for much of the theological reflection on just war, Vitoria (who was himself a student of Aquinas's thought) stands at the beginning of a trajectory that will blossom into international law. Vitoria and the school of theologians that developed around him are known for the way they discussed just war not only by drawing on Scripture and tradition but also by appealing to the customary laws of people or nations. It is the significance given to these customary laws of peoples, which are not self-evidently dependent on Christian convictions, that will, in time, bear fruit as international law.

The first thing to be said about Vitoria's work on the discipline of just war is that he was a consolidator. He drew the various components of the tradition together such that for the first time the principal elements of what would later come to be known under the headings of *jus ad bellum* and *jus in bello* are clearly articulated. That is, in Vitoria we find spelled out in rather clear and systematic fashion what it means to do justice both in going to war and in waging war. For this reason, many characterize Vitoria's work as the classic expression of just war.[12]

Yet even as he was a consolidator, Vitoria also contributed to the development of the tradition in four primary ways. The first concerns legitimate authority. For the most part, what Vitoria says is in keeping with the tradition as we have already unpacked it; namely, the prince has been delegated the authority to wage just wars by God. Furthermore, in keeping with the tradition, he admonishes the princes that as they exercise their authority to wage wars they do so not simply to enlarge their empires or for the sake of their personal glory or aggrandizement. At this point, however, he adds a significant nuance when he argues that even as the sovereign prince has the authority to wage war, it is not sufficient to go to war on the word or judgment of the prince alone. In response to the question, is it sufficient for a just war that the prince believe his cause to be just? Vitoria answers no and goes on to explain: "It is possible that they act in vincible error, or under the influence of some passion. Any man's opinion is not sufficient to make an action good; it must be an opinion formed according to the judgment of a wise man."[13] Specifically, Vitoria has in mind that princes should surround themselves with wise counselors and advisors, and that they should seek out and heed the advice of these wise persons. (Failing to consult and heed the wise is itself an immoral act.[14]) Vitoria goes so far as to oblige all those who are admitted, called, or of their own accord attend to public governance to examine the causes of a war and to advise the prince against unjust actions, explaining, "the king is not capable of examining the causes of war on his own, and it is likely that he may make many mistakes, or rather he *will* make mistakes, to the detriment and ruin of many. So war should not be declared on the sole dictates of the prince, nor even on the opinion of the few, but on the opinion of the many, and of the wise and reliable."[15]

This is not to suggest that the average person, or even the wise, should approach the prince's judgments automatically with skepticism or suspicion. Rather, it is born of an honest appraisal of the frailty of human nature as well as of the character of some of the rulers of his day. Therefore, notwithstanding his cautionary advice and the way this could be misconstrued in our contemporary political climate as a counsel of fundamental suspicion, Vitoria adheres to and repeats what had come to be the consensus of the tradition at this point: the ordinary subject and soldier are under no particular obligation to investigate the justice of a war. To the contrary, they owe the prince the benefit of the doubt. The ordinary subject is to follow the judgment of the prince even when the justice of a war is doubtful. Only when one is convinced that a war is unjust is the ordinary subject or soldier to refuse to fight. Moreover, Vitoria notes, a prince neither can nor ought always to explain the reasons of war to his subjects.[16] None of this, of course, excuses willful ignorance or deliberately turning a blind eye to injustice, which Vitoria makes clear is wrong.[17]

The second of Vitoria's contributions to just war concerns just cause. Vitoria repeats the standard account of what qualifies as a just cause for war, namely, repelling active aggression, recovering that which has been unjustly taken, and punishment (understood primarily as restoring the moral order). Yet Vitoria, replicating a tendency among many who wrote about just war in his day and age, tends to discuss just cause in terms of defensive and offensive/aggressive wars. Hence, according to Vitoria, just wars can either be defensive (defending or recovering possessions) or offensive (undertaken to avenge losses). This choice of framing just cause is significant insofar as in future centuries the specific causes for just wars will be forgotten, and instead people will speak only of wars that are either defensive or aggressive, with aggressive wars eventually being judged wrong.

Also with regard to just cause, Vitoria is sometimes credited with being among the first to declare that wars may no longer be fought over religion. While Vitoria does declare "difference of religion cannot be a cause of just war,"[18] in truth he is simply repeating what had been the official line about wars and religion since at least the time of Aquinas. Unbelief was not grounds for waging a just war; belief could not be coerced. But a refusal to permit the proclamation of the gospel, a refusal to hear the gospel, or attacking the Christian faith were all just causes for war.[19] If there is anything novel in Vitoria's exposition of religious causes for war, it was his steadfast adherence to the tradition and his rigorous interpretation of it in the face of tremendous pressure to use religion as a pretext for the conquest of the Americas. Thus, when others were suggesting that unbelief or immorality legitimated conquest, Vitoria held fast to the tradition and condemned those clergy who were too eager to salve consciences and praise butchery,[20] boldly denouncing the injustice of conquest in the name of Christianity. While this may not constitute an unequivocal break with the crusading strand of just war, it is a clear move in that direction.

One of Vitoria's novel perspectives on just cause is the notion that there can be a just cause on both sides of a just war, or at least it can *appear* that way. The unspoken assumption of the tradition thus far was that the just cause of a war could belong to only one party in a conflict. It was assumed that if two parties had mutual claims of justice against each other, they would work out those differences in good faith by means other than war, such as negotiation or even simply relinquishing claims. Vitoria argues that it is possible for two sides to go to war with both sides sincerely believing that justice is on their side. Vitoria is clear that in such a situation both sides do not actually have just cause. Rather, one side merely thinks that it does due to invincible ignorance.[21] As a result, Vitoria says, it is possible for people to fight on both sides of a war and for neither to incur moral guilt. Moreover, the possibility that all sides in a war could in good faith believe that they were fighting on behalf of a just cause, in Vitoria's mind, was all the more reason to wage wars with moderation, even renouncing some of the rights of vengeance and so forth that normally accrue to the just party in a conflict. As we shall see shortly, the recognition of simultaneous ostensive justice, as it came to be called, did not have the effect Vitoria hoped it would.

The third of Vitoria's contributions to the development of just war that I wish to mention is that of proportionality. Thus far, not much has been said about weighing the costs of a just war against the benefits. Indeed, one could be excused for thinking that in a just war, because one is fighting for a high moral principle like justice, questions of the cost, of proportionality, would be largely beside the point. This was certainly the case with the Crusades, where one was typically fighting for the highest goods, such as defense of the faith. As the just war tradition develops, however, the concept of proportionality emerges as a matter of weighing the benefits against the tremendous costs (material, financial, human, and otherwise) involved in even a just war. The roots of this idea were present in earlier thinkers. Aquinas, for example, (when he discusses not war but sedition) notes that sometimes one should refrain from taking just actions against a tyrant because the harms that inevitably occur in the midst of deposing a tyrant may actually surpass the harms of the tyrant remaining in power.[22]

Vitoria, however, grants the notion of proportionality real prominence in his work. On one hand, he raises the question of proportionality with regard to decisions of going to war, arguing that care must be taken to ensure that the bad effects of a war do not outweigh the possible benefits sought by waging it: "since all the effects of war are cruel and horrible—slaughter, fire, devastation—it is not lawful to persecute those responsible for trivial offenses by waging war upon them."[23] He even asserts that although one might have a right to reclaim a city or province, that right may be nullified by the risk of provoking greater conflict.[24] On the other hand, he asserts the importance of proportionality in the way one wages battle. Proportionality means that one use only the force necessary to attain the just purposes of the war. (And, he notes but does not elaborate, just because something is advantageous does not mean it is necessary.[25]) In other words, to wage a just war proportionately is to wage war without wanton or excessive violence and destruction. Wanton destruction, Vitoria says, is "diabolical" and "the fire of hell."[26] Thus even as he affirms the right of just warriors to kill, destroy, and so forth, Vitoria cautions that the right to kill that is extended to just warriors extends only as far as that killing and destruction serves the purpose of the just war. In other words, proportionality assures that the sanctioning of death and destruction in a just war does not become mere license for terror and rampage, that the violence of a just war does not become an obstacle to the very justice and peace that are the cause and end of the war.[27]

The fourth of Vitoria's contributions that merit attention concerns his treatment of justice in waging war. Although this was an area of concern that was not completely missing from earlier accounts, Vitoria's work stands out for the way he addressed "what may be done in a just war" in a much more substantial and systematic manner. His treatment of justice in waging war begins with a reaffirmation of the immunity of the innocent from attack, including women, children, clergy, travelers, and so forth.[28] We have already seen how the protection of certain classes of people had increasingly become a concern of the church in the Middle Ages. What is novel about Vitoria's treatment is that he picks up on Aquinas's observation that an action can have both intended and unintended effects ("double effect") and uses it to qualify the immunity of noncombatants.[29] Thus he argues that although one can never intentionally kill the innocent in war, one may nevertheless engage in actions that will in all likelihood kill the innocent so long as those deaths are accidental in the sense of not being intended. He gives the example of besieging a city and attacking it with artillery and fire. Such actions, he asserts, will cause the death of innocents, but they are permissible so long as they are necessary to attain victory (recall the notion of "proportionality" mentioned above) and the death of the innocents is neither intended nor desired.

With regard to what may be done in war, Vitoria next turns his attention to the question of the moral propriety of plundering and looting in war. Vitoria wrote at a time when large standing armies consisting of persons not formed by the knightly code of chivalry were beginning to be used, and the funding for those armies was not yet firmly established in a stable national treasury. As a result, there was significant pressure in these mass armies to loot as a means of supplementing their income. Vitoria attempts to bring this practice under the just war discipline by arguing that goods may be seized, even from the innocent, as a kind of pledge, only in accord with what justice dictates is appropriate for reparations and punishment of the enemy. Indeed, he encourages victors to be merciful and moderate in exercising their rights in this regard and, where possible, not to exact all that they lawfully might. In other words, not everything is liable to seizure, and wanton destruction and killing are prohibited. Likewise, Vitoria acknowledges the reality of rape and so forth, denouncing such horrible crimes and reminding officers of their obligation to discourage those crimes. Moreover, Vitoria insists that reparations are to occur only under the supervision of officers and that where looting occurs without authorization, those responsible should make restitution to the victims.

Vitoria then addresses the proper treatment of enemy combatants, prisoners of war, and enemy civilians at the conclusion of a war. He argues that enemies who have fought justly and quit the fight may not be pursued and slain, whereas enemies who have fought wickedly or who are fleeing only to regroup and threaten again may be pursued and slain. Here we see displayed what is sometimes called the "moral equality of soldiers," that is, the notion that soldiers who fight justly and in good faith—sincerely believing their cause is just, or at least having no grounds to overrule the benefit of a doubt they owed their prince—in a losing or unjust war are nevertheless not punished for fighting or for the actions of the governing authorities. The same holds true, generally, for noncombatants. They are not to be slain. But as we have noted, the innocent may be plundered as part of a just victor's efforts to recoup both the cost of injuries done that precipitated the war and the cost of waging the war itself. Indeed, in what appears to be a holdover from chivalry, captives—including the innocent—may be held for ransom. The point here is not simply greed or war-profiteering but instead holding persons and property as a kind of pledge until those who are responsible for the injustice that led to the war can themselves be made accountable.[30] Finally, Vitoria addresses the matter of deposing princes, taking over governments, and dissolving kingdoms.[31] He acknowledges that there are situations where these drastic measures may be justified, such as when the character of the prince or government is such that their continued rule poses a threat to the peace and security of the common-wealth. Nevertheless, he cautions against such measures on the grounds that the punishment must fit the crime, and even then it is a good thing to temper the punishment with mercy.

One significant caveat to Vitoria's guidance on waging war justly that bears noting is that these limitations with regard to both combatants and noncom-batants apply specifically to Christians. Thus Vitoria notes, for example, that whereas at a war's conclusion Christians can only be held for ransom, non-Christians may be enslaved. Likewise, whereas he asserts that one should not slay all the enemy combatants at the end of war, he admits that this applies to Christians and that in a war with infidels "from whom peace can never be hoped for on any terms," the only solution may be to eliminate all who could bear arms.[32]

Such is the state of just war as the Middle Ages come to a close and the modern world takes shape. We now turn to some of the major thinkers and developments in just war during that age.

Modernity and the So-Called Wars of Religion

As we turn to consider just war in the modern era, there are two principal developments to be highlighted. The first is the shift from a Christian context to a secular, international context. How just war was understood and practiced changed as reflection on justice and war moved out of the distinctly Christian theological context of the Middle Ages and into a secular and international setting, where the guidelines and limitations on war were cast in terms of in-ternational law and so did not require one to accept the Christian faith in order to understand them. The second major development to be considered is the eclipse and eventual revival of just war. Even as lawyers were busy attempting to articulate an international and legal framework for the limitation of war, just war as a recognizable discipline effectively disappeared from the battlefield in the modern world. This was the era of what is commonly called "total war," and it spans the nineteenth and part of the twentieth century. By the second half of the twentieth century, however, just war underwent a revival. We will consider both the eclipse of the tradition and the state of its recovery.

With the work of the Dutch Protestant lawyer Hugo Grotius (1583–1645 CE) we enter the modern era of reflection on just war. That we have entered the modern world is nowhere made clearer than by Grotius himself when in the preface to his classic work, *The Law of War and Peace*, he writes:

> I have had many and weighty reasons for undertaking to write upon this subject. Throughout the Christian world I observed a lack of restraint in relation to war, such as even barbarous races should be ashamed of; I observed that men rush to arms for slight causes, or no cause at all, and that when arms have once been taken up there is no longer any respect for law, divine or human; it is as if, in accordance with a general decree, frenzy had been let loose for the committing of all crimes.[33]

Grotius writes at the outbreak of and in response to the Thirty Years' War (1618–48 CE), a war that by its end was particularly vicious and unrestrained.

It is commonplace today in both scholarly circles and popular culture to refer to the conflicts that riddled this transitional time between the medieval and modern worlds collectively as the "wars of religion." As the story is typically told, the centuries of war that plagued late medieval and early modern Europe were the result of fanatical religious folks going to war and butchering one another in the name of various confessional and doctrinal differences. The problem is that this collective memory is a false one. This way of telling the story of those centuries of war has been shown to be a myth.[34] The Thirty Years' War, for example, was not a battle over how Jesus is present in the Mass/Communion, infant versus adult baptism, or forms of prayer and the veneration of the saints. Rather it was an effort by a great political dynasty to solidify and expand its power, and the bloodiest and most brutal part of the war was actually a struggle between two dynastic families who shared the same faith![35]

The point of this brief history lesson is that Grotius writes as the last remnants of the medieval world are passing, and he seeks to put just war on a foundation that is more suitable to this new historical situation. I noted earlier that the church and the secular princes had been locked in a centuries-long battle for authority. The transition from the Middle Ages to the modern world marks the end of that struggle. The Thirty Years' War and the other wars like it created a new political order that reflects the church's defeat. The age-old battle between pope and prince for the upper hand in this temporal realm had been won by the prince. This is nowhere clearer than in the passage from Grotius. The just war discipline that was part and parcel of the medieval world no longer held. As the church's public authority diminished, the moral force of its disciplines, like just war, also declined. As a consequence, wars became more brutal and destructive. Christians now acted as if war gave them a license for all sorts of crime. What is worse, princes could use the faith to pit Christians against one another, Protestants against Catholics, and vice versa, which showed how far the church's authority had diminished and its just war discipline eroded.

In other words, what today typically gets cast as an example of what happens when religion gets involved in politics—the so-called wars of religion—is actually an example of what happens when Christianity's moral force is diminished by its own internal problems, as well as by secular political pressures, and it is no longer able to form and shape its members according to the just war discipline. Although the church's reflection on just war as we have traced it thus far may not be without its problems and shortcomings, it clearly did not sanction or bless (to paraphrase Grotius) going to war without a just cause or for slight injury and without any restraint. The problem that just war faced at the outset of modernity, then, was *not* that of how to disarm Christianity and square it away safely in an apolitical box so that it would not disturb an otherwise peaceful society and politics. Rather, the question that thinkers like Grotius sought to answer was how to articulate just war in the wake of the collapse and fragmentation of the Christian vision. How is war restrained in a world where Christian convictions do not seem to hold or where they are not shared?

Hugo Grotius: Father of International Law

The solution pursued was to deemphasize (and eventually replace) the distinctively or particularly Christian features in favor of what was thought to be a more universal norm that in principle could be known by and applicable to everyone, regardless of their faith affiliation or lack thereof. For his efforts to develop this more universal foundation for just war, Hugo Grotius is often referred to as the father of international law.

A Two-Tier Ethic

Grotius's efforts in this regard, however, did not begin by simply discarding Christianity and starting over. His faith would not permit that. Instead, he followed the lead of early Christians (called "apologists") who attempted to reach out to pagans by showing that even though they did not know Christ, in their various philosophical systems they nevertheless had glimpses of the truth that found its completion in Christ. Thus, like a modern-day apologist, Grotius drew on a wide range of sources for his account of just war, including the Roman legal and philosophical tradition, Western history, the natural law, and the customary law of peoples or nations that had slowly developed over the centuries.

What is remarkable in the finished product is the way that the law of just war becomes a kind of two-tier ethic; in other words, Grotius's account of just war articulates two related but clearly distinct standards of morality in war. On the one hand, there are the precepts of the natural law and the law of nations. On the other hand, there are the demands of the new law embodied in the gospel. As his work unfolds it becomes clear that the natural law/law of nations functions as a kind of moral minimum, embodying the minimum standards of justice in war by which everyone—Christian and non-Christian, Westerner and non-Westerner—can be expected to abide. In contrast to this are the precepts of the gospel, which are more demanding and are applicable primarily to Christians. For example, after considering the nature of the punishment that natural law permits one to inflict on an aggressor, Grotius writes:

> Now we must see whether the law of the Gospel has more narrowly restricted freedom of action in this regard. Surely . . . it is not strange that some things which are permissible according to nature and by municipal law are forbidden by divine law, since this is most perfect and sets forth a reward greater than human nature; to obtain this reward there are justly demanded virtues which surpass the bare precepts of nature.[36]

Throughout this work, Grotius lays out the demands of natural law with regard to justice and then follows that with the higher demands of the gospel.

Insofar as Grotius was imitating the early Christian apologists, we can assume that his intent in making this strong distinction between the natural law and the gospel was actually that of leading people from the moral minimum to the more perfect way. His intent was not to separate just war from Christianity but to reconnect the two in a situation where he deemed that the link between Christian morality and war had been weakened. In the centuries that followed, however, the distinction that Grotius made between natural law and Christianity was taken up by others who did not share his hope for reviving the Christian ethic in war. In the process, what was a distinction in Grotius became a separation in others. International law is built on the foundation of natural law and the law of nations that Grotius articulated. He is remembered and lauded for the work he did only with regard to the first tier of his ethic, that universal moral minimum. The importance of this shift in just war thinking will be taken up in more detail in the next chapter.

Preemptive Strikes

Facilitating the shift of just war from its theological foundation in the Christian faith to a secular and juridical/legal framework in international law is the chief, but not the only, reason Grotius is worth mentioning. There are two other dimensions of his account of just war that bear considering. The first is his treatment of preemptive strikes in war. In defining what constitutes a just cause for war, the tradition thus far tended to emphasize that a just cause depended on an actual injury being suffered. The general assumption was that just war is always a "second strike," a response to an injury that was not merely looming but had already been suffered. Grotius, however, expands the notion of just cause slightly when he states that "an injury not yet inflicted, which menaces either person or property" constitutes a just cause for war.[37] Perhaps recognizing the potential for abuse inherent in such a claim, he goes on to clarify what he means by an injury that menaces. Speaking in particular of private self-defense, which is frequently treated as a kind of private war, Grotius notes that the danger must be grave—one's existence must be in peril— and imminent.[38] Noting the difference between private self-defense and public wars, he then grants the state more leeway with regard to the immediacy of the threat than he permits private individuals. But he qualifies this preemptive permission, noting that mere fear of the neighbor alone is insufficient for a preemptive attack. Instead, we must not merely fear them but also possess certainty with regard to the prospective enemy's power and intention.[39] He exhorts those contemplating a preemptive attack: "But that the possibility of being attacked confers the right to attack is abhorrent to every principle of equity. Human life exists under such conditions that complete security is never guaranteed to us. For protection against uncertain fears we must rely on Divine Providence, and on a wariness free from reproach, not force."[40]

Right Intent

The second additional feature of Grotius's treatment of just war that merits attention is the way he deals with right intent. Recall that as the tradition developed to this point, it had typically been organized around the criteria of legitimate authority, just cause, and right intent. And in the later medieval period there was significant attention devoted to issues surrounding what could be done in waging a just war. Grotius's work is divided into three books that address, respectively, issues of authority, just cause, and matters of just conduct of war. What is missing from this list is right intent, a significant development. Grotius does not ignore the question of proper intent in going to war altogether. He begins his treatment of causes that render a war unjust, for example, with the recognition that wars can and even frequently are waged for motives other than those attached to the presumptive just cause. That is, just cause is often a pretext concealing other motives. Nevertheless, Grotius clearly diminishes the importance of right intent in just war when he observes that a war begun with a just cause often suffers a defect because of the intent of the party waging the just war. This happens, he says, either because some other legitimate intention—such as some advantage anticipated from the war—overrides the just intention of a war or because some vicious intention—such as delight in the harm befalling another—does so. Either way, Grotius declares, "when a justifiable cause is not wanting, while these things do indeed convict of wrong the party that makes war, yet they do not render the war itself, properly speaking, unlawful."[41]

What we see here is the clear beginning of a trend in much modern reflection on just war. The importance of right intention is diminished. At the same time, the importance of just cause is elevated. (Grotius's treatment of just cause dwarfs his treatment of the other criteria of the tradition.)

The Eclipse of Just War

Grotius was prompted to write because in the seventeenth century it was obvious that the medieval just war tradition was not holding. The temporal or worldly authority of the church had been substantially diminished and, in his memorable words, Christians were using war as a license for ferocity and crime. His efforts to reestablish justice in war would eventually give birth to the laws of war codified in international law. Before this was to happen, however, things had to get worse.

The wars that dominated Grotius's life—and Europe for almost 150 years after his death—are sometimes referred to as "limited wars." These wars were effectively dynastic wars fought between great political families and figures. They were wars limited not only by a moral code but also by natural and material limitations. With the passing of medieval Christendom and erosion of the church's public authority, a way of war that had been (imperfectly) defined by a (imperfect) theological and moral code passed as well. The generally small temporary armies comprised predominantly of knights who had been trained to fight virtuously and who had taken an oath to uphold a rigorous moral code of chivalry and justice gave way to larger standing armies whose principal motive in fighting was economic. Notwithstanding the changing moral ethos and less honorable motives of these armies, wars of this time remained limited because of a number of factors, among them being the technological limits of their weapons, the finite and sometimes very strained resources of the sovereigns who hired them, and the reluctance of the same sovereigns to run the political risks associated with exhausting their armies in either costly losses or victories.

This changed in the nineteenth century as the styles and means of warfare underwent dramatic development.[42] The nineteenth century saw the advent of "total war," a term that can be misleading. In the popular imagination, total war is frequently associated with all-out war, or war with no limits, particularly with regard to the means used to wage war. But such a war is a fiction. War untempered by restraint is not total war but more akin to an imaginary ideal that the famous military strategist Carl von Clausewitz called "pure war."[43]

Napoleon

The shift toward total war began with Napoleon, who in the midst of his military campaigns across Europe and Russia in the early nineteenth century succeeded in capitalizing on trends that had already been underway for several centuries. Specifically, Napoleon raised a massive army by means of conscription (the draft) that was able to draw on the strength and resources of the whole nation in a sustained manner. By itself, however, this does not constitute a change in the type of warfare, only the scale; Napoleon was able to wage larger and longer wars than his predecessors. What makes Napoleon a marker for the beginning of a change is the way he waged war. Specifically, in his campaigns Napoleon freed his army (not always voluntarily) from depending on supply magazines and storage depots; instead, it lived off the land. "Living off the land" is, of course, another way of saying that the army lived off the resources produced by civilians in the lands the army passed through. In other words, the new kind of war that is developing is war that places a significant burden on noncombatants, not only because the enemy seizes supplies but also because one's own forces may destroy civilian resources in order to prevent them from falling into the hands of the enemy army.

Although this was an important change in the way war was waged, Napoleon does not yet mark the advent of total war. Napoleon continued to wage war in what was then a fairly traditional manner. The emphasis was on obtaining victory by indirect means—not destroying the enemy but convincing them to withdraw or surrender. One did this by seizing the advantage, construed either as capturing strategic points or outnumbering the enemy, thereby convincing the enemy of the futility of fighting. These were wars of attrition, and, although "living off the land" could place a tremendous burden on noncombatants, the focus of the war was still on wearing down enemy combatants until enemy leaders deemed it no longer worth fighting.

US Civil War

The US Civil War is generally recognized as the real watershed in the birth of "total war."[44] The conflict was initially waged in accord with the basic precepts of Napoleonic war, with the exception that "living off the land" was prohibited and that where civilian supplies were inadvertently destroyed, the civilians were compensated for their losses. The leading generals of both the North and South had attended the US military academy and learned the Napoleonic style of fighting, waging wars of attrition by strategic capture and maneuver.

This changed, however, as the Union forces encountered stiff resistance, often in the form of guerrilla attacks on their supply lines and depots. Consequently, as the Union generals Grant, Sherman, and Sheridan became increasingly frustrated both with the guerrilla tactics that hindered their advance and with the South's general failure to capitulate, they began "living off the land" and eventually destroyed resources not only in the hopes of crippling the Confederate army's ability to provision itself but also as a direct attack on the civilian population in the hope of undermining Southern morale and weakening its determination to continue the fight. Simultaneous with these developments was a shift in the perceived purpose of battles. No longer was it a matter of maneuver and capture for the sake of convincing the enemy to capitulate. Rather, the end became destruction—destruction of the enemy forces—and this by the most destructive means available. As Francis Lieber, a significant voice in US military policy at the time, wrote: "When nations are transgressed in their good rights, and threatened with the moral and physical calamities of conquest, they are bound to resort to all means of destruction."[45] Elsewhere he adds, "If destruction of the enemy is my object, it is not only right, but my duty, to resort to the most destructive means."[46]

Thus was total war born, and over the course of the next seventy-five years war was waged as if to prove that Lieber's sentiments were right and true.

The First and Second World Wars, each in their own way, were waged as total wars, with little practical regard (irrespective of the rhetoric) given to the combatant/noncombatant distinction and with a tremendous escalation in the nature of and willingness to use destructive force in war. This was evident in the strategic or terror bombing of civilian population centers in World War II by both Allied and Axis forces and culminated in the nuclear bombing of Hiroshima and Nagasaki. This in turn gave way to the Cold War and what is perhaps the pinnacle of total war—the threat of nuclear-enabled mutually assured destruction.

The Rise of International Law

Even as the tide of total war was rising, the voices of persons like Grotius were not silent. Alongside the slide into total war, there was an effort to (re)assert moral control over war. When the US Civil War witnessed the full flowering of total war, Francis Lieber—the same Lieber who could voice the sentiments of total war—was asked to draft a code of laws pertaining to land warfare. The result was a document that goes by the title "General Orders No. 100" or, informally, the "Lieber Code." Published in 1863, it is a landmark as the first effort by a modern nation to draw up and enforce a formal code regulating the conduct of its military. In a sense, it can be understood as a response to the collapse of the culture of chivalry, where conduct in war was regulated as much by internal character and social formation as by "military discipline." In the absence of such internal controls on the conduct of war, external disciplines became more necessary and more prominent. Indeed, the Lieber Code is the forerunner of a long line of military manuals intended specifically to regulate soldiers' conduct in battle.

About the same time that Lieber was drawing up his code, a Genevan named Jean-Henri Dunant, reacting to the horror of the modern battlefield, was forming a committee of Swiss citizens that would become the International Committee of the Red Cross. Shortly thereafter, the Swiss government agreed to host a meeting of representatives from sixteen countries for the sake of drawing up regulations concerning the protections and care due those wounded on the field of battle. Following in the footsteps of Grotius, this gathering attempted to codify into positive law the widely recognized but largely unwritten customary rules, principles, and practices of war. This gathering sought to spell out in positive law what was the customary law of nations with regard to the treatment of the wounded. This effort resulted in the Geneva Convention of 1864.

Thus began the effort to formally establish the international laws of war. Since then, there have been numerous other meetings, which have resulted in conventions and protocols that address both right in going to war and right in waging war. Among the more notable of these are the Geneva Conventions of 1925, 1929, 1949, and 1977; the Hague Conventions of 1899, 1907, and 1954; and various United Nations conventions.

Although the specifics regarding what international law says about matters such as just cause, legitimate authority, and justice in waging war need not detain us here, it is worth mentioning several features of international law that are important with regard to just war. First, international law represents the culmination of the movement of the moral regulation of war away from a theological foundation. Recall the way the father of international law, Grotius, drew a distinction between the secular and the Christian bases of the laws of war. With the formal codification of international law we see the distinction that Grotius drew transformed into a full-fledged separation. The customary law that the shapers of international law drew on is the sum of the practice and principles thought to be universally available to all (reasonable, right-thinking) persons. Theology, faith, and religion are no longer authoritative sources for the laws of war. You will search in vain, for example, for references to Scripture, Augustine, Aquinas, or Vitoria in international law. Justice in war is now a thoroughly secular matter.

Second, related to this, we see that, with the rise of secular international law, the dominant forum for discussing justice in war is the international community of nation-states. Justice in war is now primarily a matter of diplomacy and politics between nations, a matter of politicians and public policy. No longer is justice in war significantly determined by church councils, the judgments of bishops, and the wisdom of confessors.

Third, as imposing as "international law" sounds and in spite of the authority with which it is sometimes invoked, it is not a particularly firm foundation for the moral regulation of war. There are a host of difficulties that work to undermine its authority and hinder its effective implementation. Among these are matters of interpretation. Unlike domestic law, for which there is a final, authoritative interpretation, no such finality accompanies international law. Countries can and do interpret this law in divergent and sometimes conflicting ways. For example, even as international law outlawed the use of poison in the early twentieth century, some countries argued that gases were not poisons.[47] There are also issues of coverage. Some of the laws of war are unrealistic or overly ambitious, as in the law that says prisoners of war should be permitted scientific equipment for educational purposes and athletic uniforms.[48] Other laws are rendered irrelevant and/or inadequate insofar as technology and tactics evolve beyond them. One might consider here the laws regulating the use of hot air balloons in war or the absence of laws addressing some of the cutting-edge high-tech forms of electronic warfare. Issues of implementation and enforcement continue to hobble international law as well insofar as it remains captive to the whims and purse strings of the very powers it is intended to regulate. Additionally, international law frequently is not absolutely binding. Much international law regarding the conduct of war is qualified by "necessity" or what is "reasonable." Thus, what at first glance appear to be strict prohibitions may end up being overridden in a particular situation where it is deemed "necessary" or where adherence is not thought "reasonable." We might note here as well that even as countries sign on to international treaties and conventions on the regulation of war, they may qualify the binding character of that convention by means of official declarations, reservations, and objections, thereby further weakening the binding character of international law.

The Recovery of the Just War Tradition

One response to the advent of total war was the rise of international law. Yet that effort was divorced from the theological tradition from which it sprang. In fact, there is very little evidence in international law of the tradition of reflection on just war that we have traced in this chapter. Indeed, it has been argued that the just war tradition all but disappeared from the time of Grotius's death to the mid-twentieth century.[49] At that time, in the wake of the world wars, just war began to garner renewed attention. Christian theologians like John Courtney Murray, SJ, and Paul Ramsey appealed to the tradition in the course of morally evaluating the postwar international scene, particularly the challenges presented by the destructive potential of nuclear weapons and the threat of nuclear war that hovered over the Cold War. Attention to just war increased during the years of the Vietnam War as persons opposed to that conflict began using language like "just cause" and "proportionality," which in turn prompted a deeper examination of those terms and hence of the tradition. In the years since, there has been a blossoming of research and writing on just war, with one of the significant developments being the 1983 release of *The Challenge of Peace* by the US Catholic bishops, which prompted an outpouring of reflection on the nature of just war in both Christian and secular circles.[50] In recent decades, the language of just war has begun to appear more prominently in the discourse of political leaders, playing a prominent role in debates around both the 1991 Gulf War and the 2003 invasion of Iraq.[51]

Has There Ever Been a Just War?

Such is the history, in brief, of the just war tradition since its adoption and adaptation by Christianity. What the history reflects is that war is not one thing always and forever, that it is not necessarily and inevitably "hell" as Sherman and others would have it. To the contrary, it is a human practice and as such is capable of being waged in different ways, from the highly ritualized and almost game-like wars of medieval chivalry that were minimally lethal (my favorite example being a yearlong war involving one thousand knights in the year 1127 CE during which five died, four of those being the result of accidents),[52] to the limited wars of attrition of the seventeenth and eighteenth centuries, to the total wars that characterized significant wars of the late-nineteenth and early-twentieth centuries.

At the outset of this chapter, the question was raised as to whether war could ever be just. Both pacifists and realists suggest the answer is no. While the historical overview suggests that war need not be total, it does not provide an entirely satisfactory answer to the question of whether war can in fact be just. By itself it does not refute the skeptics. These skeptics sometimes pose the question of just war in a more pointed manner by asking, Has there ever been a just war?

Such a question threatens to plunge us into the midst of the culture wars and the ideological battles of the current moment. After all, there is no short-age of persons willing to proclaim this or that war just or unjust in a manner that appears to be driven more by the political fortunes of the moment than by any deep familiarity with the just war tradition. From the longer perspective of history, there are historians of war and of just war who have argued that there have indeed been just wars.[53]

From a Christian theological perspective, however, the question of whether there has ever been a just war is largely beside the point. From the standpoint of the Christian moral life, it is the wrong question. After all, the Christian moral life does not depend on whether that life has ever been lived faithfully before or not. If Christians are called to be a just war people by God then the proper response to that call is not to step back and ask, Has anyone else done it before us? Rather, even if it means going forth like Abram and his family into the unknown and unprecedented (Heb. 11:8), the proper, faithful response is to discern how our life should be so ordered in response to that call that we might be a people who wage war or refrain from waging war in accord with the precepts of just war. In other words, the proper response to the call to just war is not, Has it been done before? but, How then should we order our lives so that we might respond to the call faithfully?

Perhaps the misguided nature of the question will be clearer if we put a similar challenge to another facet of the Christian life. Take, for example, the Ten Commandments. We might ask if there has there ever been a Christian community that has embodied those commandments perfectly. Has there ever been a Christian church that has succeeded in living out even one of them perfectly? Or take the Great Commandment that we love God and our neighbor. Has there ever been a church that has followed that commandment without flaw or failure? That the answer to these questions is no does not in itself render the commandments invalid, irrelevant, or unrealistic.[54] That the Christian church has displayed and in the course of its life continues to display terrible failures with regard to both love of God and of neighbor does not abolish that calling or erase the reality of that love in its life. That we miss the mark, that we continue to struggle with sin, does not diminish either the high calling to or the reality of holiness and virtue in the life of the church. Our failure as a people does not disprove God's call; neither does our repeated failure establish that we are not in fact capable of accepting and embodying that call. All of this means that even *if* one could definitively show that the church had never even once embodied the just war discipline in war, that in itself would not prove that just war was neither the church's calling nor a real possibility in its life.

The Challenge for the Church: How Then Should We Live?

That the question of whether just war is possible is the wrong one does not mean that it is entirely without its usefulness. To the contrary, it gestures toward the challenges that the history of just war puts to the church. To begin with, if the preceding claims are correct, if our failures to uphold just war may not reflect the impracticality of just war, then we are pressed to ask what a failure to abide by the just war tradition reflects. The frailty and failure of just war may be a symptom of a people's refusal to let their actions in war be guided and limited by the parameters of the tradition. The brief history of just war suggests that the nature of war is not set in stone, that it can and does change for the better or for the worse.

The historical overview suggests, in other words, that war is not something that simply happens to humanity, like a hurricane or earthquake, but is a human practice. War is not an act of nature that strikes randomly and lies beyond human control. Quite the contrary, war is the product of human choices, decisions, and responses. Someone decides to have bronze foundries cease making church bells and start making cannon balls. Someone decides to seize church property and then mine it for the ore needed for weaponry. Someone decides to give the orders to the archers to cut down the prisoners of war. Someone decides to conquer the whole of Europe in order to improve the continent, and so on. Humans decide to bomb cities or burn down villages or rape and pillage. Humans decide to use nuclear weapons or poison or land mines. This is part of what Carl von Clausewitz meant when he penned his now famous (and frequently misunderstood) statement that war is the continuation of politics by other means. War is not something that is imposed on humanity by forces outside itself, nor is war simply an outburst of an irrational and impulsive primordial inner beast that lurks just below the surface in the breast of humanity, always threatening to burst forth in an uncontrollable spasm of rage and violence. War is not simply a relapse into an extramoral, prehuman state. Rather, it is a thoroughly human practice, subject to human control. Therefore, given the flexibility of warfare as a human practice, if war is waged in ways that are not disciplined by the tradition then one has to ask if those who wage war are indeed seriously committed to just war. Are they truly a just war people?

Accordingly, the challenge to the church is that of looking in the mirror, of deep soul searching, of putting to ourselves the question, Do we truly desire to be a just war people? Are we willing to let the just war tradition guide, limit, and shape our actions around warfare? Will we embrace the discipline? Moreover, insofar as just war is understood as a form of Christian discipleship, as a form of faithfully following Jesus, we can and ought to ask if we are willing to respond to the call of God by waging war justly and only justly. If just war is a form of faithfully following Jesus, then we must ask, Are we willing to follow Jesus?

But we cannot stop here because the historical overview suggests that the form war takes and the limitations to which it adheres are not simply a matter of the willpower and good intentions of either individuals or communities. Rather, even if one has the desire or intention to act in accord with just war, the history of just war suggests that the ability to act on and abide by those desires and intentions depends on many factors. The history of just war shows that the form war takes depends not only on the intentions that individuals harbor in their hearts but also on cultural forces and political forms and the character of institutions, like the church, nation, and army. We see that some cultural and political forms, as well as some institutional arrangements, lend themselves to certain kinds of warfare. Thus in Grotius's time we see that the church's retreat from politics and its division into quarreling denominations contributed to the weakening of moral restraints on war. Or we see that a weak central government might be able to gather an army but cannot pay it and so has to acquiesce to soldierly plundering as a means of compensation. Or we see that with the passing of chivalry, the virtues like honor, charity, and justice no longer could be counted on to restrain soldiers who were not formed in those virtues, and so a harsh external discipline had to be imposed as a feeble replacement for those virtues. We see that with the passing of feudalism the communal bonds that obliged military service for the community dissolved and rulers had to resort to mercenaries and forced conscription to raise armies. We see that with the loss of the connection of truth, beauty, and goodness (displayed, for example, in the ornate armaments and fortifications of the Middle Ages), warmaking became more utilitarian, a mere means regulated primarily by efficiency in attaining a government's ends (as displayed, for example, in Sherman and others' arguments on behalf of waging total war against the South in the US Civil War).

All of this is to say that in asking ourselves about the extent or depth of our commitment to just war, we should not stop with examining our desires or intentions. Instead, this examination of conscience must extend to our asking about the culture and politics and institutions to which we belong and to which we are committed. Do they enable and enhance our ability to be a just war people, or do they obstruct that commitment from becoming reality? What kind of culture, politics, churches, and institutions do we need to be about shaping if we are to be formed and sustained as a just war people?

Later chapters will raise more specific questions and at least begin to suggest some answers. I will conclude this chapter by raising two related "big picture" questions for reflection. The first concerns our ecclesial or churchly culture and institutions. The question that framed this chapter was, Can war be just? and in answering it I raised the issue of intentions. Are we committed to just war? Do we really want to be a just war people? But at least ever since Paul penned Romans 7:14–25, crying out in lamentation, "I do not understand my own actions. For I do not do what I want, but I do the very thing I hate," Christians have recognized that we do not always act on our best intentions and desires. For this reason, God has given various means of grace, including the spiritual disciplines and practices of the church, to aid us in living out our best intentions.

The question I wish to raise at this point is whether our church culture is conducive to the kind of supportive, accountable discipline that just war entails. Do we take advantage of the gifts God has given to make us better than we otherwise would be? Are we open to the kinds of supportive and accountable relations with our sisters and brothers in the congregation of the faithful that might indeed make it possible to sustain just war commitments and practices even in the midst of the stresses and temptations of war? Or have our churches drunk, perhaps too deeply, from the therapeutic mindset that in the midst of quickly and blithely announcing "all is forgiven" inadvertently implies "all is permitted"? Have we embraced the individualism of the surrounding culture to the extent that the folks next to us in the pews on Sunday mornings are as likely to be strangers or mere acquaintances as persons who know us and are involved in our lives to the degree that they actually could support and hold us accountable for our discipleship? Although my experience is far from comprehensive, many of the churches I am familiar with lack almost any sense of the propriety or helpfulness of a holy discipline. Many churches are populated with veritable strangers, and even where there is friendship, it is often of a kind that does not expect or even permit a discipline of support and accountability. (How many of the Christian readers of this paragraph would be willing to show their bank statement or checkbook to the person in the next pew on any given Sunday?) Indeed, in many mainline churches what remnants are left of any sense of a disciplined life are largely confined to the leadership of the church.

Granted, the institutions and organizations that make up the churches may offer a host of opportunities—programs, studies, retreats, and so forth—designed to foster the spiritual growth of their members. But most of these offerings are not particularly disciplined or demanding, and as voluntary offerings that one may take or leave like the vegetables on a salad bar, they by definition cannot foster the supportive and accountable culture needed to sustain the kinds of convictions that underwrite just war. The best they can do is make just war one option among many that can be discarded as easily as it was picked up.

If I am right, at least in the broad strokes regarding the sense of disciplined discipleship in many congregations, then the challenge that just war puts to the church is not simply that of fostering the intention or desire to be a just war people. It is also that of developing the kinds of supportive and accountable relationships—as well as the institutions and practices that nurture them (e.g., catechesis, mandatory small group participation, more emphasis on the meaning and seriousness of membership vows, etc.)—that would help all of us contribute to and abide by the church's call to be a just war people. As I stated in the first chapter, we need to teach the just war tradition to the young and the old, to the soldiers and civilians in our midst, and we need churches organized in ways that enable the church to care for and assist its members in abiding by that tradition.

If the first "big picture" challenge that the historical overview of just war presents is that of nurturing the desire to be a just war people, as well as the church culture and institutions to support it, then the second "big picture" challenge prompts us to look outward, toward the wider society and world.

After all, the church is not an island but exists in the midst of a confluence of cultures and a host of institutions, all of which may contribute to or hinder the church's effort to embody just war. Hence, as we contemplate how the church might be so ordered as to nurture and sustain just war we would do well to also consider the kinds of institutions and cultures that we should encourage and support in the wider society.

As we will see in the chapters that follow, just war requires certain political forms and institutions. It also requires that militaries be organized in certain ways. Beyond this, however, and perhaps not as obvious, there are some cultural forms and practices that lend themselves to just war and others that do not. For example, during the US Civil War the generals and politicians who decided that destroying the civilian infrastructure of the South was an acceptable way to wage war did so in accord with a consequentialist logic that says the ends justify the means. The means of destroying the civilian infrastructure (crops, other food sources, cities) were justified on the grounds that such means would bring about a good end, that is, the war's successful conclusion, more quickly. Making such a decision—indeed, even thinking according to such a logic— was made easier by the fact that culture and society were already permeated by a consequentialist logic.

Accordingly, the challenge to the church presented by just war includes that of discerning those forms and forces in the wider world that work for or against just war, even when those forms and forces may not appear to have anything directly to do with war at all. As the case of the US Civil War reminds us, even something as seemingly distant from war as a cultural logic that says actions that lead to a good result are morally justified can have a profound impact on our ability to think and act in accord with the precepts of just war. For example, if the wider culture teaches that lying, promise-breaking, or cheating are permissible when they lead to a good end or result, then persons formed in and by that culture may find it very difficult to abide by the just war tradition's prohibition of directly targeting civilians in war. According to such a consequentialist logic, after all, in a situation where targeting civilians could contribute to the good end of victory and the cessation of war there would be no moral reason not to do so.

❧

Having surveyed the history of just war and at least raised to the fore the significance of practices, institutions, and cultures for living out just war, we now turn to a constructive account of what just war as a form of Christian discipleship involves.

3

Just War as Christian Discipleship

Presuppositions and Presumptions

It is commonplace in popular culture as well as scholarly circles to refer to the "just war theory" or even the "just war doctrine." As popular as it is, such a habit is misleading at best and simply wrong at worst. This is the case for a number of reasons, not the least of which is that while many churches may identify themselves with just war, no church has produced a single, definitive "doctrine" of just war. Moreover, as the historical overview of the previous two chapters makes clear, just war is not a theory that was spelled out and widely accepted, once and for all. It is not as if Augustine drew up something called a just war theory or doctrine, which was set in stone and to which the church has adhered without deviation or change ever since.

Rather, Christians adopted a rudimentary vision of just war from the ancient Romans and then began a long process of developing it that has not stopped to this day. For this reason, it is more accurate to refer to the just war *tradition* than to a just war *doctrine* or *theory*. Christian reflection on and practice of just war is a living tradition that more closely resembles an ongoing conversation about what it means to love and seek justice for our neighbors in war. Accordingly, there is no single, universally accepted account of what constitutes just war. Each of the criteria, and even what the criteria are, is subject to debate and a range of interpretations.

This is perhaps worth lingering over for a moment because in some ways it gets to the heart of what I hope this book accomplishes. To refer to just war as a tradition may not sound any more fluid and flexible to modern ears than if we called it a theory or a doctrine. After all, for many of us, tradition brings to mind that obstacle we run into any time we suggest doing things differently. Tradition names "the way we have always done things around here" and it is about as flexible and open to change as a brick wall. While it is certainly the case that tradition can be used (I would say, abused) in this manner, at its best, tradition is not a nostalgic effort to freeze one moment or to capture a particular understanding or practice like a relic and then simply repeat it over and over. It is not a narrow line that one must toe, with little room for movement or innovation. Rather, at its best tradition is a conversation extended over time about the goods that make up a community's life and the best ways of inhabiting or living out those goods. The confessions and disciplines that define the church today, for example, like the Apostles' Creed or the practice of confession, did not simply fall from heaven like a stone two thousand years ago but have developed in the course of time as the church, under the Spirit's guidance, went about the business of discerning what it means to live faithfully as followers of Christ. Accordingly, tradition is not best equated with a narrow line or straitjacket; rather, a better image might be that of an expansive playing field where the participants in the game are in constant conversation about the best ways to define the game as well as the boundaries of the field on which they play the game in a given time and place.

In the case of just war, as the historical overview showed, the field stretches across almost two millennia and is populated by a diversity of voices in a variety of social and historical settings and involves a number of ways of construing the practice called just war. In what follows I add one more voice to the conversation as it continues to advance in the present day. And I do so in the hopes not of settling things once and for all, thus ending the conversation, but of prompting a host of additional voices (including yours) to join the conversation for the benefit of the whole church and the neighbors we are called to serve through just war. I begin this prompting in this chapter by distinguishing two broad if overlapping strands within the larger tradition of reflection on just war, which I identify as Just War as Christian Discipleship—hereafter referred to as Just War (CD)—and Just War as Public Policy Checklist—hereafter referred to as Just War (PPC).

From the outset, this book promised to spell out just war as a form of Christian discipleship. What this means precisely has been hinted at it in the previous chapters. In this chapter I begin to unpack what I mean by Just War (CD) as a constructive, coherent whole. After sketching these two broad strands within the just war tradition, I turn to the presuppositions and presumptions that underwrite Just War (CD). Here I wade into an ongoing debate in scholarly circles concerning whether just war is best understood as embodying a "presumption for justice" or a "presumption against violence or war." I risk wading into this largely fruitless academic debate in order to show how the vision of Just War (CD) that I propose largely renders the debate beside the point. The debate over the supposed founding presumption of just war provides an opportunity to display the difference that conceiving of just war as a form of Christian discipleship instead of as a public policy checklist makes. Next I identify a number of ways that just war is properly used and improperly abused. Finally, the chapter concludes with a consideration of more challenges that Just War (CD) presents to the church today.

Two Strands in the Tradition: Christian Discipleship and Public Policy Checklist

The distinction I draw in the tradition between just war conceived as a faithful form of Christian discipleship and just war as a public policy checklist could be characterized in several ways. One could cast it as the difference between just war in its medieval and modern forms, for there is no question that what I am calling Just War (CD) shares more than a few similarities with medieval just war and runs against the grain of certain trends in modern just war thinking. Casting the distinction in this way, however, would be a mistake. For the account I offer is not driven by nostalgia for a past that is long gone and well beyond restoration. Additionally, even at its climax in the work of Vitoria, the medieval just war tradition remains problematic in several features and hence ought not simply be recovered.

Alternatively, one could draw this distinction as between distinctively Christian and basically secular visions of just war. Again, drawing the distinction in this way would not be entirely off the mark, for in fact the difference that theological convictions make plays a crucial role in how just war can be articulated as a faithful form of Christian discipleship. But this too would be misleading to the extent that there are many contemporary Christians who conceive of just war in ways that have more in common with what I am calling the public policy checklist approach than with what I am calling the Christian discipleship approach. And while I think the public policy checklist approach flawed, I would not want thereby to suggest that those erring sisters and brothers were somehow outside the fold of the faith.

So, how should this distinction between the two forms of just war be drawn and unpacked? To begin with, I offer a baseline summary of the two visions of just war, which will then be unpacked in more detail in what follows in this chapter as well as throughout the remainder of the book. On one hand, there is what I am calling Just War (CD). This vision focuses on how just war is an expression of the character of the Christian community; an outgrowth of its fundamental confessions, convictions, and practices; and an extension of its consistent, day-to-day life and work on behalf of justice and love of neighbor (even enemies) in the time and realm of war. Just as Christians are called to be about the business of justice and loving others as we raise families, interact with friends, encounter strangers, serve the poor and needy, work, and worship, so too we are concerned to love and seek justice and peace for our neighbors, including our enemy neighbors, when we wage war. In other words, Just War (CD) highlights just war as a distinctively Christian practice that is but a manifestation of the same faithful discipleship that is on display in our life in times and places of peace.

On the other hand, there is what I am calling Just War (PPC). This vision of just war has as its starting point not Christian convictions and the Christian community but modern nation-states and international law. While it is not synonymous with formal, positive international law—because international law is not in any simple and straightforward manner the same as just war—this approach to just war thinks primarily in terms of the laws and rules that do and/ or should regulate the behavior of modern nation-states in war. This vision is decidedly secular, having no intrinsic connection to the Christian community and its confessions. Hence Just War (PPC) is cast not as an aid to discipleship but as an instrument of public policy, a checklist of criteria that aspires to guide politicians, rulers, and military leadership in times of war. Moreover, as a checklist of criteria, this vision of just war does not concern itself with daily life outside of war. Whether a people or nation typically and usually care about justice and their neighbors is largely irrelevant to the use of the checklist. All that matters is that in going to war one is able to check off the criteria. Thus, for example, a people or government could be thoroughly vicious and unjust, normally and characteristically displaying little regard for its neighbors, but as long as it can check off the criteria on the list, it can claim to be waging a just war.

To flesh out these initial descriptions and comparisons a bit more fully, we can approach them in terms of how they differ with regard to the *source* of the moral norms that regulate the conduct of a just war, the *purpose* that the just war discipline is intended to serve, and the *nature* of the moral norms and guidance that it articulates.

The Source of Just War Norms

The Christian community, with its particular confessions and convictions and practices, is the starting point for reflection on the nature and expectations of waging war justly in Just War (CD). When we want to know what just war entails, according to this vision, the first place we look is not to international law, what the politicians or political scientists assert, what the military field manuals tell us, or what our favorite pundit, talking head, or nongovernmental organization claims but what the Christian faith teaches. In other words, in order to understand and practice Just War (CD) it is necessary to be part of the Christian community. Just War (CD) is—and can only be—the practice of a community, specifically the Christian community. It is intrinsically, and not merely accidentally or incidentally, connected to the faith and life of the church. At the heart of Just War (CD) is the claim that what Christians confess about who God is and how God acts in the church and the world makes a difference in how just war is both understood and lived out.

Although such a claim may at first glance strike one as unduly narrow and even exclusivistic, in reality it is neither; it is only common sense. Such a claim does not preclude non-Christians from being just warriors; as the previous chapters displayed, the just war tradition is deep and broad. Just war as a distinctly Christian practice is only one dimension of the tradition. Neither does it prohibit non-Christians from joining the church; it only states the obvious—that as a form of Christian discipleship, just war is intrinsically connected with Christian convictions and community. Granted, the intrinsic connection between just war and Christian community presupposed by Just War (CD) is perhaps not *immediately* obvious, but it is the case that war, and especially just war, cannot be engaged in by solitary individuals. Despite the way the likes of Rambo or Schwarzenegger are portrayed by Hollywood as one-man armies, and notwithstanding the terribly misleading "Army of One" marketing campaign of recent years, war is a communal practice. (Militaries know this, which is why they work so hard to break down the individualism of inductees.) Just War (CD) is a practice of the Christian community. Therefore, the Christian faith is the primary source of moral guidance for what constitutes justice and injustice in waging war.

The moral norms for Just War (PPC) are, broadly speaking, those rules and norms that are recognized to govern modern nations and states in war. The most obvious sources are, of course, the laws of war that have developed in international law. But because the international laws of war are not simply synonymous with just war and because there is no single, set-in-stone account of just war, the sources for Just War (PPC) can be quite diverse, drawing from the length of the tradition outlined in the previous chapters as well as leaning heavily on prominent contemporary just war theorists. For example, many people take the work of political philosopher Michael Walzer, whose excellent book *Just and Unjust Wars*[1] has become something of a contemporary classic, as the starting point for understanding just war.

What is noteworthy about Just War (PPC) and what distinguishes it from Just War (CD) is that its sources, even if they are explicitly Christian thinkers such as Augustine or Grotius, are shorn of any intrinsic connection to Christian faith and practice. Even if a Christian theologian or bishop is the source of some particular aspect of just war, the fact that that person was a Christian who prayed regularly to the blessed Trinity, went to confession, or partook with some frequency of the Lord's Supper is thought to be completely irrelevant for understanding what they said about just war. Thus, for example, even if Augustine is the source of the criterion of, say, just cause, what just cause looks like is completely secularized. To understand what just cause means, one need not be a part of or even pay attention to the Christian faith that animated Augustine. And this holds for all the criteria. Just war can be articulated without any reference to or regard for the Christian community and its faith. Faith, theology, and the church are thought to make no positive difference for understanding just war.[2] The sources of Just War (PPC) are either secular or thoroughly secularized.

The Purpose of Just War Norms

The second way we might distinguish the two strands in the just war tradition is in terms of how each conceives of the purpose that the just war discipline is meant to serve. According to Just War (CD), the purpose of just war is finally no different from the purpose of the rest of the Christian life, which is to faithfully follow Christ in this world, loving God and serving our neighbors. Thus the just war discipline is first and foremost an aid to discipleship, to growing in the life of faith even in a time of war. In other words, the primary purpose of the just war discipline is not to guide princes, presidents, and politicians who stand at the helm of nations and states; it is decidedly not a public policy checklist. Rather, it is a rule of life (and death) in the face of war. The first function of Just War (CD) is not to guide modern states through the turbulent waters of international politics; rather, its primary function is to guide Christians (including Christian politicians) in loving God and serving their neighbors faithfully in the midst of wars and rumors of wars. To put the matter perhaps a bit more bluntly, the principal concern that drives Just War (CD) is not, Are nations doing the right thing? but, Is the church? Are the People of God? The purpose of the just war discipline is to guide the church in faithfully following Christ.

Hence, Just War (CD) is an explicitly church-centered instead of state-centered approach to just war. It does not assume that the nation-state is either the primary anchor of Christians' identity or the most important ensemble of institutions in times of war. Having said this, however, Just War (CD) does not pretend that nations and states do not exist. It does not pretend that nations have no significance in shaping the identity of Christians, that states are irrelevant in times of war, or that the faith has nothing to say about nations and their relations. To the contrary, Just War (CD) embodies a substantial understanding of political community, government, and the proper exercise of political authority, including coercive and deadly force. This is not a vision that effectively withdraws from politics as we know it and thus has nothing to say to politicians, presidents, and others who form public policy and make decisions about war for nations in this day and age. This church-centered vision offers a particular way of envisioning politics and the church's participation in politics, as well as its influence on heads of state and other shapers of public policy.

As we shall see, Just War (CD) has plenty to say to rulers and to nations. (Indeed, I anticipate some critics asserting that this vision has too much to say!) But what it says, it says in a particular way. It speaks as a disciplined body that actually lives out what it asks of others. What it encourages others to do, it displays in its own disciplined life. In other words, this is not a vision where the church tells others what to do while its own members do not do or believe the very things they are telling others to do and believe. For example, this church-centered vision does not simply approach politicians and generals with a request, perhaps in the form of a petition, social statement, or letter signed by the church leadership, along the lines of, "We want you to act in accord with just cause or proportionality." Rather, it approaches politicians and generals and so forth with such a request backed up, if you will, by a body of people who have been formed to act in war only in accord with just cause and proportionality along with the other precepts of just war. To put it crassly, this is a vision of the church's influence that goes beyond words that are effectively hollow because the politicians know that there are few if any bodies backing them up. It is the end of the "do as I say, not as I do" form of (non)influence. It is a vision of influence that begins with embodying our convictions so that when we speak to others, they may see not only how what we ask is possible but that we mean what we say. It is a form of politics that begins with witness. We are a just war people and we invite the nations to join us.

With regard to Just War (PPC), the purpose of just war discipline is predominantly that of guiding heads of state and those who formulate public policy. It provides decision makers and their advisors with a checklist of criteria to limit and legitimate the resort to war. It is meant to guide the decisions that initiate as well as steer the conduct of war, and it is meant to structure the way governments publicly justify their resort to war. In this regard, think of the way just war was used in the run up to the war in Iraq that began in 2003. In a host of contexts—print media and airwaves, political speeches and church publications—just war was presented as a list of criteria that could be used to evaluate the decisions and actions of politicians and nations. As such, Just War (PPC) is clearly state-centered. Its point is first and foremost to guide nations in their deliberations and actions around war.

In its most extreme form, Just War (PPC) is all but removed from the hands of ordinary citizens. The criteria are said to be only for politicians, political leaders, and their advisors. If the logic of this presumption is accepted then everyone else should simply permit the political authorities to do their job and abide by the decisions those authorities make. More typically, however, Just War (PPC) is used in a manner that is meant to aid citizens in deciding on the justness of a war and then attempting to sway the politicians and political leaders to act accordingly. Here again, unlike Just War (CD), the image of politics is thoroughly state-centered. The purpose of the criteria is to shape what citizens tell those who are at the helm of the state to do. Incidentally, but not inconsequentially, this use of just war does not require those who use it to abide by it themselves. I may use just war as a checklist for public policy without actually being committed to it myself. I or my church may ask politicians to act in accord with the parameters of just war or to make decisions in a given situation in accord with its precepts without thereby committing myself or my church to act with that same sense of justice in other areas of life and/or public policy. This fact leads to the third way these two strands within the just war tradition may be compared.

The Nature of Just War Norms

The final way I will introduce these two strands of just war is by distinguishing between the ways they characterize the moral life. By this I mean that each vision of just war presupposes that the moral life has a particular shape. While both strands unpack just war in terms of the traditional criteria, how those criteria function—the work that they do in the moral life—and the kinds of people and institutions that are needed to embody and abide by them are very different.

Just War (PPC): Law Centered

The moral vision that underwrites Just War (PPC) is law or rule centered. It presumes that the basic problem of the moral life is that of the individual knowing what is the right thing to do and then mustering the willpower to do it. Thus, in the case of war, the problem is that of knowing what the rules and laws of justice are and then obeying them. Just War (PPC) addresses this problem by providing a rather succinct list of the principles that should be enshrined in the laws of war. Accordingly, an individual is able to determine if a war is just or not by measuring it against the list of rules or norms provided by the just war tradition. Thus are born the slew of editorials that in the space of a few hundred words purport to evaluate the justice or injustice of a given conflict. Here are the criteria for a just war, and here is how war X measures or fails to measure up. Here are the rules, and here is how they were obeyed or disobeyed.

Of course, knowing the rules is only part of the moral equation. The other part is summoning the willpower to obey the rules. After all, we can know the right thing to do and still not do it because of a failure of our willpower. So, essential to this vision of the moral life as a matter of knowing the rules and then following them is the centrality of obedience and the discipline to enforce it. Recall from the historical overview that when the medieval world collapsed, military discipline was created to fill the void left by the passing of the moral formation of medieval chivalry. In the absence of a kind of internalized moral formation militaries had to impose a morality on their members, and they did so by stressing obedience and discipline. (It is worth noting that a similar sense of moral deficiency in civilian culture coupled with the military's sense that it needs to instill moral discipline has fueled debate over a growing military/civilian divide in the US.)[3] This is the source of the popular vision of military morality as a matter of instantaneous and unquestioned obedience to commands. It is also part of the rationale given for the military training offered to foreign armed forces with a questionable reputation: professionalizing them, meaning among other things teaching them to obey orders without hesitation, so they will be more likely to obey the rules of just war when they are ordered to do so.

Just War (CD): Character and Virtue

By way of contrast, the moral vision that underwrites Just War (CD) is character- or virtue-based. Its ethical focus is on the character and virtues or habits that should distinguish the Christian life in war as well as in peace. This is not to say that rules, laws, commands, and the virtue of obedience are unimportant, only that focusing narrowly on them is insufficient. While rules and commands are important in the moral life generally, as well as in just war specifically, the moral life is more complex than the rule- or law-centered ethic of Just War (PPC) suggests. For example, the moral life, particularly in the midst of the fog of war, is rarely as straightforward as the "know-the-rules-and-follow-them" approach suggests. For one thing, there is no rule for every situation. Try as we might, we will never anticipate every possible situation that could arise in war and then spell out how the laws and rules apply. This is implicitly acknowledged by those who argued in the wake of the Vietnam War, as well as by some contemporary voices commenting on the Iraq war, that the war was/is a new kind of war, one that we have not seen before, and so we should not be surprised nor can we blame those who commit terrible acts precisely because it is not yet clear how the rules apply in this new situation. In other words, a rule-based ethic is insufficient because war is not a static thing but always changing, while the rules of war are inevitably written for the last war. A rule-based ethic is always playing catch-up.

A second difficulty with the rule-centered approach is that it is not always clear which rule or rules apply in a given situation. For example, when person A shoots person B, it is often not self-evident which rule or law applies. Is it manslaughter? Assisted suicide? Homicide? If so, which degree of homicide? This is why we have a complex legal system—to determine which rules are applicable and how—and that determination, as anyone who has served on a jury knows, is not simply a matter of knowing the rules and then obeying them. There is more at stake even in following rules than simply being told what the rules are and being determined to obey them. It is this "more" that just war as a character- or virtue-centered ethic addresses and that the public policy checklist approach lacks.

A third difficulty with the rule-centered approach is its effectiveness. We have already referred to the struggle St. Paul describes in Romans 7 regarding the frustrating inability to actually do what one desires and instead doing what one does not desire. The struggle he describes suggests that living the moral life is not as easy as simply knowing the right thing to do and then willing to do it. In relation to war particularly, there are serious questions about the effectiveness of a moral vision that centers on learning rules and then willing oneself to follow them is, especially under the extraordinary stresses one can face in combat.[4] And it should be noted that this concern holds not only for those who face combat directly but also for those who care deeply about those who face combat and about the just outcome of conflict. Although the stresses are different for those who do not face combat directly, they are no less real. For example, for those who care deeply about the victims of unjust aggression, the possibility that an aggressor may prevail in war puts tremendous pressure on the will to abide by the parameters of just war. Indeed, there are many prominent people today who assert that, in the face of possible defeat, one cannot be expected to abide by just war rules. Thus, in the face of war and the possibility of the death of loved ones in combat, or the possibility of defeat, waging war justly requires more than promulgating the rules and expecting people (soldiers and civilians) to summon the will to follow them. Abiding by the just war discipline requires more than just knowledge and willpower.

This "more" is precisely the virtues that make up what we would call a person—or in the case of the church, a people—of character. Virtues, in turn, might be described as those dispositions and habits to act in a particular, consistent way. Thus a person who displays the virtue of justice is not someone who only occasionally or accidentally does what justice demands but is one who characteristically or habitually acts justly. In the same way, we would not call someone who frequently lied truthful. Instead, we call truthful and honest someone who habitually and normally abides in the truth. Likewise, a courageous community is not one that occasionally does what courage demands but instead is a community for whom courage is an integral part of their very character. It is the normal way they act; it is what people come to expect from them. Perhaps an example or two will make this clearer.

Imagine you have a friend with whom you frequently spend time on the weekends. Every single time you are with this friend, who is married, he invariably shares with you his desire to cheat on his spouse and is constantly flirting with people you encounter on your weekend outings. Now, to the best of your knowledge, this friend has not in fact cheated on his spouse. Would you say that this friend displayed the virtue of fidelity? Would you say he was an example or model of fidelity? No. Even if this friend had not cheated, perhaps because you always managed to intervene or cajole or because he was afraid of, say, the financial repercussions of the messy divorce that would result if the infidelity were discovered, we would not say that this person's disposition was that of fidelity. In fact, many of us might be inclined to think it is only a matter of time before the talk becomes reality and thus we would be unsurprised (if saddened) to hear on one of our weekend outings that indeed a divorce was in the works because of infidelity. Furthermore, some of us might be inclined to say that our friend's character would better be described not by the virtue of fidelity but by the vice of infidelity, even if that vice had yet to come to full fruition in the commission of adultery. Contrast this with the person who has been married to the same person for forty years (or four years), who may on occasion feel the pangs of temptation, but for whom infidelity has never been a serious option. The virtuous person, the person of character, is one for whom virtue—in this case, fidelity—is the normal condition of their soul; it is the ruling temper of their heart and life. Unlike the friend in the first example, virtuous persons are persons who do not have to constantly ask themselves what the moral thing to do is and then convince themselves (or be convinced by others) to do it. A spouse whose character is marked by the virtue of fidelity does not have to go through each day reminding themselves over and over not to cheat. (Although reminders are not a bad thing, and can be very helpful.) Instead, fidelity becomes habitual, a second nature. It becomes not merely something you do but who you are.

A person or community of character is one that has internalized what rules and laws, in their irreplaceable if incomplete ways, point to. This internalization is not something that comes about simply by memorizing rules and then willing oneself to follow them. Although rules and laws are a helpful part of this process of becoming a person or community of character, they are insufficient. Instead, one learns the virtues, one becomes a person of character, by being surrounded by a community of persons whose lives embody the virtues and whose characters reflect them. In the wider culture, such persons are called role models, although in our individualistic culture we rarely see communities recognized as such. In the church we call such persons saints, a category which includes not just the famous persons who stare at us from the stained glass windows and statuary, but all the local saints as well. These are people who greet us every week in worship: the woman who is known for her generosity to the poor, the elderly man known for his patience and wisdom, the business owner known for her compassion. In short, we cannot learn the virtues on our own. Nor do we learn to be virtuous from exceptional individuals but from the many persons who make up the communion of saints, the great cloud of witnesses, the church. We learn the virtues by imitating those whose lives display the virtues. In a manner not unlike that of learning a craft, hobby, or sport, we learn the virtues by learning rules, to be sure, but also by taking the time to observe, imitate, and practice what we see the saints do. We are then corrected by those saints, until the character that rules point to becomes the normal disposition of our lives.

Unlike Just War (PPC), which operates on the assumption that individuals can know what justice in war is simply by both learning a list of criteria and following it if they are able to drum up the sheer willpower, Just War (CD) recognizes that one cannot know what just war entails simply by memorizing a checklist of criteria. Nor is following the just war discipline merely a matter of willing oneself (perhaps with the assistance of an intimidating, forward-leaning commanding officer or pastor) to follow the rules. Indeed, according to Just War (CD), the criteria that constitute the moral parameters of just war are not in any simple or straightforward sense a list of rules, norms, or principles that could be used as a public policy checklist. They are even less amenable to being pared down to the brief space allotted them in the typical editorial or church social statement. Instead, the criteria are a kind of shorthand for a way of life. They are signposts for an ensemble of practices that give rise to and sustain, and in turn are sustained by, particular virtues. As a form of faithful discipleship they are shorthand for the convictions, practices, and virtues that constitute the character of the Christian community. And learning just war entails not merely learning some rules but being immersed in that way of life. Learning and living Just War (CD) entails becoming people of a certain kind of character who are, among other things, habitually disposed to love and seek justice for their neighbors as if such a disposition were a second nature.

And as we might expect, this acquiring of a second nature does not happen overnight. Becoming virtuous and unlearning the vices cannot occur at the pace of one of the ubiquitous TV makeover shows. Nor does it happen in the space of a class or two on the just war criteria or in the time it takes to read a checklist of criteria on the editorial page and commit them to memory. Acquiring the virtues and becoming part of a people who have the character that is necessary to sustain just war as a faithful form of Christian discipleship takes time. It takes a lifetime—or even several lifetimes, if we consider how long the church has been wrestling with becoming a just war people. But it is precisely in the midst of the Christian community that we have the gracious opportunity to learn from the lives of the saints around us as well as from the lifetimes of the saints who have gone before us.

The Difference that Virtue and Character Make

Exploring the difference that having a virtuous character makes for how we think about and embody just war is the task of the remainder of this book. But a few comments can be offered now by way of further explanation of what a character or virtue ethic is. Consider the difficulties with the rule-centered approach that were mentioned above. How does the virtue- or character-centered approach address those issues? The first two problems with a rule-centered approach to just war concerned the applicability of rules. On one hand, there is simply not a rule for every conceivable situation, and any effort to actually articulate such a comprehensive list of rules would quickly become unmanageable. This is perhaps nowhere more evident than in the chronic sense that the rules are always on the verge of being out of date as the nature and conditions of war continue to evolve in response to social, political, and technological changes. On the other hand, there is the problem of knowing which rules are applicable in a given situation and how to apply those that are.

Adapting to the Changing Face of War: Equity

While the continually changing face of war presents a challenge to every ethic, a virtue or character ethic is particularly equipped to address this situation. In fact, there is a virtue that is of use specifically in situations where the letter of existing law proves to be either inadequate or inappropriate. This virtue is frequently given the name "equity," although that hardly captures all that this virtue is about. We might describe one who displays this virtue as possessing insight into how to act in a novel situation that is "beyond the rules," yet in a manner that is consistent with the spirit and goal of existing rules and laws. Mundane examples of this kind of virtue abound. As an engineer once explained to me, those who know only the rules that make up the building code make lousy engineers and, if permitted, would build unsafe structures precisely because they lack the virtues—among them what is classically called "equity"—that are truly essential to the craft of engineering. Likewise, skilled assembly line workers who manage to retain a sense of their work as a craft know the difference between "working to rule" and producing good products. In both instances, merely knowing and following the rules is insufficient and perhaps even detrimental to the good the rules aim at. Instead, what is needed is a kind of practical wisdom that knows when and how to exceed the rule in a given, perhaps novel, circumstance, a wisdom akin to what is sometimes indentified with the "spirit" of a law as opposed to the mere letter. More to the point of just war, the virtue described here, although rarely named as such, is frequently associated with good leadership. It is not uncommon in the memoirs of soldiers to find "by the book" officers, particularly green lieutenants just out of college ROTC programs, viewed with suspicion precisely because they may know the rules but have not acquired the virtues necessary to lead well in situations where the rules do not exactly fit.

Indeed, despite the stereotypes and myths that frequently revolve around military training, at least some militaries recognize that effective war fighting is not a matter of blind obedience but requires soldiers whose character is such that they can be given objectives and then trusted to exercise proper discernment and judgment regarding how best to accomplish those objectives in a manner consistent with the moral character of the community they serve. In this regard, obedience is less about mindlessly following orders than it is a virtue related to the pursuit of a shared good. We might say that as a virtue, obedience is about the delegation of authority for the sake of attaining a common goal. As such, it is more akin to a disposition of mutual trust in a community that shares a common pursuit than it is simply about coercing the will to fall in line with the dictates of a higher authority. Moreover, one might be surprised at the degree of "flexibility" in the authority exercised and obedience expected in some military organizations[5]—perhaps not unlike the surprise some Protestants express when they discover that the authority of the teaching office in Roman Catholicism allows for a latitude of opinions as well as degrees of disagreement and dissent. It is worth noting as well that even where instantaneous obedience is demanded, it may be more about the *instantaneous* than about the unthinking nature of the act. In battle, any hesitation in acting may hinder success and/or unnecessarily endanger lives.

Seeing Which Rules Apply: Prudence

Closely related to this is the way a virtue or character ethic deals with the matter of knowing which rules apply when, as well as how they apply. Here again there is a virtue associated with this skill: prudence. It is a kind of judgment that is able to assess a situation, identifying what is at stake and how various rules and virtues come into play. In the popular imagination, prudence is often equated with a certain cautious deliberation in acting, a kind of careful application of the rules. This is a fair description of the virtue as far as it goes—particularly if "cautious" is not rendered the equivalent of "slow," for there is nothing necessarily slow about being prudent. What this understanding lacks, though, is a sense of how prudence is more than mere deliberation but also involves "seeing," in the sense that prudence involves recognizing the morally important features of a situation in order to determine what acts are appropriate and what rules applicable. For example, it is a prudent soldier who, on seeing a small child pushed out into a street in the middle of a firefight to recover a weapon, is able to discern whether and how the decision to shoot that child involves questions of proportionality or discrimination. Likewise, it is the virtue of prudence that names the church's ability to cut through the myriad of justifications and rationales given for a possible war so it can be determined if and how they relate to such matters as just cause and right intent.

Resisting Brutality: Character

Finally, there is the question raised about the effectiveness of a rule-centered approach to just war. Although it has not caught on in any significant manner in civilian culture (where moral instruction, when it has not capitulated entirely to an ends-justify-the-means approach, too often remains at the level of "just say no"), in some military cultures it has been recognized that a moral vision built around simply knowing the rules and then mustering the will to follow them is insufficient for sustaining moral behavior in the midst of war. This is particularly evident in the memoirs of Vietnam veterans and the work of those who have counseled them. In the midst of battle, which can frequently feel like an ethical wilderness, what checks a person's descent into brutality is character.[6] Those who lack the requisite character, even if they know the rules and are charged with enforcing them, are not likely to abide by their moral commitments in the face of the extreme stresses of combat. In other words, there is a certain character that is needed to sustain one's commitment to moral rules in the midst of experiences like war. And people who lack that particular moral character—for example, those who are not committed to justice for their neighbors in their everyday life or whose politics do not nurture prudence—will not be able to wage a war justly, even if there is just cause for war, because they lack the kind of character that would be able to rightly embody and sustain the moral commitments that make war just.[7]

Recognizing this, some militaries now think about training less in terms of duties and rules (although neither is absent) and more in terms of character and virtues. Thus, for example, it is not unheard of for a drill sergeant to introduce Marine recruits to Aristotle and the virtues during basic training.[8] Likewise, whether they mention Aristotle and other classic advocates of a virtue/character ethic or not, many militaries devote much time and attention to shaping the character of and instilling particular virtues, such as honor and courage, in their members.[9]

It would be grossly simplistic to attribute the brutality of modern warfare entirely to the collapse of the moral vision of virtue/character that marked just war as a Christian discipline and the subsequent failure of the rule-centered vision of just war that replaced it. Nevertheless, there is some truth to the charge. As those who actually fight the wars increasingly recognize, the moral guidance and limitation of war hinges on more than just knowing the rules; it depends on more than following a list of criteria that can be checked off.

Just War (CD) attends to the "more" that Just War (PPC) is missing. Without dismissing the usefulness of rules or the importance of public policy guidelines, it focuses on the questions of character and the kinds of practices needed to instill the virtues necessary to sustain justice in war. It focuses on the practices of the Christian life whereby God graciously forms the church into a community of disciples who love and seek justice for their neighbors (including their enemy neighbors) in war.

As we shall see, the way just war functions—the kinds of demands it makes and the kind of people it requires to embody it—depends a great deal on whether it is rooted in the character and discipleship of the Christian community or in policy decisions of modern nation-states and international law.

A Presumption for Justice or against Violence?

As an opportunity to further display what I mean by Just War (CD) and how it differs from Just War (PPC), let us consider a perennial debate in scholarly circles about the foundational presumption of just war.[10] The contours of the debate are not always easy to follow because the terms of the debate sometimes shift even within the writing of a single author and because some of the prominent figures in the debate have changed their position over the years. Nevertheless, in simplified form the debate revolves around just war being rightly understood as beginning from either a presumption for justice or against war/violence/force.[11]

The origins of this debate can be traced back to the reemergence of the just war tradition in the late twentieth century and the claim that was advanced first by individuals and then by the US Catholic bishops in their 1983 *The Challenge of Peace*, namely that just war and pacifism shared a common presumption against violence and war.[12] This prompted others to argue that in fact just war and pacifism do not share such a presumption, that just war is established instead on a presumption for justice and against injustice.

This matters to the advocates of various sides of this debate because each side fears that the presumption championed by the other side will result in people and nations being either too quick or too slow to wage war. On the one hand, those who argue that just war is established on a presumption for justice and against injustice are convinced that accepting the presumption against war or violence amounts to adopting a pacifist position. If we are predisposed to think of war as intrinsically bad, then we will inevitably exaggerate the evils of war and so keep raising the bar of the presumption, such that no war could ever reach its standards. The presumption functions, in practice, as a prohibition of war. On the other hand, those who argue that just war embodies a presumption against war or violence believe that the alternative position inclines persons and nations to be too quick to wage war. In a reverse image of their opponents, these folks argue that by minimizing the harm of violence and war, the bar is inevitably lowered and war, in practice, becomes accepted as inevitable.

From the standpoint of Just War (CD), the entire debate over the proper "presumption" that founds just war is misguided. It is misguided because the concept of a "presumption" is inadequate to the task of describing the fundamental convictions and commitments that rightly characterize the Christian life. For example, contrary to the claims of some, Christianity does not hold a presumption for justice. Rather, Christianity's commitment to justice is absolute and unwavering.[13] To couch the Christian commitment to justice in terms of a "presumption" is to make that commitment too tentative, too weak. To talk of a presumption for justice suggests that the Christian commitment to justice is limited; the very language of presumption suggests that under certain circumstances our commitment to justice can be overridden, with the result that Christians would at that point no longer be committed to justice. In reality, Christians are called to an absolute and consistent commitment to justice. The only thing that changes with regard to that commitment is not its strength or constancy but how it is lived out in a given situation. To put this in terms of the just war tradition, there are times when the church's pursuit of justice is rightly embodied in war, and there are times when the pursuit of justice takes forms other than war. Moreover, when the church's commitment to justice leads it to abstain from war on just war grounds, it is not thereby relinquishing or curtailing its commitment to justice. Deciding on just war grounds not to wage war is itself an act of justice; moreover, abstaining from war as a means of pursuing justice does not in any way release Christians from pursuing justice for their neighbors by other means. While the form that it takes may change, the commitment to justice remains steadfast.

Furthermore, when the presumption is cast in terms of a presumption against violence or against war, it has the effect of rendering just war a lesser evil. Conceived of in terms of a presumption against violence or against war, just war casts war as fundamentally problematic. This is why there is a presumption against it. But it recognizes that at some point the alternative evil of letting injustice go unchecked is worse than the evil of war, and at that point the just war presumption against war is overridden. Confronted with a worse evil, the presumption against war is overcome and just war becomes a legitimate "lesser evil" in the face of the greater evil of unchecked aggression or injustice. Yet the Christian adoption and adaptation of just war was not a matter of accepting a lesser evil but was understood as a positive act of love directed toward both the innocent or unjustly attacked as well as the aggressor. While this lesser-evil interpretation of just war is popular in some modern theological circles, the bulk of the Christian tradition, including the principal figures in the development of just war in Christianity, could not imagine or sanction doing an evil—even a lesser evil—that a good may result.

In this way, the debate concerning the proper presumption is misguided. Neither conceiving of just war in terms of a presumption for justice nor conceiving of it in terms of a presumption against war or violence accurately captures the character of the Christian life and how just war emerged and is sustained as part of that life.

This having been said, however, the underlying concern that appears to drive the debate over the proper presumption is a legitimate one and actually points us toward Just War (CD). The underlying concern is that beginning with the wrong presumption will result in war being initiated either too slowly (the error of those holding the presumption against war or violence) or too quickly (the error of those holding the presumption for justice and against injustice). This is an appropriate concern insofar as just war does indeed involve a mean between the two extremes—going to war too hastily and going to war too hesitantly.

The problem with the whole debate concerning the proper presumption is that although it rightly brings to our attention the importance of the appropriate timing in going to war (neither too quickly nor too slowly), the language of presumption is not adequate to the task of helping us get our timing right. Endorsing one presumption or the other is not finally what prevents us from going to war either too hastily or too hesitantly. Rather, what guides our timing, our appropriately holding back or leaning forward in a given situation, are the character and virtues that underwrite the just war criteria. It is not embracing one presumption or the other that either restrains or prompts our going to war but a certain character and virtues that are manifest in the just war criteria.

In the end, the whole debate over the proper presumption ends up circumscribing the criteria. Instead of letting the criteria that deal with going to war do their work, the debate tries to add a presumption to the criteria that would incline us to use the criteria one way or another. But, we might ask, why do those engaged in this endless and fruitless debate feel the need to add a presumption to the criteria? Why is it that the criteria themselves are not thought adequate to the task of appropriately guiding our disposition toward entering into war? The whole debate, although it provides the wrong solution, points to the inadequacy of just war construed as a public policy checklist. In its own way, this debate reinforces the claims made earlier about the problems with Just War (PPC). Conceiving of just war simply as a checklist of rules or principles that can be learned quickly and used by anyone, irrespective of their character, is inadequate. The checklist approach, for example, leaves just war open to manipulation and abuse such that it can be misused to hinder going to war when one should, or, conversely, it can be misused to encourage going to war when one should not. Born of the recognition of this weakness, the debate attempts to address this susceptibility to abuse by establishing a presumption. Although embracing a presumption is the wrong way to fix the problem, just by identifying the problem the debate points to the need for a vision of just war and the criteria that are rooted in a character- and virtue-centered ethic.

The Tradition and Its Teeth: The Use and Abuse of Just War

The debate over the proper presumption that orients the use of the criteria, misguided though it is, does raise the specter of the abuse and proper use of the criteria. In the introduction, several ways the tradition as a whole might be abused were mentioned, all of which entailed "just war" language legitimating forms of warfare that in fact do not conform to the tradition. The argument over the starting presumption suggests that just war can be abused in another way as well, namely, by manipulating the criteria themselves such that war is made either too easy to justify or impossible to justify. In this section, we will consider three common ways the criteria are abused and then consider their proper use. This is sometimes cast in terms of the tradition having teeth or not having teeth.[14]

Just War without Teeth

The first way the criteria can be abused may be called "just war without teeth." Abused in this way, the just war criteria are invoked and perhaps even permitted to discipline one's actions in war for awhile, but in the end their moral force is drained. The guidance they offer and the restraint they impose are discarded. This is just war with its teeth pulled. In the worst case, the tradition and the criteria are invoked and acknowledged but the criteria are not actually used to guide or limit one's actions related to war. This is, perhaps, what the ancient Christian writer Lactantius had in mind when he offered this criticism of the "just wars" of the Romans: "they solemnly declared wars and legally inflicted injuries and eternally desired and appropriated other men's goods, and thereby gained for themselves possession of the whole world."[15] Just war without teeth may invoke the criteria, but it does so in a shallow or superficial manner that is something less than actually engaging, wrestling with, and being disciplined by the criteria. It may acknowledge the criteria and give lip service to their authority, but it does not really take them seriously such that the criteria are permitted to actually shape how one wages or refrains from waging war. To put it in contemporary parlance, it may talk the talk but it does not walk the walk.

A slightly different form of just war without teeth begins by actually taking the criteria seriously, by engaging the criteria and letting them discipline one's war fighting, but then it eventually pulls the teeth by ignoring or dismissing the binding force of the criteria. Typically, this discarding of the teeth of the tradition, this overruling of the criteria, is done in the name of "necessity." This is to say, one follows the criteria until necessity dictates that the criteria be discarded. Perhaps this "necessity" is a matter of survival; perhaps it is a matter of victory. One adheres to the criteria until it becomes clear that continuing to do so may result in death and/or defeat, at which point it becomes necessary to discard the criteria in favor of doing whatever it takes to achieve victory or ensure survival. One follows the just war criteria, but not at all costs. At some point the cost of following the criteria becomes too high, so the teeth are pulled in order to avoid paying that cost. For example, Michael Walzer, one of the leading secular just war thinkers today, argues that when a community is faced by a "supreme emergency" it may be necessary to violate the just war criteria.[16] By supreme emergency, he means a situation where a community's very way of life is at stake. He argues that when a community's existence is at stake, when the values that animate its way of life are at mortal risk, necessity entails incurring the moral guilt of breaking the rules, of violating the just war criteria for the sake of survival.

Just War with Too Many Teeth

The second way that the just war criteria can be abused may be called "just war with too many teeth." This form of abuse is the mirror image of just war without teeth. Whereas just war without teeth effectively erases the moral force of the tradition, just war with too many teeth exaggerates the bite, or moral force, of the criteria by strengthening them in a manner that renders them all but impossible to meet. If the first abuse effectively abolished the moral bar, this abuse raises the moral bar too high. One form that this takes with some regularity concerns last resort. In the run up to any given war, inevitably some argue that there is always one more thing that can be tried for the sake of resolving the situation short of war. By arguing that last resort requires every possible and conceivable tactic—including my grandmother baking cookies for a potential adversary—to be exhausted before we are indeed in a situation of "last resort," this criterion is bolstered to the point that it is literally unattainable. Although the cookie example is a facetious exaggeration, there is indeed always one more thing that could be tried. If I have begged and pleaded diplomatically fifty-six times, well, I could beg and plead a fifty-seventh time and then a fifty-eighth time and so on and so forth. After all, the fifty-seventh time or the fifty-eighth time might be the charm! Another form this takes that is heard on occasion is the ratcheting up of the criterion of discrimination or noncombatant immunity. As it is sometimes used, discrimination is enhanced to mean that no noncombatant deaths are permissible in war. Thus, if noncombatants die, the war in question is judged unjust. While prohibiting any noncombatant deaths does not render just war impossible, such a rigorous standard is, as we shall see, not in fact what is meant by the traditional criterion of discrimination. This improper strengthening can happen to any of the criteria. For example, "legitimate authority" can be equated with unanimous domestic and international consent and authorization, or "right intent" can be defined in such a way that only those who have never committed an injustice may engage in a just war. Without going through each of the criteria, the point should be clear. Abused in this manner, the criteria no longer function as the signposts of a viable, livable discipline but instead are transformed into a set of principles whose purpose is to disqualify war, one war at a time.[17]

Just War with a Few Teeth Pulled

The third form of abuse to be considered might be understood as inhabiting the moral mean between just war with no teeth and just war with too many teeth. This abuse is what could be called, to stick with the dental metaphor, "just war with a few teeth pulled." This form of abuse recognizes some of the criteria while ignoring or diminishing other criteria. Insofar as it does not uniformly recognize the moral force of all the criteria, it pulls some of the teeth out of the tradition. This can take different forms. It can be simply a matter of paying attention to only some of the criteria. For example, it has been argued that historically the US has a tendency to concentrate almost exclusively on the criteria of just cause.[18] The North American moral ethos is such that the US believes itself to be engaged in a just war anytime it is responding, by whatever means necessary, to an unjust attack. Or it might entail a kind of ranking of the criteria in importance and then asserting that violating or ignoring the lesser criteria does not render a war unjust. Francisco Suárez, a theologian writing on the eve of the birth of modernity, does this when he effectively reduces the importance of right intention by arguing that if a war springs from hatred, it may well violate the virtue of charity but that does not thereby undermine the justice of a war.[19] In a similar manner, Hugo Grotius, who was influenced by the work of Suárez, argued that in some cases a just cause for war may exist, but the party initiating or leading the war is motivated by a sinful intent. While such a wicked intent is indeed a sin, Grotius asserts, the presence of such an intent does not render the war itself unjust or immoral.[20] Again what we see here is a kind of ranking of the criteria, with right intent being effectively stripped of its determinative role in defining what constitutes a just war. Whether one goes to war with right intention or not may make a moral difference to the individual, but it has no bearing on whether war can rightly be called just or not. In this way, one of the teeth of the tradition has been pulled.

Another way that teeth are pulled from the tradition concerns the way different moral weight is given to the criteria that are commonly identified with justice in going to war (*jus ad bellum*) and justice in waging war (*jus in bello*). Teeth are pulled from the tradition as pride of place is given to one set of criteria or the other, with the result that the set of criteria taking second place is stripped of power to exercise moral authority in war. There are two ways this happens. First, the *jus ad bellum* criteria are all but dismissed as the other criteria, concerning justice in waging war, are highlighted. In the years after Vitoria, the criteria that had to do with going to war, such as legitimate authority, just cause, and so forth, took a backseat to the criteria that addressed how one wages war justly, namely discrimination or noncombatant immunity and proportionality. Although the reasons for this concentration are complex, the logic of this development is not. Once Vitoria declared that it was possible for both sides in a war to believe sincerely that they have justice on their side, the possibility of actually settling a dispute short of going to war was significantly reduced. After all, as Vitoria pointed out, the tradition could not be guaranteed to determine which (if either) party in a potential conflict actually had just cause. Instead, one could sincerely abide by the tradition, be lacking a just cause, and still believe that one had a just cause. Or, to put this a little differently, after Vitoria the moralists lost confidence in the ability of humans to adjudicate questions of justice in going to war. As a result, the criteria associated with justice in going to war lost moral force and the focus shifted to those aspects of just war where it was still thought that the tradition could help us distinguish between justice and injustice, where it was still thought possible to adjudicate right and wrong. The focus shifted to the criteria concerned with justice in waging war.

The second way the teeth are pulled from the tradition in this manner is by granting primacy to the question of justice in going to war and diminishing the moral force of the criteria concerned with justice in waging war. The way this is typically done today is by arguing that the real core of the just war tradition consists of the criteria concerned with going to war. These are the criteria that really matter, must be satisfied, and cannot be ignored. The criteria concerned with justice in waging war, on the other hand, are not that important. Sometimes it is argued that those criteria are really just prudential guidelines. It is a good idea to follow them; but, if you do not follow them, although you may be unwise, you are not immoral or unjust.[21] Sometimes it is argued that the justice-in-war criteria are not as important because it is so difficult to make judgments about them, whereas judgments about the justice-in-going-to-war criteria are much clearer.[22] This, we may note, is a simple reversal of the argument made after Vitoria for why the justice in going to war criteria could not be used effectively. Either way, whichever set of criteria is privileged, the other criteria are weakened and the just war discipline loses some teeth.

A third way that just war loses some of its teeth involves a kind of weighing or balancing the criteria against each other. Instead of viewing the criteria as a whole in which all of them together make up the justness of a war, the criteria are viewed independently as if they were each weights that were to be placed on one side or the other of a scale, depending on whether the criteria were followed or violated. A war is said to be just, according to this vision, when the scale tilts toward justice. What this means is that the violation of some criteria are measured against the strength of the other criteria to determine if the violations are significant enough to render an otherwise just war unjust. The significance, scale, and gravity of the violation of one or more criteria are measured against the strength or weight of the criteria that are upheld. Thus, it might be argued in a particular case that significant and widespread violations of the criteria for justice in war are not enough to overcome the strength of the just cause. Given the tremendous justness of the cause in a particular case, the violations of justice in war would not weigh enough to tilt the scale and make the war unjust. For example, in a war against a particularly heinous dictator, the widespread targeting and destruction of enemy civilians would not be enough to outweigh the justness of defeating that particularly wicked dictator. In this case, violating the criterion of discrimination would not negatively affect the moral justice of that war.[23] And so the discipline loses a tooth.

Just War with All Its Teeth

Against these various ways of abusing the tradition stands the just war discipline with all of its teeth. A just war is a war waged in accord with *all* of the criteria. There can be no cherry-picking from among the criteria, discarding those that for whatever reason do not appeal. There is no constructing of a hierarchy of importance among the criteria, with some carrying more moral weight than others. There is no weighing the justness of the just cause or the rightness of the right intent over against the gravity of ignoring discrimination and directly killing civilians. A war is just when it is disciplined by all of the criteria. A war is not just when it meets only some of the criteria. Just cause alone does not make a war just. It is the whole discipline that makes a war just. As Paul Ramsey, one of the principal architects of the recovery of just war in the late twentieth century, said, just war is "twin-born."[24] By this he meant that the discipline provides at the same time both justification for and limitation of war. This does not mean that some of the criteria—namely, those pertaining to justice in going to war—grant permission and make war just while other criteria—namely, those pertaining to justice in waging war—then function only to limit or take back that permission. Rather, each of the criteria contributes to the justification and the limitation. If any of the criteria are ignored or dismissed, the justice of the whole discipline is undermined. As Thomas Aquinas notes, a moral act is not good unless it is good in all its components. Thus, evil results from a single defect, whereas good is the effect of a complete cause.[25] In other words, a war is just when it is waged in accord with all the criteria, whereas a war is unjust if it is waged without regard for any one of the criteria.

The Challenge for the Church

The challenge that conceiving of just war as a form of faithful discipleship presents to the church will be considered in more detail in the chapters that follow as we look at the different criteria and the particular difficulties involved. At this point we continue the trend of the previous chapters and consider more general challenges put to the church by the discipline as a whole. More specifically, we will take up three challenges that arise from this chapter's treatment of Just War (CD) as well as its presumptions and presuppositions.

Who We Are: The Question of Identity

The first of these challenges concerns identity. Distinguishing between a distinctly Christian and a modern secular strand of the just war tradition brings to the fore the question of who we are. What is the most basic reality, the fundamental story that anchors our identity? What is the first thing that comes to mind when we ask ourselves who we are? Do we think that we are fundamentally self-made, self-sufficient, independent individuals? At the core of our identity do we identify ourselves as citizens of a nation, party, or some interest or lifestyle group? Am I first and foremost a North American, a Democrat, a Marine, the bearer of a family name, a neo-conservative, a mother, a Braves fan, a hunter, an athlete, a teacher? In a similar manner, when we think of politics, do we think first in terms of nations, states, and secular governments? Do we assume that the primary and most important instruments of public and political life are nations and governments? This is to say, to what do we anchor not only our personal identity but also our political identity?

Just War (CD) starts from the premise that our identity, who we are, is anchored first and foremost in Christ. The center of our identity, the story that makes sense of all the other things we say about ourselves, the ultimate authority for our life, is Christ and the good news of what God in Christ has done, is doing, and will do in history. The most important thing that could be said about any of us is that we belong to Christ, and as members of Christ's body we share Christ's mission and ministry in and for the world. This does not mean that all the other things we might say about ourselves, all the other ways we would identify ourselves, or all the other groups to which we belong are unimportant, only that those other marks of our identity are secondary to our identity as members of Christ's body, the church. It does not mean that all other sources of moral guidance and authority are dismissed and ignored. Rather, it means that if or when those secondary authorities conflict with the moral vision that is ours in Christ, then like the apostles and saints before us we will say that we must obey God rather than any merely human authority (Acts 5:17).

Moreover, essential to the centrality of Christ and Christ's body to our identity is the recognition that the church is the first form of our politics. As suggested earlier, Just War (CD) is church centered. This means that when we think of political action and social change we do not think primarily in terms of public policy directives aimed at governments; rather, our politics are first embodied in our life together as a church body. Just War (CD) does not depend on persuading politicians and public policy shapers to embrace it; rather, it depends on the body of Christ embracing it. While we would certainly be happy to see politicians and governments embrace this just war discipline, our commitment to it does not depend on such an outcome. The viability or possibility of our living out Just War (CD) does not depend on governments endorsing it. This is the case because our primary political identity is rooted not in governments and nations but in Christ's body, the church. What is publicly or politically possible for us depends not on the policies of a given government but on the kind of life the body of Christ lives.

The challenge to the church, then, is to claim this public, political identity. It is who we are; do we recognize and affirm it? Do we believe, teach, and live as if our baptisms were more determinative of our identities than our passports? Do we remind one another that *whose* we are is the single most important mark of *who* we are? Do we as the body of Christ acknowledge and claim this kind of moral, public, and political authority? If not, why not? What are the obstacles to a robust Christian identity? Why do we grant to so many lesser authorities and groups a power over us that rightly belongs to Christ, to whom we belong? The list of reasons and obstacles is a long one. Contemporary culture tends to celebrate individualism and independence. Modern politics has reduced Christianity to an apolitical, spiritual, private reality. The church itself is broken and divided into squabbling and competing factions. The church has too often abused or squandered the public moral authority that it has had. The church itself has accepted its apolitical and privatized role and largely surrendered its moral authority. If we are to be a just war people who live just war as a form of faithful discipleship, then we will be about the task not only of learning the tradition but also of working to recover the centrality of the faith and, more specifically, the community of faith to who we are and how we live in the world. Only as we do this will just war be viable as a faithful form of discipleship.

Forming Character

The second challenge that arises from this chapter concerns how we envision the moral life and form people in it. Just War (CD) rests on a vision of character and virtue. While rules and laws are certainly an important part of the moral life, by themselves they are insufficient. Thus, Just War (CD) entails more than simply teaching people rules and laws and then exhorting them to muster the willpower to obey them. Rather, it involves forming character and instilling certain virtues that might sustain persons in their moral commitments even under the extraordinary stress of wartime and warfare. In this regard, Just War (CD) is more like learning a hobby or a craft than it is like memorizing multiplication tables.

Consider how one learns a craft or a hobby. Certainly one is required to learn the rules—like never sand against the grain of the wood, always preheat the oven, or the outfielder can call off an infielder on a pop fly—but to truly master a craft or hobby requires much more than merely learning the rules. It is as much a matter of mentoring and apprenticeship as memorization. Learning a craft or a hobby involves watching and imitating those who are masters of the craft. One must observe, imitate, practice, be corrected, and practice some more. And by means of the observation, imitation, practice, and correction, following the rules eventually becomes habitual, almost a second nature. When this happens, one no longer has to think about the rules and instead is freed to concentrate on those things that make the difference between a merely adequate performance and an excellent one. For example, one no longer has to think about dropping the elbow before swinging at a softball or lightly thumbing the reel at the end of the cast of a fishing lure. Instead, one's attention is freed to attend to the particular pitch or the contours of the shoreline, to the kinds of things that distinguish a novice from a master.

Thus, the challenge to the church is to reflect on how we conceive and implement moral training and formation. Particularly in recent centuries, Christianity has tended to conceive of the moral life as a matter of learning and abiding by certain rules and laws. Accordingly, the Christian life in general, and just war in particular, has been taught (if and when it has been taught) primarily as a matter of memorization and willpower. Learn the rules and will yourself to obey them. And so learning the Christian life has often been a matter of sitting around a dinner table, or in a classroom or a pew, being told the rules and exhorted to obey them (perhaps reinforced with threats or promises of dire consequences if one fails to obey). Relatively less attention has been given to character, virtue, and the mentoring/apprenticeship that is integral to growing in character and acquiring the virtues.

If we are serious about being a just war people who live out just war as a form of faithful discipleship, then we will need to be intentional about recovering moral formation and training in the church as a matter of mentoring and apprenticeship. If we are to be just in war, then not only will we need to learn the criteria that make war just, but we will also need to imitate those persons of virtue and character in our midst, thereby becoming virtuous and inhabiting the character that is necessary to sustain our moral commitments to the criteria in the midst of war. In addition to learning what the "rules" are (the criteria), we will need to practice being just, so to speak, in times of peace. By seeking justice and acting prudently in times of peace, we will be better prepared to do so in times of war. All of which means that moral training in the church must move beyond memorizing lessons and rules in the pews or Sunday school classrooms. Just as some churches have begun to recover the practice of mentoring young persons in the faith, a practice that exceeds mere memorization of rules and facts in the space of a Sunday school hour or youth group meeting, taking just war seriously as a faithful form of Christian discipleship requires a different approach to learning the moral life.

Living the Tradition

The third challenge arises out of the discussion of the tradition and its teeth. Recall that the tradition is abused when its teeth are either pulled or supplemented (as in "just war with too many teeth"). The challenge for the church in this regard is to embody the tradition with all of its teeth as a kind of mean between the errors of either too much or too little. In part this is the challenge of education, that is, learning the tradition with all of its teeth.

A just war people know the criteria and know when they are being ignored or manipulated. In part the challenge is that of being honest. Those who are opposed to all war should not attempt to manipulate just war criteria to condemn all war one war at a time. They would do better simply to make the case that just war is not morally or theologically justifiable. Likewise, those whose commitment to just war is conditional, holding only so long as just war does not jeopardize victory or survival or some other value, should not claim to be just warriors; for indeed, so long as they are ready and willing to discard the just war discipline when the costs of adhering to it are deemed too high, they are not.

This last comment brings to the fore the heart of the challenge presented by just war with teeth. Just War (CD) is a difficult discipline. It is a demanding tradition to embody. It asks a great deal of those who would be a just war people. After all, fighting a war justly may well be more costly in terms of both material resources and lives (friend and foe, combatant and noncombatant) and may take longer to conclude than some ways of fighting unjustly. Indeed, just war may require that one accept surrender and military defeat, if a war cannot be waged or won justly. It is not easy to be a just warrior or a just war people.

Among those Christians who profess to be pacifists, it is sometimes recognized that the call to live nonviolently in this world is a call to take up the cross. Indeed anyone, pacifist or not, who reflects on what it might be like to live nonviolently in this world knows how extraordinarily difficult that would be. Living the just war discipline as a genuine discipline with all its teeth, living it as a form of faithful discipleship, is no less difficult. To face the myriad challenges, risks, and terrors that personify war in accord with the discipline—abiding by its limitations when disregarding them might diminish the challenges, reduce the risks, and temper its terror—is an extraordinary thing. And in this way the just war discipline with all its teeth, as a form of faithful discipleship, may also be a form of taking up the cross.

The challenge to the church, then, is that of taking up this cross. Are we prepared to abide by the parameters of just war and to maintain its discipline—with all of its teeth—even when pulling some of those teeth and ignoring its strictures might reduce the risk, suffering, and loss that we and those we love would otherwise face? Or do we flee from the cross? Have we capitulated to a risk and suffering adverse culture that finally finds it difficult to name anything worth suffering and dying for, that is quick to surrender principle to expediency and survival? In the midst of a culture where everything is relative and all that is solid appears to melt into air, do we encourage one another to stand fast in our convictions, no matter the cost? Do we model for one another the courage to abide by our convictions and maintain the discipline of discipleship even when the path is steep and narrow? And do we comfort, support, and aid those who suffer much for courageously keeping the faith? Will we not only support but also encourage and embrace our sisters and brothers in the faith who speak and act for justice and against injustice in times of war?

4

Who's in Charge?

Legitimate Authority

The previous three chapters could be read as a kind of introduction to the moral life, for in each chapter we considered an important facet of what it means to follow Christ in the way of discipleship. Looking at the emergence of just war in the Christian tradition by way of Augustine, I argued that the Christian life is oriented by love. Discipleship is not a matter of resigning ourselves to sin and evil and merely attempting to pick from the available bad options for what we hope is the lesser evil. To the contrary, God in Christ has gathered a body of people and given them all they need to follow Christ faithfully in this world. This means we need not wage war as if it were inevitably hell but can abide by the just war discipline. In Christ, as Christ's body, we can be a just war people. Moreover, this way of discipleship is not first and foremost a matter of memorizing a list of rules and then summoning the willpower to abide by them. Although rules are important, they are only one part of a life that is finally a matter of character and virtue, about being a certain kind of people—a people who are graciously disposed by their very habits and instincts to love and seek justice for their neighbors.

So as we turn to the particular criteria that constitute the formal shape of Just War (CD), we are not suddenly lapsing back into a vision of rules, raw willpower, and public policy checklists. Although, as we have noted, the criteria are commonly used in exactly that manner as we consider them as part of Just War (CD), the criteria are not simply rules. Rather, they function more as markers that indicate the contours of a way of life. They are knots in the tapestry of the church's life; if you tug on them and follow them they will lead you deeper into the life of a people and their God. They are shorthand, if you will, for some of the central features of the way of life of the Christian community in a time of wars and rumors of wars as it seeks to faithfully follow its Lord in loving our neighbors.

In the chapters that follow we will examine each of the criteria with an eye to the contours of the way of life they outline and the challenges they present to the church's current way of life. The complete list of criteria is:

1. legitimate authority
2. just cause
3. right intent
4. last resort
5. reasonable chance of success
6. discrimination or noncombatant immunity
7. proportionality

This is a fairly standard way of listing the criteria, although as noted previously, because it is a fluid and living tradition there are variations, particularly with regard to the first five criteria. Sometimes, for example, what I treat under five headings will be presented by another in six or even seven headings. Furthermore, it is worth noting that it is not uncommon for the criteria to be divided into those that deal primarily with initiating or entering into war (commonly collectively referred to as *jus ad bellum* and encompassing the first five criteria) and those that deal with how one actually wages or fights a war justly (commonly collectively referred to as *jus in bello* and encompassing the last two criteria). To the first criterion that addresses justice in initiating or entering into war, namely legitimate authority, we now turn.

Who May Wage War?

The criterion of legitimate authority—or as it is sometimes called, "competent authority"—can be considered under two aspects. First, the criterion of legitimate authority addresses who may *wage* war, and second, it addresses who *determines* if waging war in a particular situation is just.

Just War (PPC)

The modern public policy checklist approach to just war holds that nation-states may legitimately declare and wage war. Granted it is not uncommon to hear claims that the Kellogg-Briand Pact of 1928 outlawed war or that the United Nations Charter strips states of the right to wage war, but the fact remains that the dominant vision of just war not only (rightly) disputes those claims but holds that nation-states are the only legitimate agents of war.[1] Ever since the Peace of Westphalia (1648) definitively marked the end of the Middle Ages and the establishment of the modern political order of nations and states, just war reflection has granted to nation-states, and only to nation-states, the right to wage war. Indeed, this monopoly on the legitimate use of violence has come to be essential to the very definition of a modern nation-state.[2]

That modernity ceded to nation-states a monopoly on violence and the right to declare war does not mean that either that monopoly or that right went entirely unchallenged. Even before the right to wage war was lodged solely in the hands of the nation-state, in the Middle Ages the question of revolution was raised. And the issue of a just or legitimate revolution continued to be pressed in the modern world. If anything, the question of the legitimacy of revolution has intensified in the modern world as anticolonial movements emerged and as peoples rose up against oppressive regimes and brutal tyrants. In other words, the restriction of legitimate authority to states has been challenged in the name of a host of non-state actors and entities. There have been efforts made at the level of international law to recognize what are commonly referred to as "irregulars" as legitimate combatants who are entitled to all the protections accorded regular national soldiers and combatants, but such efforts have not borne much fruit.[3]

In recent decades, the monopoly on the legitimate use of force granted to nation-states has been challenged from another direction as well. As the national and international debates surrounding the Gulf War in 1991 and the more recent war in Iraq revealed, there is a significant movement for reformulating legitimate authority in distinctly international terms. There is a push toward making legitimate authority a matter of international deliberation and authorization. This push is intensified by the recent and seemingly increasing calls for humanitarian interventions in the internal affairs of a host of nation-states, from Serbia to Sudan. The calls for humanitarian intervention affect the criterion of legitimate authority because the monopoly on violence granted to modern nation-states is closely linked with the notion of territorial sovereignty. In the modern world it is held, in theory if not always in practice, that the territory of a sovereign nation is inviolable. Nations are not to interfere in the internal affairs of other nations. Humanitarian interventions violate this principle of territorial sovereignty and thus undermine or diminish the authority of nations, frequently in the name of what is claimed as a higher international authority, such as universal human rights, the United

Nations, or NATO. In other words, humanitarian interventions subordinate national authority to an international authority backed by armed force and thus contribute to weakening the link between legitimate authority and the nation-state

Having named several forces that are currently putting pressure on the linkage of legitimate authority to wage war with the nation-state, it should be stated clearly that to this point, just war does not *require* international authorization or support. But because the tradition is a dynamic and living thing, it may well be the case that the tradition is moving in that direction, though it is not there yet.

Just War (CD)

At first glance and on the surface, Just War (CD) does not differ from the dominant vision of Just War (PPC) with regard to the legitimate authority to wage war. Legitimate authority to wage war resides in nation-states. As we dig below the surface, however, differences appear. To begin with, there is a difference in how that authority is conferred on nation-states.

Source of Authority

Just War (PPC)

As a thoroughly secular vision, Just War (PPC) anchors the legitimate authority of states to wage war in a natural right of self-preservation. In the modern world it is simply taken for granted that nations have a right to pursue and preserve their rights and interests against the encroachments and violations of those rights and interests by their neighbors. Granted, according to the just war tradition, nations do not have a right to pursue and protect *any* interest by means of war—the particular limitations and permissions in this regard will be considered under "just cause" as well as the other criteria. Nevertheless, legitimate authority is anchored in a natural right of self-preservation.

Just War (CD)

In contrast to this "naturally" derived authority to wage war, Just War (CD) asserts that there is a theological foundation for this legitimate authority. This is to say, humanity is not naturally endowed with the authority to wage war. Instead, this authority is conferred by God. The foundation for the authority to wage war is not natural but theological. Here we may recall Augustine's account of this authority. Discussing the commandment, "Thou shall not kill," Augustine argued that God is sovereign over life and death. God alone has final authority over life and death. Thus, we do not have a natural right to kill in self-defense. Yet, Augustine argued, God does share that authority over life and death with human beings.[4] Specifically, God shares that authority with those who have the responsibility of governing. As this came to be articulated in the tradition by the likes of Aquinas, Luther, and Calvin, among others, this delegation of authority over life and death was associated with Romans 13, where the apostle Paul wrote about the governing authorities, "there is no authority except from God, and those authorities that exist have been instituted by God. . . . It is the servant of God to execute wrath on the wrongdoer" (13:1, 4).

Anchored as it is in God's ordering of human life, the criteria of legitimate authority is integral to a larger theological vision of how human life is to be rightly ordered. To put this in the simplest of terms, in Just War (CD), "legitimate authority" arises out of and is irreducibly tied to a vision of God's political hopes and providential care for humanity. I say political hopes because politics in its proper form is about the right ordering of human community, and God created humanity to be in communion with God, one another, and all of creation. But with the irruption of sin ("the fall") the harmony of this original communion was shattered and a kind of civil war took its place. Instead of communion, human life under the sign of sin is marked by estrangement and conflict—with God, one another, and creation, something that the third chapter of Genesis portrays with powerful simplicity. Yet God in God's grace does not abandon us to our sin. Just as God clothed Adam and Eve and protected Cain after he slew his brother, God uses the governing authority to protect and preserve human life from its own worst depredations. This ordering of governing authorities to preserve with the sword of just war a kind of civic peace, a degree of what Augustine refers to as the "tranquility of order," is, of course, not all that God does to redeem humanity and restore us to the communion for which we were created. Rather, the pinnacle of God's redemptive activity takes shape in Jesus Christ and the communion of saints that he gathers. Nevertheless, God uses governing authorities to establish an earthly peace. God desires humanity to live in communion and not perish in the throes of constant civil war, so God uses governing authorities to restrain wickedness and keep the peace for the sake of the renewal and restoration of communion. The importance of this theological foundation of legitimate authority will become apparent as we proceed.

Even as Just War (CD) recognizes that the authority to declare war resides with nation-states, it is not immune from the pressures that challenge the restriction of this authority to nation-states. Like Just War (PPC), it too faces contemporary currents and trends that would diminish the authority of states in favor of the authority of the international community. This is not the first time that the Christian tradition has faced this kind of debate. In the Middle Ages, a similar discussion went on for several centuries regarding where, among the various feudal authorities, authority to declare war rests. As was the case with the secular vision of just war, there is not yet a just war requirement that nation-states seek and obtain international approval for waging war.

The Question of Revolution

The question of revolution also challenged the location of legitimate authority to declare or wage war solely in the hands of nation-states. The Christian tradition of reflection on just war has been reluctant to sanction what might be called "just revolution."[5] Within the tradition, however, there has developed a slight opening to the possibility of a just revolution. This slight opening is seen in the work of Thomas Aquinas, where he addresses the sin of sedition.[6] That he simply takes for granted that sedition is a very grave sin would at first glance appear to rule out revolution or civil war against the governing authorities. Yet as he unpacks the sin of sedition it becomes clear that there is a small space for a revolution. To understand his reasoning we need to recall the theological foundation of legitimate authority. God establishes the governing authorities for the sake of preserving and protecting the unity of peoples. We might say that God orders government for the sake of the common good. What makes sedition a sin is that it is an attack on this unity, communion, or common good. Hence, when a faction of persons rises up against the governing authorities who are doing their appointed job of safeguarding the common good of all, that faction is guilty of the sin of sedition, or undermining the common good of the community. So where is the space for revolution? It emerges in Aquinas when the governing authorities are tyrannical, by which he means that they govern not in accord with the common good of all but rather in accord with their own private, individual good. In such a situation there is no sedition in disturbing a government if it can be done without giving rise to even greater harm. In fact, Aquinas notes, it is the tyrant who is actually guilty of sedition, precisely for betraying his office and attacking the common good.[7]

In the centuries after Aquinas this space for a just revolution has not expanded significantly. For the remainder of the Middle Ages, theologians essentially affirmed Aquinas's conclusions, adding only the clarification that a just revolt must adhere to the other precepts of the just war tradition.[8] The

Protestant theologian John Calvin (1509–64) made a noteworthy contribution to this conversation when he argued that in the face of tyranny, private individuals do not have legitimate authority to revolt but that other magistrates—others who have been given governing authority either directly by God or by virtue of their appointed position in civil government—do have the authority to initiate resistance to a tyrannical government. Calvin goes so far as to suggest that the failure to withstand the "fierce licentiousness of kings" who "violently fall upon and assault the lowly common folk" is itself a "nefarious perfidy" that is nothing less than a betrayal of God's ordinance.[9] In more recent years, in the face of various revolutionary movements, a note of caution has been struck in church teaching. As Pope Paul VI wrote in 1967, "We know . . . that a revolutionary uprising—save where there is a manifest, long-standing tyranny which would do great damage to fundamental personal rights and dangerous harm to the common good of the country—produces new injustices, throws more elements out of balance and brings on new disasters. A real evil should not be fought against at the cost of greater misery."[10] This statement does not rule out just revolution, but in light of the grave temptations and difficulties that confront those who would venture down that path, it certainly puts a damper on revolutionary enthusiasm. In doing so, it is largely in keeping with the spirit of the tradition since Aquinas, who first acknowledged the possibility of a legitimate revolution against a tyrannical government but cautioned that revolution would not be legitimate if it led to greater harm than that which followed from enduring the tribulations of the tyrant.

Who Determines the Justice of War?

The second aspect of legitimate authority concerns who decides if a war is indeed just. Here again Just War (PPC) posits this authority in the hands of the nation-state. Sometimes it is argued that no one else has access to the information that is needed to make such a determination; in a similar vein, sometimes it is argued that persons who are not politicians lack the particular skills or expertise necessary for making such judgments. Sometimes it is argued that nongovernmental organizations such as the church can only offer general guidelines or remind the politicians of the moral rules but cannot themselves make any kind of judgment regarding how those rules apply in a particular situation.

As was the case with the assertion that the nation-state may wage a just war, the claim that the governing authorities of a nation-state decide the justice of a war has been tested by recent developments. In particular, there is some pressure to shift this authority in an international direction. But, as was the case with the question of who wages war, this shift has not (yet) happened. The authority to determine the justice of a war remains in the hands of national authorities.

This question of who determines the justice of a war is one place where the difference between Just War (PPC) and Just War (CD) is significant and important. To begin with, the *nature* of the authority granted to the state by Just War (CD) differs from that of Just War (PPC). Furthermore, whereas the standard checklist approach posits the power of decision in the state alone, the Christian tradition holds that there are actually three nodes of decision, including not only the state but also the individual and the church.

The State

Just War (PPC) grants to heads of state the authority to decide on the appropriateness of war on the basis of *power*. Just war was effectively secularized beginning in the seventeenth and eighteenth centuries, which unsurprisingly downplayed the moral or theological dimension of the prince's authority to wage war. In place of the moral or theological foundation arose what is called the doctrine of *compétence de guerre*.[11] It was simply assumed that if the prince had the power to make war and get away with it, then he had the authority. Even today, the argument for the authority of the state in matters of war is largely an argument about power. Thus the calls for a shift in the locus of legitimate authority to the international level are resisted, in part, on the grounds that there are no international agents that can reliably or competently exercise the power to effectively pursue justice. The UN, for example, does not possess that kind of effective power.

In contrast, Just War (CD) grants the state or heads of state legitimate authority to determine the justice of war based on the moral and theological vision previously spelled out. This is to say, the authority granted the head of state in matters of war is intrinsically related not simply to *power* but to the *responsibility* the governing authorities have for attending to the common good (recall Aquinas's account of sedition and tyranny, in which a tyrant is a ruler who pursues a private good instead of safeguarding the common good of the whole). In this regard, we might say that authority in matters of war is granted to particular persons on the basis of their holding a particular *office*. The authority to make determinations with regard to the justice of war is granted to holders of an office that is by definition responsible for preserving the common good. In other words, authority does not accrue to the head of state simply because it just so happens that is the place where the power to actually wage war is to be found, given the nature of politics today. In this regard, Just War (CD) does not understand governing authority to be a kind of prize that is fought over by two parties, with the winning party free to treat that authority as a prize that is now theirs to use as they wish to implement their private good/partisan agenda. Rather, in keeping with the Christian tradition's constant teaching in this regard, Just War (CD) acknowledges the proper role of governing authorities in determining the justice of war because God has delegated to the governing authorities the responsibility for looking after the common good. Furthermore, while it is the case that every vocation, calling, or office in society should contribute to the common good—from parent to single person to accountant to teacher to assembly line worker to retiree—not every office is charged with overseeing the common good as is the office of government.

If Just War (CD) differs from Just War (PPC) in that it connects legitimate authority with responsibility for the common good, it also differs with regard to the expectations of both character and counsel it places on the governing authority. As for the former, the expectation is that persons who fill the office of ruler will be persons of character. As Aquinas writes, "To discharge well the office of a king is . . . a work of extraordinary virtue."[12] In other words, the office of governing authority requires more than the ability to manage information and administer power; it requires a certain kind of character, a certain kind of moral formation such that those who would rule are capable of using the resources of the office well, that is, for the sake of the common good. For this reason Aquinas urges those responsible for filling the office of ruler to attend carefully to the character of the potential rulers.[13] In particular, the virtue that is paramount in a ruler is justice, since justice is the name of the virtue that oversees the common good of the whole community.

In so arguing, Aquinas reflects the heart of the Christian tradition, which anchors just war in a vision of how God desires human life to be ordered so that communion may flourish. And again we see that legitimate authority with regard to just war rightly attaches not simply to whoever happens to win a contest and seize a position like a prize. After all, as Aquinas notes, such a one might well lack the requisite character, become a tyrant, and so lose their claim to exercise legitimate authority. In other words, not only does Just War (CD) recognize legitimate authority attached to an office charged with overseeing the common good, but it also recognizes that authority attaches to a person or persons of well-formed character who care for the common good.

One might immediately object that such an expectation is unrealistic or utopian. Few would dispute that governing authority has often been exercised by persons of questionable character who have dismissed the common good in favor of private or partisan interests. The Christian tradition is not oblivious to this sad state of affairs. Hence, many in the Christian tradition have argued that such rulers are but punishment for a people's sins. At the very least, we might acknowledge Martin Luther's insight that we get the politicians we deserve, that rulers frequently reflect the character and virtues (or lack thereof) of their subjects.[14] Regardless of how we interpret the rule of the unjust and vicious, the point is that the Christian tradition is not oblivious to or unrealistic concerning the fallen nature of humanity or the difficulties that confront those who would rule and exercise legitimate authority.

Accordingly, the Christian tradition frequently has argued that the heads of state should not exercise the legitimate authority of their office without first heeding the counsel of wise advisors. As Vitoria says, a ruler, no less than a private subject, may act in error or under the sway of some passion, and so a person's opinion is not sufficient to make an action good. Rather, he says, opinions must be formed in accord with the judgment of the wise. For this reason, rulers are encouraged to listen to the arguments of opponents and to seek out the counsel of reliable and wise persons who can speak freely, without anger, hate, or greed.[15] He writes, "Besides, the king is not capable of examining the causes of war on his own, and it is likely that he may make mistakes, or rather that he *will* make mistakes, to the detriment and ruin of the many. So war should not be declared on the sole dictates of the prince, nor even on the opinion of the few, but on the opinion of the many, and of the wise and reliable."[16] In a similar manner, Grotius observes that sovereign princes are so consumed by the affairs of ruling that they have little time for the study and deliberation that are necessary to exercising sound judgment, and so he too exhorts rulers to consult the wise and experienced.[17] Francisco Suárez points out that it is precisely this access to public counsel that distinguishes public judgment from private inclination and assists the ruler in avoiding the problems that befall the judgments of individuals.[18] Vitoria goes even further and declares that in uncertain cases, it is a *requirement* that the wise be consulted and that a failure to heed the wise exacerbates the injustice of a wrong act or tarnishes the propriety of a good act.[19]

The Individual

The second node of decision in Just War (CD) involves individual subjects or citizens, be they soldier or civilian.[20] With regard to the standard public policy checklist approach, it is the case that some states do permit individuals to decide whether or not they will participate in a direct military manner in a war.[21] One form of such permission is the state's decision to forgo conscription and instead rely on an all-volunteer army. Individuals who are opposed to war may simply refrain from enlisting. A second form of permitting individuals to exercise some authority over their participation in war is the recognition by some states of what is called conscientious objection and/or the provision of alternative forms of service for those individuals who decide war is unjust or immoral. That states may permit this, however, does not mean that individuals have a *right* to make that determination for themselves and so opt out. Rather, such an option is a *privilege* granted and maintained solely at the state's discretion. In other words, even where states may permit individuals to decide, they are not required to do so. The privilege can be rescinded at any time. The public policy checklist approach does not hold that individuals should be permitted to exercise such judgment on war.

Just War (CD) holds that individual citizens—soldiers and civilians—are responsible for making a determination of the justice of a given war. To be sure, the extent of the responsibility that individuals hold differs according to their position in society. "Generals and other chief men of the kingdom," that is, persons who advise the governing authorities and shape public opinion, have a responsibility to investigate the justice of a war.[22] Lesser subjects, including ordinary soldiers, who neither advise the governing authorities nor shape public opinion, may simply follow the governing authorities, unless the injustice of a war is patently obvious.

From this hierarchy of responsibility for discerning the justice or injustice of war we can extract two complementary claims that form the bedrock of the Christian tradition with regard to the right and responsibility of the ordinary citizen to determine the justice of war. First, in the words of Vitoria, "if the war seems patently unjust to the subject, he must not fight, even if he is ordered to do so by the prince."[23] This is a strong statement that is made even stronger when Vitoria goes on to argue that persons must not go to war when their conscience convicts them of the war's injustice, even when their conscience is wrong.[24] At first glance, this claim might appear to thoroughly undercut the legitimate authority of the prince to wage war. After all, if everyone is permitted to decide for themselves whether to fight and their decision has to be honored even when it is obviously wrong, then the prince's authority is effectively reduced to nothing. Such a conclusion does not follow, however, for several reasons. To begin with, there is the second basic claim of the tradition, namely, that subjects owe the prince the benefit of a doubt. This is to say, if a subject or citizen considers a war and thinks it may not be just, then that subject should give the prince the benefit of a doubt. After all, Vitoria notes, a prince neither can nor ought always to explain the reasons for war to his subjects; there are times when the delay involved in offering such an explanation would put the state in grave danger.[25]

Thus, to summarize Just War (CD) on this point of individual responsibility for determining the justice or injustice of a war, we can say that subjects owe the governing authorities the benefit of a doubt. But when persons are certain that a war is unjust, they are not to fight, even if they are ordered to do so, and even if their judgment is wrong.[26] Furthermore, persons who contribute to the direction of the governing authorities and/or public opinion have a responsibility to examine the justice of a war while those who do not exert any influence on the governing or public mind do not.

The Church

The third node of decision in Just War (CD) is the church. The standard public policy checklist approach does not permit the church any say in the deliberations of state. At best, some proponents of this approach will concede to the church an indirect role that entails reminding the governing authorities of the moral values or criteria involved, but they do not recognize the church's authority to render a verdict on the justice or injustice of a war. This limitation on the church's public voice is part of the marginalization that the church suffered (which was in some ways self-inflicted) in the wake of the collapse of medieval Christendom and the birth of the modern world.

Just War (CD), being rooted as it is not in modern nation-states but in the church, does not accept this marginalization of the voice of faith. Indeed, it only makes sense that just war as a faithful form of following Christ would acknowledge the authority of Christ's body, the church. After all, it is the church and not the state that is our principal guide, along with the Holy Spirit, on the way of discipleship.

In upholding the authority of the church to speak publicly and politically about justice in war, Just War (CD) is again only following the mainstream of the Christian tradition. Augustine was not shy when it came to advising the governing authorities, not all of whom shared his faith.[27] Throughout the Middle Ages, the pope, bishops, and priests interceded, intervened, mediated, and sometimes issued blunt judgments regarding the justice or injustice of various wars.[28] Sometimes this exercise of authority took the form of public statements; sometimes it took the form of actually mediating between conflicting parties; sometimes it was a matter of hearing confession and imposing penance on returning soldiers; sometimes it took the form of advice given while serving as chaplains or spiritual directors to princes; sometimes it was a matter of declaring certain weapons unlawful or particular times, places, and persons off-limits to war. Such was the public influence of the church at its height that one historian could refer to the civil authorities as "merely the police department of the church."[29]

This strong role for the church in discerning the justice or injustice of war is reflected in the teaching of the church. So Aquinas writes that it is the duty of clerics to dispose and counsel others to engage in just wars;[30] Vitoria declares that the pope can act as judge between princes who are on the brink of war, inquire into their claims, and deliver a judgment that is binding;[31] and Suárez notes that if the pope issues a judgment against a war, the prince is thereby deprived of all right to make war.[32]

This robust vision of the church's direct role in political judgment has not simply vanished with the rise of modernity. The Roman Catholic Church continues to espouse the authority of the church to rule on matters of war.[33] Pope John Paul II's public remarks on the war in Iraq is a case in point.[34] The situation in Protestantism is a bit more complex. Many contemporary Protestant churches have at least formally all but relinquished this kind of direct public political authority. The actual practice of Protestantism, however, is more ambiguous when we consider the role it played in such matters as prohibition, the civil rights movement, and, more recently, the various causes championed by what is called the "religious right." Moreover, even as many Protestant churches espouse a kind of apolitical neutrality, the fact remains that many continue to expect that their pastors will follow Aquinas's instruction—they are expected to counsel their parishioners regarding military service, which could be interpreted as advising at the level of general principles but could also be interpreted in the more direct and concrete manner that is in keeping with the church's historic practice.

Taken as a whole, the tradition clearly recognizes the legitimate authority of the church to evaluate the justness of a war in its particulars and not simply at the level of abstract principles and norms. The church is well within its proper role when it speaks to the other two nodes of legitimate authority. It rightly speaks to the governing authorities, even to the point of issuing at times blunt pronouncements on the justice or injustice of a given war. It can do this not simply because it claims technical expertise in every aspect of modern war and geopolitics, although the church may well include within its communion persons who do have just such expertise and on which it can draw in offering its judgments. It can do this not simply because it claims to have all the information that governing authorities have, although as I will suggest in the next section, it should have that information and perhaps even more. It exercises legitimate authority because at least as important as information and expertise are character and formation in the virtues that make sound judgment possible, and the church is where God has promised to form persons and raise up leaders to render such judgments. It is through the church, if not *only* through the church, that God has chosen to make God's wisdom known to the rulers and authorities (Eph. 3:10).

In this regard the church addresses not only the first node of legitimate authority, the governing authorities, but the second node, individuals, as well. It rightly instructs individuals and forms consciences, so that disciples do not decide for or against a particular war on just any grounds. Thus, when Vitoria said that subjects should follow their consciences, he was not opening the door to a kind of relativism that would justify opposing a war for any reason at all, from its interfering with one's vocational plans to an inability to see a war in a distant land contributing anything to our national interest to an inarticulate and vague "feeling" that it is wrong. In the Christian tradition, conscience is not synonymous with what contemporary culture calls personal feeling or opinion. Indeed, integral to the Christian faith is the recognition that the pervasiveness of sin precludes our simply trusting our personal feelings, opinions, or "gut instinct." We are told to follow our consciences because it is assumed by the church that the consciences of disciples will be shaped by the grace of God through the various practices of the church, in accord with justice and righteousness. Immersed in the Word and the life of faith, our consciences are redeemed and become an extension of the character and virtues we graciously acquire in Christ.

Challenge for the Church

The criterion of legitimate authority is rich with challenges for the contemporary church that emerge out of our consideration of each locus of decision for the justice of war. We begin with the challenges that arise out of the legitimate authority that is lodged by God in the hands of the governing authority.

Supporting Good Leaders

Just War (CD) suggests that the kind of leaders we have has everything to do with whether or not we will be able to wage a war justly. This immediately raises the question, what kind of politicians and politics do we support? Insofar as legitimate authority is associated with responsibility for the common good, we might ask ourselves if we support persons who display a commitment to govern with an eye toward the common good. Do we encourage the governing authorities to pursue the common good rather than national interest narrowly conceived? Do we approach and endorse politics as a kind of prize fight, where the winner takes all with the expectation that they may use the "prize" of political office as an instrument to advance particular instead of common interests? Have we embraced interest group politics whereby contemporary political parties and movements frequently identify with a narrow range of interests to the exclusion of others: business versus environment, labor versus management, black versus white, Christian versus secular, young versus old, living versus unborn, rich versus poor, and so forth?

We might also ask ourselves whether we preach, teach, and otherwise embody in our own life a passion for the common good, such that politicians know that if they desire our support then they must be committed to the common good. Or does the church present itself as just another "interest group" out to advance its own private good or goods in competition with other interest groups? Do we perpetuate a kind of politics that might be cast as "war by other means" (to invert Clausewitz's famous aphorism), or does our political life point to a kind of politics that is what politics is actually supposed to be about—the nurturing of human community? Said differently, do we embrace a political stance that is little more than a continuation of the civil war begun in the fall, or do we embody a new kind of politics, appropriate to our new life in Christ, the One in whom all things hold together (Col. 1:17)?

Do we raise up leaders both in the church and in the wider society who are persons of character, who display the virtues such as justice that are integral to working on behalf of the common good and to inspiring others to do so as well? Or do we settle for those who will doggedly pursue some partisan agenda or private good (especially if it is our own private good) with little regard for the good of all? Do we expect our leaders to be wise, prudent persons capable of exercising sound judgment in difficult and demanding circumstances? Or do we sanction governing authorities who resemble weather vanes, shifting (flip-flopping) to and fro with every swing of the opinion polls? Do we expect our leaders to be temperate, neither asking of us nor promising to give us more than is possible or appropriate? Or do we fall in line behind those who promise what we want to hear with little regard for what they can or should deliver? Do we nurture and endorse political leaders who will be courageous, doing the right thing, even in the face of shifting opinion polls and partisan attacks?

Beyond what we expect of the character of the leaders themselves, do we ask that they surround themselves with and heed, not partisan hacks and ideological sycophants who toe a party line or simply echo and amplify judgments of the governing authorities, but advisors who display virtue and who, as Vitoria noted, will share their wisdom, insight, and judgment without fear of disagreement?

Granted, the connection between each of these virtues and just war may not be obvious, especially when we are used to thinking of just war as a kind of public policy checklist that can be used by anyone, with little regard for character. But, as we will see, these virtues in leaders and advisors are crucial to our ability to be a just war people. For example, the virtue of justice, unsurprisingly, is crucial to executing a war that well serves not simply a narrow national interest but the common good of all peoples—citizens, neighbors, and enemies alike. Likewise, given the grave consequences and difficult circumstances that surround decisions in times of war and rumors of war, prudence is of utmost importance. Similarly, temperance is necessary so that just warriors do not overreach, either inflicting more harm than justice would require or exacting more in restitution than justice would permit, thereby falling into the vice of vindictive revenge. And courage or fortitude is required in order to abide by the just war tradition in the face of the manifold pressures (rising casualties, shifting opinion polls, national pride that refuses to accept defeat or surrender, etc.) that would tempt one to stray from its parameters.

Forming Faithful Disciples

With regard to the second point of decision, that of individual soldiers and citizens, the challenges to the church are similar insofar as the body is challenged to teach, preach, and form it members in the virtues so that they might duly serve the common good by supporting only just wars. Here I reiterate and expand on challenges stated previously. The challenge to the church is to teach the tradition as a discipline, as a faithful form of discipleship, instead of leaving our formation in this regard up to the talking heads, newspaper columns, and so forth that treat just war like a public policy checklist. The challenge is to be intentional about forming faithful consciences instead of leaving such formation principally in the hands of the vast array of voices and visions present in contemporary society that advocate a moral vision very different than that of the faith. The challenge is to be deliberately about the work of cultivating the virtues, like justice, prudence, courage, and obedience, that are crucial for soldiers and subjects to inhabit the tradition as a faithful form of discipleship. The challenge is to foster a theological vision of political life and the proper role of governing authorities in that life, to form a people who recognize both the legitimate authority that God delegates to governing authorities as well as the limits of that authority, which, as we have seen, are a matter of the common good, the benefit of the doubt, and heeding one's conscience. We must do all of this not only in times of war but also in times of peace, since Just War (CD) is part of a way of life that cannot be learned in an instant on the eve of or in the midst of war.

Furthermore, the challenge facing the church is that of assuring those of us who would be governing authorities, their advisors, or soldiers that such persons will have the spiritual and material support of the church as they abide by the tradition, whether that takes the form of refusing to support or fight in an unjust war or of supporting or fighting in a war, but only in accord with the just war discipline. In this regard, intrinsic to the just war discipline is what is commonly called selective conscientious objection (SCO). Being a just war people entails actively supporting and advocating that the governing authorities recognize SCO. Just War (PPC) lodges legitimate authority solely in the hands of heads of state but allows that states might grant individuals the privilege of refusing to fight in *all* wars. The renunciation of all war is referred to legally as "conscientious objection," and some nation-states, such as the US, currently excuse conscientious objectors from military service. Conscientious objector status, linked as it is to a renunciation of *all* war, however, is not adequate for dealing with just war because being committed to just war does not entail a refusal to participate in *all* wars.[35] Rather, a just war people will support and fight in just wars even as they will refuse to support and fight in unjust wars. This *selective* support of or opposition to a particular war based on the justice or injustice of that specific war necessarily expresses itself in the call for the governing authorities to recognize *selective* conscientious objection, which would recognize the right of persons to refuse to fight in a war they conscientiously deem unjust. Granted, determining how to go about recognizing SCO would not be easy, just as recognizing a principled or virtuous opposition to all war along the lines of conscientious objection is not easy. Shortly I will offer one possible way to think about this.

Where the state refuses to heed such a call, in the absence of the legal recognition of SCO by the governing authorities, the church is put in a position where it will have little choice but to confess with the early disciples, "we must obey God rather than any human authority" (Acts 5:29). In such a situation, being a faithful just war people and supporting our sisters and brothers who are committed to being just warriors entails our encouraging and supporting them as they resist being compelled to fight unjustly. Such support and encouragement might take several forms, including advocating on behalf of changes in military and/or political policy to bring such policies in line with justice, as well as offering spiritual and material support to our Christian sisters and brothers who are soldiers or advisors to the governing authorities (and their families) as they confront and deal with the manifold repercussions for their faithfully abiding by Christian just war convictions and refusing to fight an unjust war.

Reasserting Church Authority

The challenges associated with the third point of decision, the church, may well be the most daunting of all, for the expectation that the church should exercise legitimate public, political authority moves against the tide of hundreds of years of the church's history in the West. Indeed, modernity's depoliticizing of the church and cordoning it off safely in a disembodied realm of the spirit, where it trades in abstract values and principles, is often celebrated by Christians and non-Christians alike as a great accomplishment. Of course, this political marginalization of the church is not *uniformly* celebrated because persons on all points of the politics-and-faith spectrum have on occasion shown themselves to be quite amenable to the church recovering from its political laryngitis when doing so has meant the church sounded the proper political note, as per the civil rights movement in the 1960s or the anti-abortion movement more recently.

Nevertheless, that Just War (CD) recognizes a legitimate, authoritative, immediately political role for the church presents a significant set of challenges to the church. To begin with, there is the problem presented by the brokenness of the church. The division of the church undermines its public political authority in at least two ways. First, the fractured nature of the church diminishes the authority of its words and judgments to the extent that what one part of the body does, another part may undo. Thus, even as one part of the church may determine a war to be just, another part may declare that same war to be unjust, or vice versa. In either case, the viability of just war as a faithful form of discipleship is undermined as the governing authorities are no longer faced with a worthy conversation partner that must be taken seriously but instead may merely shop around until they find a church that will inevitably sign on to the particular war favored by the governing authorities. Historically, to the extent that the just war tradition functioned, it did so at least in part because the church was able to speak with a unified voice. In this respect, recall Grotius's lamentation on the failure of Christian discipline in war, a lamentation that coincided with the breakup of the church into factions that, far from speaking with one voice, were now fighting each other.

Second, the division of the church undermines its political authority because what the governing authorities may do, namely shop around for a church that agrees with them, Christians may do as well. Not only does the division of the church diminish its authoritative voice before the governing authorities, but it also reduces the weight of its words with its own members. If I do not agree with what a particular church says, I do not have to stay there and wrestle with it; all I have to do is go down the street to another church more to my liking—not unlike the way I surf the dial looking for the news that suits my particular ideological disposition.

Therefore, one challenge presented to the church by Just War (CD) is that of working to overcome the divisions of the church so that we may speak both to the world and to ourselves about justice in war in a manner that may carry some authority and thus be heeded.

A second challenge to the church is that of facing the displeasure of the nation-state with the courage of our convictions. Although nations may proclaim their hospitality to the faith, it is not unreasonable and certainly not unprecedented to expect that the church may face unwelcome consequences for coming out of the apolitical shadows and reasserting its legitimate public authority, especially with concrete judgments of war and peace, where for several centuries states have held nearly unchallenged authority. The spectrum of anticipated possible consequences spans from persecution and martyrdom (recall Jägerstätter) to the loss of favorable tax status to the sudden closing of channels that provided access to and influence on matters of government. Whatever the costs, great or small, the challenge is to face them with the same faith and fortitude displayed by the saints who have gone before us.

Another challenge presented by the recognition of the legitimate political authority of the church with regard to just war is that of the character of the church's leaders. Earlier it was argued that Just War (CD) implies certain expectations with regard to the kinds of persons who serve in the offices of governing authority—they should be persons of character, who serve the common good instead of private or partisan goods and so forth. In like manner, the public political authority exercised by the church carries with it certain expectations about the kinds of leaders the church calls to order its own life. Just War (CD) presupposes the presence in the church of faithful leaders who are persons of character, know the tradition, and are capable of exercising sound moral judgment with regard to matters of war and peace. This, of course, does not mean that they necessarily must be technical experts in military or geopolitical affairs, only that they are the kinds of persons who would surround themselves with wise and faithful advisors in such matters.

Hence, insofar as we truly desire to be a faithful just war people, we might ask ourselves how the church calls its leaders. By what criteria are they selected? Do the qualities of character, the virtues commensurate with leading the church faithfully in just war, play a significant part in their selection? Or do managerial, bureaucratic, therapeutic, or partisan values tend to carry more weight? Another way to approach this might be by asking if we encourage, support, and call leaders whose judgment on such matters we would trust and obey, even to the point of going ourselves or sending our loved ones to fight in a war they declared just or, conversely, even to the point of refusing to fight—and facing the consequences of such a refusal, no matter how dire—in a war those leaders declared unjust. The challenge of Just War (CD) to the church is that of raising up the kinds of leaders we would trust not only with our own lives but with those of our loved ones.

Gathering Reliable Information

Related to the nature of church leadership is the question of information. Already I have attempted to distance Just War (CD) from those who would tie legitimate authority and the right to make judgments on war primarily to information, as if what underwrites the legitimate authority of the governing powers is their privileged access to the information necessary to make decisions regarding war and peace. After all, access to information does not ensure its proper use or sound decisions. Instead, I have suggested that mere access to information is not sufficient; at least as important as information is formation in the kind of character and habits of discernment and judgment that would dispose one to use information appropriately, considering it carefully, neither neglecting nor manipulating nor distorting it for partisan or ideological ends. Having said this, it must also be said that information is not unimportant or irrelevant to sound judgments, and so if the church, no less than the individual subject or soldier, is to make sound decisions, it needs to consider its sources of information regarding situations of war and rumors of war.

Many have noted the difficulty of discerning what really is the case in an age of terminal spin, public relations, propaganda, plausible deniability, and what is politely given the euphemism "disinformation."[36] Modern war is more than a clash of warriors, wills, wits, and weapons; it is war that is advertised, marketed, and relentlessly sold to the domestic public as well as the rest of the world.[37] The difficulty of discerning "what is the case" in the face of such control of information by governments and militaries has reached the point that some suggest that the "benefit of a doubt" traditionally owed to the governing authorities by the just war discipline no longer holds. It is argued that continuing to grant the benefit of a doubt to a system that does not have truthfulness as its baseline and has within its reach powerful resources for masking its lies all but ensures that the just war discipline will not be able to exercise its proper discerning function.[38] In effect, the suggestion is that a posture of suspicion replace the earlier posture. Others take an even harder line, asserting that given the nature of the control and manipulation of information operating in modern nation-states, Christians *cannot* know what they would need to know in order to determine that a war or prospective war is just and thus ought to be supported, and therefore Christians cannot fight.[39]

The challenge for the church, then, is this: If the just war discipline is to avoid the conclusion that we cannot know what is going on and therefore cannot exercise the legitimate authority necessary for declaring and waging a just war, then the church must carefully and diligently reflect on the sources from which it draws knowledge of what is the case in matters of war and peace. How reliable are those sources? To what extent can they be trusted? Furthermore, part of the challenge put to the church by the issue of the need for reliable information is that of developing new and/or existing channels of information that may better circumvent the various spin machines that launder and distort the picture of reality we are given. In this regard, it should not be overlooked or undervalued that the church is truly a transnational entity. Indeed, this was true long before talk of "globalization" and "transnational corporations" became popular. Thus, perhaps exercising legitimate authority in just wars will require the church to be more intentional about fostering the ties that bind us to our sisters and brothers around the world in one faith, one hope, one baptism. If we are indeed one great body, then there is no reason the church needs to rely solely on the (dis)information provided by governing authorities, their PR machines, and embedded media. In fact, there is in principle no reason why we cannot rely on the hospitality of each other not only to hear about what is the case but also to go and see for ourselves, in a kind of church fact-finding mission or "church-exchange" program. Of course, the success of such efforts will depend in part on the church's working to overcome the various confessional, cultural, and national barriers to our unity.

Critically considering our current sources of information and developing new sources, especially by means of strengthening the ties between Christians around the world, is all well and good. Such efforts would no doubt aid the church in properly exercising its legitimate authority over just wars. But it cannot be denied that governing authorities can, by virtue of their particular combination of political authority and resources, have information that may not be readily available elsewhere. Hence, it would be good if the church had access to that information as it deliberated about war. Granted, no government is a vault and so there are always unofficial means of gaining access to the same information that states have. In the context of Just War (CD)'s criterion of legitimate authority, however, both the church and the state would be better served if this sharing of information were formal and official.

This is the case because Just War (CD) does not set out to be antagonistic to the governing authorities and their judgments concerning war. As the theological vision of politics we considered earlier suggested, the church recognizes that God has delegated authority to wield the sword in just wars to the governing authorities, and the church has no desire to impede that God-given task. The church also recognizes that the authority to determine the justice of wars is a shared responsibility. It is in the spirit of this shared responsibility that the church should have access to the information the governing authorities are using in their deliberations concerning war. Not only would this aid the church in its discernment but it would also permit the church to maintain the posture of the "benefit of a doubt" that the tradition grants to the governing authorities. While it is true that permitting the church to see what the rulers know and letting those rulers make the case for the justice or injustice of a war might result in the church rejecting the rulers' judgments, if the governing authorities were indeed wrong in their judgment, then there is no harm done. On the contrary, it is to the benefit of the state that it refrain from waging unjust wars or that it be encouraged to wage just wars (for example, in a situation where perhaps a state selfishly or unjustly refused to intervene in a genocidal conflict in a neighboring state). But such consultation need not necessarily result in a rejection of the state's case. It could result in the church agreeing with the argument, supporting the just war, and forming the consciences of its members accordingly. Or it might result in a disagreement, but with the church recognizing that the case in question is a difficult call and that the government's argument is not obviously morally flawed, and so granting the government the benefit of a doubt.

But, we might ask, does not this suggestion run afoul of the tradition's recognition that the prince need not always explain himself or his decisions to his subjects? Certainly it might if it entailed state secrets being revealed wholesale and the legitimacy of a war being put to a church-wide referendum. There is another way to think about this, however. Specifically, something like this sharing and consultation might happen if the church were to select a few leaders to carry out this consultation who could then be granted the necessary security clearances and so forth. The viability of such a proposal would hinge on many things, not the least being the character of the church leaders so chosen, which only further highlights the previous challenge regarding the nature of the leaders the church calls and our willingness to follow their judgments.

For some this challenge of sharing information will undoubtedly sound rather startlingly novel if not a bit farfetched; yet for others this will sound like old hat. Why? Because there is already a practice in place in some churches and militaries that, at its best, permits and encourages some form of moral consultation and advising. That practice is military chaplaincy. Since the early Middle Ages when Christian ministers accompanied units attached to the Roman army in order to lead worship and offer the sacraments to soldiers, the church has consistently been engaged in ministry in the midst of war and warriors.[40] This, in turn, has prompted theological reflection on the proper role of clergy in the midst of war. While the church has typically—although not unanimously—prohibited its clergy from shedding blood or encouraging slaughter, it has consistently blessed tending to the spiritual needs of soldiers, exhorting soldiers to be courageous and stand fast in their moral commitments, and morally evaluating the conduct of soldiers through the practice of confession and penance.[41] In more recent times, some military chaplains have been permitted to function as moral advisers to military commanders, offering an ethical evaluation of the justice or injustice of various proposed courses of actions. This suggests that the proposal for sharing and consultation is not that far-fetched.

Although the practice of chaplaincy gestures toward the possibility of the kind of consultation or advisement suggested here, chaplaincy itself does not in any simple and straightforward manner provide a model for how such consultation might occur. It is far from clear that chaplaincy, as it has been practiced thus far, is capable of sustaining the kind of independent theological judgments that Just War (CD) calls on the church to make. The historical record reflects, and many chaplains confirm, that the chaplaincy has with unsettling frequency fallen prey to nationalistic rhetoric that has overwhelmed theological reflection, with the result that chaplains (sometimes unwittingly and often unwillingly) have blessed brutality and injustice, thereby serving neither the nation nor the church well.[42]

Accordingly, Just War (CD) may challenge the church's practice of chaplaincy in favor of developing models that strengthen the hand of chaplains such that they are able to better withstand the multitude of personal and institutional factors that work against their moral voices being heard and respected. In this regard, from time to time suggestions have been raised about the propriety of chaplains serving in uniform, as officers subject to the military chain of command, paid by the military, and so forth. It may be the case that, if the church wishes to exert its legitimate authority regarding the justice of wars in which its members fight, such proposals need to be seriously considered.

The real issue that drives these and similar questions is that of the chaplain's ability to exercise sound theological judgment without it being distorted by or subordinated to narrow nationalistic or partisan interests and objectives. Such a concern is born not of a suspicion of chaplains but of the recognition that Christian discipleship cannot be sustained by solitary individuals, particularly amidst the stresses of war. Thus proposals to make chaplaincy more independent of the military are not about further isolating chaplains but instead about reconnecting them more substantially and supportively to the church that calls and should actively support them.

Toward this end, perhaps the church's exercise of its legitimate authority with regard to war should be conceived institutionally as a kind of ellipse with two foci—the political and the military. Thus, the church would engage in consultation and advisement with the governing authorities at two principal points. Consultation and advisement would begin outside the military in the political realm with church leaders in conversation with governing authorities, but would extend in and to the military through the chaplaincy. Some such practice of legitimate authority could strengthen the hand of chaplains in the military, particularly insofar as it was part of the church's reclaiming its legitimate moral authority over war and peace such that any governing authority who desired Christian soldiers to fight in a war would need to have the church's leadership on board. Backed up by the church's public authority in this way, chaplains could not so easily be bypassed or bullied. Additionally, such a conception and practice of moral oversight might enhance chaplains' voices in the church as well, allowing them to play a crucial role in the church's discernment process as well as helping them maintain their proper theological priorities.

In the final analysis, the criterion of legitimate authority as part of Just War (CD) challenges the church to reclaim its identity as an exemplary form of human community. The criterion of legitimate authority calls the church to recover its political voice, not only shaping the character and consciences of its members, but reminding the governing authorities of this world of their responsibility to work for the common good by making concrete judgments about justice and war. If earlier chapters challenged Christians to reclaim the centrality of the faith to our way of seeing and acting in the world, such that our baptisms are more determinative of who we are than our passports, this chapter puts that challenge to Christians collectively as the body of Christ, the church.

If this is a rather unsettling suggestion, it is understandably so, given that for several centuries Christianity has more or less viewed itself as a sort of apolitical spiritual custodian of the values that underwrite modern civilization. For centuries, the church has more or less accepted its banishment from the political realm and contented itself with consoling souls instead of discipling bodies. But this cannot continue if it is to embody just war as a form of faithful discipleship. The church must pray for the wisdom to discern and the courage to speak not merely about abstract values, principles, and guidelines but about concrete practices of justice and injustice in the midst of wars and rumors of wars. It must risk speaking the wisdom of God to the rulers and powers of this world, not for the sake of thwarting them at every turn but so that those rulers and powers might be about their appointed work of serving the common good. And it must act in accord with its own insight by teaching, encouraging, and supporting its own members to fight just wars and to refrain from fighting unjust ones, whether or not the nations agree.

In essence, Just War (CD) calls the church to reassert its theological and political independence from the nation-states that succeeded in domesticating it with the arrival of modernity. At the end of the Middle Ages, when the church's political presence was slowly but surely evaporating, theologians and other church leaders discussed the appearance of what were then commonly called mercenaries but what today might be called "independent contractors." These were small political entities that existed alongside and within other political bodies and that would offer themselves in service to others. Theologians such as Suárez argued that this practice was permissible so long as such units were oriented not toward profit and gain but toward justice. And indeed the Vatican itself hired mercenaries to protect its grounds. In a sense, this is what the church in this postmodern age is called to be, a kind of independent contractor. Legitimate authority presumes the presence of the church as an independent political body that would not fight to defend itself (recall Augustine and company's rejection of lethal self-defense), but who out of love for our neighbors will serve the governing authorities in their proper, just efforts to protect and preserve the common good. This—the reasons why we will fight—brings us to the next criterion, just cause, and the challenges it offers the church.

Why Fight?

Just Cause

Having considered who may wage a just war and who determines if a war is just, we now turn to the question of *why* one wages just war. The answer to this question encompasses two criteria, the first of which is just cause, the subject of this chapter. Just cause focuses primarily on the enemy or potential enemy's behavior. It considers what an enemy or potential enemy must be guilty of, what offense they must commit, or what injury they must inflict in order to be rightly subject to the judgment of a just war. What offenses, when not corrected, stand as causes for a just war?

Here, the difference between Just War (PPC) and Just War (CD) is substantial. Although the two approaches share some convictions regarding what does and does not constitute a just cause for war, the basic orientations of the two approaches are quite different. One revolves around self-defense, to the point that it struggles to articulate a consistent rationale for humanitarian intervention. The other is fundamentally other-directed, to the point that self-defense is not relevant to deliberations of just cause. As a result, these two strands of just war presuppose two very different kinds of communities and politics, with different understandings and practices of justice. We begin by considering just cause according to the public policy checklist approach.

Just Cause in the Modern World: Self-Defense

With the passing of the Middle Ages and the advent of modernity, the criteria that addressed justice in going to war declined in importance to the point that the ruler or state was simply assumed to exercise a certain *compétence de guerre*. If they could wage war and get away with it, then it was assumed they had the right to do so. In a very real sense, might made right. By the late nineteenth century, however, as the intensity and destructiveness of wars increased, a movement was born to rein in the excesses of war. This movement first took shape in the codification of the international laws of war, and then in the reemergence of the just war tradition in the middle of the twentieth century.

What is of particular interest with regard to the criterion of just cause is the way in which this modern recovery of just war understood just cause. Reaching back to the earlier tradition that had been forgotten for several centuries, the modern push to restrain war recovered an ancient distinction between aggressive and defensive wars, and it identified just cause solely with defensive wars. No doubt as a reaction against the proliferation of aggressive wars over the previous centuries, Just War (PPC) construes just cause in terms of self-defense. A nation has just cause for war when it, or its allies, has been unjustly attacked.

This modern equation of just cause with self-defense is perhaps nowhere more evident than in the Charter of the United Nations. Although it is sometimes argued that the UN Charter deprives nations of the right to resort to war in self-defense, in fact the charter is clear in asserting that states may act militarily in (and only in) self-defense.[1] Article 51 of the charter states this clearly when it says, "Nothing in the present Charter shall impair the inherent right of individual or collective self-defence if an armed attack occurs against a Member of the United Nations."[2] Granted, this right of self-defense is not unlimited; the charter goes on to qualify it by adding the restriction that such a right is in play only until the UN Security Council takes the necessary measures to rectify the situation and restore international peace and security. Nevertheless, it is clear: war is permissible in self-defense.

At first glance, equating just cause with self-defense might appear rather simple and straightforward. After all, everyone knows what self-defense is. Or do we? In reality, applying the self-defense justification for military action is more complicated than one might imagine. In fact, equating just cause with self-defense requires that at least two further questions be answered.

Military Action or Police Action?

The first question concerns who or what is properly the object of defensive *military* action. Or, put more generally, when does the just *war* discipline apply? After all, a common crook or a band of robbers could be understood as engaged in an act of aggression against a nation-state and its citizens. Would such an armed attack qualify as a just cause for a military response? The point is that some acts of aggression and even some armed attacks are more properly addressed not by means of a defensive war but by police or law-enforcement action. This is why we commonly distinguish between criminal acts and acts of war and why many nations establish a legal barrier between domestic policing and the military.

What guidance does Just War (PPC) provide for determining that an armed attack is a just cause for a military response? Put simply, war is an affair of states. Yet in the previous chapter's treatment of legitimate authority we noted that this "statist" orientation of Just War (PPC) has come under pressure from a variety of non-state forces and what are called asymmetrical (that is, non-state versus state) conflicts. Guerrillas, rebellions, civil wars, and terrorist organizations all challenge the assumption that just war is solely an affair of states. We see this challenge manifest today in debates regarding who qualifies as a legitimate combatant and who is subject to the protections of the laws of war. Likewise, this issue is at the heart of numerous debates over the proper way to respond to terrorism, specifically, whether that confrontation should be guided by the rules and tactics of a police/law-enforcement approach or whether the terrorists should be engaged militarily in a war, as well as how terrorists are to be interrogated, tried, and punished.

Efforts to adapt Just War (PPC) to these old pressures and new realities have been halting at best. Efforts to broaden the protections of the laws of war to cover "irregular" or non-state actors have been resisted by the nation-states that ratify and finally enforce the laws of war. Likewise, although a few voices have asserted that a military response to acts like terrorism is justified because the international infrastructure necessary for the police/law-enforcement model to work is missing, so far there has been little serious engagement with the issue.[3] As a result, in the end Just War (PPC) does not offer much guidance in the way of determining who is rightly subject to a military response. It assumes that the just war discipline applies when nations fight other nations. Beyond this, it leaves the decision regarding military versus police action in the hands of the legitimate authority narrowly conceived as the national governing authorities.

What May Be Defended?

The second question that needs to be answered with regard to self-defense as just cause for war concerns *what* exactly merits a military defense. After all, not just any offense against a nation constitutes just cause for military self-defense. For example, the leader of one nation may insult or ridicule the leader or people of another nation, yet while such an attack on a people's honor or pride may be offensive and might merit some response, wounded pride would not constitute a just cause for *military* self-defense.

What does constitute just cause is a breach of national sovereignty or territorial integrity. The modern political order of nation-states, in theory if not always in practice, regards as sacrosanct national sovereignty and territorial integrity. Accordingly, a nation-state has just cause to defend itself militarily when either its political sovereignty or its territorial integrity is violated. For the most part, what constitutes territorial integrity is straightforward. A nation-state has just cause to respond militarily if its borders and boundaries are violated by the encroachments of another nation. Where matters get a little trickier concerns political sovereignty. On one hand, political sovereignty can be equated simply with the ability of the governing authorities to govern effectively. Thus, national sovereignty is challenged by an attempt to overthrow the government or by disrupting the government's ability to protect its citizens by, for example, launching a missile strike that kills a number of a nation's citizens. In both of these situations, military self-defense would be justified.

On the other hand, matters get a little more difficult when the meaning of national sovereignty is enlarged and equated with the preservation of values or the pursuit and protection of national interests. In such situations, the right of military self-defense can expand to include not only national territory, citizens' lives, or viable governance but also a particular way of life and all that is required to preserve it. Thus, for example, Michael Walzer argues that a just cause exists when the values constitutive of a nation's way of life are put at risk.[4] In its most extreme form, this expansion of self-defense can encompass the entire globe as a nation goes to war in defense of certain values not only when those values are threatened within its borders but even when they are threatened anywhere around the world. The same holds for national interests. When national or political sovereignty is linked to national interests, self-defense can go global as a nation seeks to protect resources and political arrangements around the world that are deemed crucial to its national interest. This is especially the case when the interests of one nation are deemed beneficial to all nations.[5] In this way, when one "indispensible nation" aggressively pursues its global interests, it can claim at the same time to be engaged in a kind of collective self-defense.

What we see here is a certain ambiguity with regard to what just cause as self-defense entails. As part of Just War (PPC), self-defense as just cause for war can cover a wide spectrum of offenses. In its narrowest sense, just cause encompasses violations of national territory or undermining the political sovereignty of a nation. In its broader sense, it may include attacks on the values that undergird a way of life and/or threatening national interests, wherever and however those interests are defined. Indeed, when self-defense expands to include defense of values and interests, the distinction between aggressive and defensive wars on which the modern understanding of just cause hinges is blurred beyond the point of being useful.

Before considering just cause according to Just War (CD), it is worth highlighting one important reality that is *not* identified as a just cause for war—religion. Given the historical developments that resulted in the secularization of just war, this should come as no surprise. Modernity continues to perpetuate the myth that it was born in part as a reaction against bloodshed in the name of religion. Insofar as Just War (PPC) buys into this myth, it holds that differences of religion cannot be a just cause for war. Just as the public policy approach does not recognize the legitimate authority of the church with regard to decisions on the justice or injustice of a war, it does not recognize religion as a just cause of war.

Just Cause and Christian Discipleship: Which Justice?

Before we can consider what offenses constitute legitimate causes for war according to Just War (CD), it is necessary to reflect for a moment on the nature of the justice that characterizes just cause. This is to say, we might begin by asking whose justice or what justice are we talking about when we talk about just cause. After all, justice can mean many different things; it can be calculated in many different ways. It could be a matter of equal opportunities or equal outcomes. It could be a matter of distributing things according to need or according to merit. It could be a matter of simply following the rules, enforcing contracts and agreements, making sure individuals get what is due them, seeing to it that the disadvantaged are given preferential aid, and so on. What is the justice of just cause?

Justice for Me: Individual Interests

According to Just War (PPC), with its emphasis so strongly on *self*-defense, the justice in question is first and foremost justice for me or my nation. Justice is about claiming and protecting the rights of my nation—its territory, political sovereignty, values, way of life, or interests. In this way, Just War (PPC) displays a notion of justice that is thoroughly modern.

Justice in the modern Western world is founded on the belief that we are all discrete individuals with our own particular ends and visions of what constitutes the meaning or purpose of life. Moreover, there is no way that all of us individuals could ever agree on or share a common good, end, or purpose in life. In this situation of almost infinite diversity, justice becomes a matter of drawing up rules or laws that can referee the interaction of all these individuals who are busy looking out for their own interests. Justice becomes a matter of protecting the rights of individuals as they go about pursuing their own private goods, making sure that they are able to pursue their own vision of the good to the extent that they do not harm other individuals as they pursue their self-interests.

As a consequence, the end result of this justice cannot be genuine peace but only a truce. Because by definition we are discrete individuals who cannot agree on a common purpose or good, justice becomes a kind of compromise, a procedure for how we might live and let live in the absence of a shared vision that alone might produce genuine peace. For this reason, modern communities, such as nations, are communities only in a very weak sense of the word. They are held together not by a common vision but by the contingent convergence of a multitude of individual self-interests backed up by lethal force.

Just War (PPC) rests on this same understanding of justice, simply transferred from the individual to the nation-state. The justice in modern just war is a matter of refereeing the interaction of nations as each pursues its own interests and values. As the account of just cause made clear, a nation has just cause for war when its right to territorial integrity and political sovereignty, its values, or its interests are attacked. Justice is first and foremost about securing a nation's *individual* good; justice is about *self*-defense. A nation has just cause for war only in defense of its *own* interests—even if it asserts that its interests are in everybody's interest. We might say that justice in Just War (PPC) is "justice for me."

That this is the case is perhaps nowhere more evident than in one of the principal difficulties that Just War (PPC) currently faces, which is the difficulty presented by humanitarian intervention. Particularly over the last decade of the last century but continuing to the present day, the difficulty that the modern just war vision has had dealing with humanitarian intervention has been painfully displayed as nations have ignored or belatedly and/or ineffectively intervened in a number of what are termed humanitarian crises. The difficulty, at least in part, arises from the way justice is conceived in terms of *self*-defense or, as was just stated, "justice for me."

When just cause is defined as *self*-defense and underwritten by the principle of noninterference in the political sovereignty and territory of other nations, any grounds for intervention evaporate. Justice means not meddling in the affairs of others, letting them pursue their own interests and vision of the good while our nation pursues ours. Justice entails leaving other nations alone, regardless of what happens internally, so long as we are left alone. Just cause is a matter of *self*-defense; justice is justice for me. After all, interfering with others, attempting to impose my vision of the good, is the very definition of injustice. As a consequence, justifying humanitarian intervention becomes very difficult, and nations struggle to frame those interventions in terms of self-defense conceived either in terms of national interests or as collective self-defense via alliances and coalitions.

Justice for All: The Common Good

In contrast, Just War (CD) rests on a much different understanding of justice. To begin with, it conceives of the justice in just cause much more broadly than merely as self-defense. It considers just cause not narrowly as justice for *me* or *us* but in terms of justice for *all*. It strives to act not on behalf of *our* right but *the* right.[6] Or as Vitoria would have it, Just War (CD) approaches the task of determining just cause not as a prosecutor in an adversarial system might, that is, by arguing only for one party. Instead, we approach just cause as a judge might, who sits in judgment between two commonwealths and seeks to do justice by all parties involved.[7] In fact, according to this account of just cause, to consider only the claims of one side, to conceive of justice only in terms of the prosecution of my rights, values, and interests, is to be guilty of hubris.[8]

To approach just cause not as a prosecutor concerned only with justice for one party in a conflict but as a judge concerned with justice for all requires a thicker, more substantive understanding of justice than that which underwrites Just War (PPC). For such a vision, Just War (CD) turns to the notion of justice in the Christian tradition. Justice prior to the advent of modernity was understood as a virtue concerned with ordering the life of all in accord with a common good. This is what makes the justice of Just War (CD) more substantial. It is not just a procedure to keep conflicting interests, whatever they are, from clashing; rather, it is a positive work of actually fostering human communion, of promoting genuine peace among peoples. Justice is not a matter of making sure that we do not interfere with one another as each pursues their own private interest, whatever that may be. Justice is not fundamentally about self-defense. Indeed, the modern vision of justice as enforcing a kind of noninterference appears as malicious neglect and thus would itself be a species of injustice.

Ultimately and eternally this common good to which justice is ordered is the shared love of God. With regard to earthly, temporal affairs and the activity of everyday life, however, it is concerned with the welfare of all, such that all may prosper in harmony with their neighbors. As such, this understanding of justice is part of the theological vision of political life previously outlined. It is about the right ordering of human life in accord with God's desire for the renewal of the community that was shattered with the irruption of sin in the fall.

Justice for Others

What all of this means for the criterion of just cause is that it is understood by Just War (CD) in a much more "other regarding" manner. This is to say, according to this vision just cause is not first and foremost a matter of *self-*defense. Rather, it is fundamentally about the defense of others, especially innocent third parties in the face of unjust aggression.

Rejecting Self-Defense

In fact, in direct contrast with the modern public policy checklist approach, self-defense is *not* a legitimate cause for Christians to wage war. With regard to self-defense, the Christian tradition has consistently, if not always unanimously, qualified the legitimacy of self-defense. Even as the just war tradition developed in Christianity, the leading advocates of just war were clear that self-defense did not constitute permissible grounds for a violent, lethal response to injustice. After all, Christians follow one who accepted the cross instead of simply slaying sinners, one who told his disciples to turn the other cheek and take up the cross. Thus, as Augustine said, we would rather be killed than kill an enemy-neighbor. Granted, not everyone took as unequivocal a stance against self-defense as Augustine did; some, like Aquinas, asserted Christians could defend themselves so long as they did not do so with the intention of killing their assailant.[9] Nevertheless, however self-defense is parsed, for Christians it is not a just cause for war.

Does such a stance leave Christians at the mercy of the unjust and the vicious, and does it mean that Christians may play no part in defending the societies in which they find themselves when those societies are unjustly attacked? No, it does not, as Augustine told the pagan authority who on studying the Christian faith wondered the same thing.[10] With regard to Christians, our refusal of lethal self-defense does not leave us at the mercy of tyrants. Rather it leaves us in the hands of God's providential care as that care is expressed both in the promise of the resurrection and in God's ordering of the governing authorities to protect good and punish evil (Rom. 13). The latter is one of the ways, Augustine noted, that Christians benefit from the peace of the earthly city as we are on pilgrimage in this world toward the eternal city of God.[11]

The foregoing of self-defense does not translate into a refusal to participate in the defense of the societies Christians inhabit. Rather, it means that Christians participating in the governing authority or serving in a society's armed forces understand themselves to be engaged not in *self*-defense but in the defense of their neighbors who collectively constitute the society in which Christians reside. Christians may serve in the government and armed forces of the nations where they live in the prosecution of a just war, not because they are trying to defend themselves but because they are called to serve their neighbors by defending them against unjust aggression.

Intervention and Responsibility

What is particularly noteworthy regarding this fundamentally other-directed vision of just cause is that, whereas at first glance it may appear to shrink just cause because it does not permit self-defense, in fact it actually broadens the range of possible just causes for war. If the modern public policy checklist approach retrieved only the notion of defensive wars from the tradition, Just War (CD) actually recovers not only the defensive dimension of the tradition but also the aggressive dimension. This means that, among other things, Just War (CD) is more amenable to the possibility of humanitarian intervention, or what more recently is referred to as "the responsibility to protect." Being fundamentally other-directed, Just War (CD) does not recognize the nearly absolute right of national sovereignty and nonintervention that are cornerstones of the modern political order. In fact, it is inclined to see the modern reduction of just cause to self-defense as providing protection for all kinds of tyrants. Against this reduction and shelter, it will argue with Martin Luther King Jr. that an injustice against one is of concern to all.[12] Thus, as Vitoria says, if it is clearly evident that subjects are suffering unjustly because of their king, it is permissible for foreign kings to wage war against that king.[13] Or, more recently, the US Catholic bishops have asserted that the "massive violation of the basic rights of whole populations" constitutes a just cause for war, appealing in defense of this claim to several statements made by Pope John Paul II, where he claims that intervention is obligatory in the face of genocide, that states do not have a "right to indifference," and that sovereignty and noninterference do not constitute a screen behind which injustice may be carried out with impunity.[14] Such sentiments correspond, we may recall, with Aquinas's treatment of sedition and tyranny. Tyrants cannot hide, untouchable, behind their borders while brutalizing the inhabitants of their country. Rather, governing authorities that no longer serve the common good may be subject to a just war; tyranny and oppression amount to a just cause for war.

Repel, Recover, and Restore

Traditionally, this other-directed account of just cause has been formally unpacked in three ways, which we might name *repelling*, *recovering*, and *restoring*. First, just cause is a matter of repulsion. One may justly go to war in order to repel an unjust attack that is underway. This is perhaps the form of just cause that comes closest to the modern account of just cause as self-defense as spelled out in the UN Charter. Second, recovering that which was unjustly taken or seized amounts to a just cause for war. If one nation occupies or seizes territory or property belonging to another nation and is unwilling to make amends, the aggrieved nation has a just cause for war. Lastly, a nation may justly go to war for the sake of restoring the moral order. Traditionally, the language used with regard to this final just cause is that of "punishment." Punishment is a legitimate cause for war.

Such a claim surprises many and offends some. After all, it is not uncommon for punishment to be associated with a kind of vindictive retribution and the infliction of compensatory suffering. In this way punishment is often associated with revenge in the modern mind and, truth be told, one may even find the language of revenge associated with this aspect of just cause in the tradition. What the tradition means by punishment, however, is very different from some of the ways it is used and invoked today. Punishment is conceived not simply as the infliction of an injury on the offender. As Grotius writes, "in punishing the guilty no injury is done to them."[15] This is in keeping with the origin of just war in the divine call to love our neighbors—even our enemy neighbors. Grotius goes on to articulate three benefits that accrue because of punishment. First, it is a corrective to the offender, a perhaps unpleasant medicine—a "harsh kindness," to use Augustine's language—the point of which is the restoration of the offender to the moral order that was breached by the act of injustice. Second, the injured party is restored insofar as the injustice is not only stopped but to some extent reversed or at least countered (since an injustice often cannot be reversed in the sense of entirely undone) by means of appropriate reparations. Third, there is the exemplary benefit whereby all are reminded of the moral order and encouraged to uphold it. Today, this is often described as "deterrence," but that does not adequately capture the positive nature of punishment as a benefit for all. Too often deterrence sounds like a utilitarian sacrifice of the guilty simply for the sake of the larger whole. Instead, we might say that this third benefit encompasses not only the offender (the focus of first benefit) or the offended (the focus of the second benefit) but the whole (which includes the first two beneficiaries but exceeds them as well). It is the fundamentally positive nature of this third aspect of just cause that has led some to speak of it not as vindictive but as vindicating[16] and that leads me to designate it as "restoration" instead of as "punishment."

Religion as Just Cause

Earlier we saw that Just War (PPC) categorically ruled out religion as a legitimate ground for just war and that this was part of modernity's marginalization of the political presence of the church. Given the emphasis that Just War (CD) places on resisting the church's marginalization in the moral life of Christians, as well as on reasserting the church's political presence, does Just War (CD) also reassert religion as a just cause for war? The answer is both yes and no. On the one hand, unlike Just War (PPC), there is a sense in which religion, more specifically Christianity, is a cause for war. On the other hand, there is a sense in which Christianity is not a legitimate or just cause for war.

Having said this, immediately a red flag will go up for many. "What? Religion could be a just cause for war? Are you leading us back to the Crusades?" Unraveling the apparent contradiction of the "yes and no" as well as diffusing the fear of religious crusades entails looking at Vitoria's renunciation of religion and the Crusades a little more closely, as well as revisiting the theological vision of politics that we have been developing gradually.

When Vitoria declared that religious differences were not legitimate grounds for war, he was not actually being the innovator that he is sometimes lauded as. In truth, he was only articulating a position that had long been espoused by a variety of voices in the church. In fact, after dismissing religious differences as a cause for war, he writes, "of all the other doctors . . . I know of no one who thinks the contrary."[17] Aquinas, for example, did not think that conversion could or should be coerced.[18] And if individuals should not be coerced, then clearly unbelief was not in itself a just cause for war against an entire population.

"But what about the Crusades?" one might ask. Although in the popular imagination they are commonly portrayed as wars against pagans and infidels simply because they were pagans and infidels, the historical reality is much more complicated, if not measurably less sordid.[19] In terms of the defense of the Crusades offered by various theologians and canon lawyers in the Middle Ages, they were not waged for the sake of conversion, nor were they waged with the goal of simply killing unbelievers because they were unbelievers. Rather, the Crusades were understood as a species of just war, and although they entailed few restrictions on what may be done to the enemy, they upheld the notion of just cause as it was articulated in terms of repulsion, recovery, and restoration. Specifically, unbelievers could be subject to attack if they attacked the faith by persecuting Christians, prevented missionaries from evangelizing, or unjustly seized goods and property. The latter was part of the public rationale given for the Crusades that so captivates the public imagination: it was argued that the Holy Land had been unjustly seized by unbelievers. As for the former rationale, Aquinas puts it well when he writes: "It is for this reason that Christ's faithful often wage wars with unbelievers, not indeed for the purpose of forcing them to believe, because even if they were to conquer them, and take them prisoners, they should still leave them free to believe, if they will, but in order to prevent them from hindering [persecuting, attacking] the faith of Christ."[20] What makes Vitoria noteworthy in his insistence that differences of religion are in themselves not grounds for just war is that he is *not* novel and was in fact attempting valiantly to uphold the just war tradition in the face of pressures to justify the conquest of the Americas on the grounds of differences of religion.[21] In renouncing religious differences as a just cause for war, Vitoria was upholding the best of the Christian tradition.

Already we have begun to articulate a theology of political life that understands God to use the governing authorities to protect good and punish evil. What we see unfolding in the discussion of religion and just cause in thinkers such as Aquinas and Vitoria is a further elaboration of that theological vision of politics. As it will come to be spelled out in the centuries after Aquinas and Vitoria, this vision asserts that God rules over this world by means of two authorities, the governing authorities and the church. Over against the modern vision of politics that relegates the church to an apolitical or strictly spiritual realm, this vision maintains a fully public, political presence for the church. Even as it maintains the church's public authority (for example, in exercising its judgment regarding just wars), it does not permit the church to wage war or call on the state to wage war for the sake of propagating the gospel. In other words, according to this vision the state may not wage war to impose the Christian faith or attack unbelief. Hence, religious differences are not a cause for just war. The governing authorities are *not* responsible for seeing to it that all persons embrace their eternal good or supernatural end, which is friendship with the blessed Trinity. That is the church's responsibility, which the church is to pursue by means of preaching and evangelism and not the sword. Instead, the state is responsible for watching over the temporal, earthly common good; it is responsible for watching over those goods that pertain to the maintenance and flourishing of civil life—so that the church can go about its business of proclamation in peace. Thus, just cause is a matter of repelling assaults on, recovering that which is taken from, and restoring the proper ordering of earthly political life toward the common good.

The last component of this theological account of the state's responsibility—maintaining the common good as an aid to the church's work of evangelism—provided the justification for declaring that the refusal of free passage to missionaries was itself a just cause for war. Although this right gradually changed into a more general right of free passage for all persons and even merchandise before it disappeared altogether (there is no intrinsic right of free passage today that if violated constitutes just cause for war), it does point to how Just War (CD) in a very particular sense posits religion as a cause for war.

Although it would not hold that the denial of free passage to missionaries constituted a just cause for war because the faith is not to be advanced with the sword, Just War (CD) is a form of war driven by religion in the sense that it is precisely because the faith calls Christians to love their neighbors that they will serve in just wars. Christians wage just wars because their faith compels them to love their neighbors in this way. After all, that is what it means to say that just war can be a faithful form of Christian discipleship. When seen in this light, Just War (PPC), by banishing religion, in a sense argues that just wars should be waged for *lesser* reasons; they should be divorced from faith and discipleship and instead be waged for secular causes. It says, in effect, do not wage war for the most important thing in life—God and faith; instead fight for merely secular things.

Insofar as faith is the motivation for Christians waging just war, it is not really a "cause" for war in the sense that we have defined just cause as pertaining to the enemy's behavior. Rather, what motivates us is properly a matter of intent, which we will take up in the next chapter. Nevertheless, to the extent that concern for the common good is central to the Christian faith, waging just wars in defense of the common good remains a practice of the faith. Christians are concerned with the common good and not simply their own private, partisan good because of what it means to follow Christ in this world. While Just War (CD) does not expect or desire that the governing authorities either enforce or defend with the sword those aspects of the faith that pertain to our eternal end, following its vision of how God uses governing authorities, it does expect those authorities to defend (understood as "repel, recover, and restore") the common good. Therefore, in the particular sense that the responsibility to defend the common good arises out of the Christian vision (although Christianity acknowledges that that is not the only way it can arise), religion is part of just cause in Just War (CD).

Several conclusions can be drawn from this brief look at religion as a cause for just war. First, one may reject religious differences as a just cause for war without embracing the modern privatization and depoliticization of the church. After all, neither Aquinas nor Vitoria (and all the voices who echoed them) had any interest in seeing the church deprived of its public influence. This means that Just War (CD) can renounce religious difference as a just cause without contradicting its claims for a public, politically present church. Second, as our brief consideration of the Crusades suggests, simply rejecting religion as a just cause for war does not necessarily prevent crusades. After all, what finally distinguishes the Crusades is not their rationale; they were not about religious differences *per se*. Rather what makes them stand out is that they were a form of just war without all of its teeth; they were just war with the criteria concerning how one wages war significantly weakened or ignored. In other words, it is an error to attribute their brutality to the nature of their cause. Rather, the source of their brutality lies in the lack of restraint regarding the means used in pursuit of the ends. Third, acknowledging that the Christian faith and its understanding of the common good is central to defining just cause does not open the door for new crusades. As long as the just war discipline is faithfully practiced with *all* of its teeth, crusades are ruled out.

Preemptive and Preventative Wars

The next aspect of just cause to be considered is the legitimacy of preemptive and preventative wars. This aspect was not mentioned under the treatment of the modern public policy checklist approach to just cause because it is one aspect of the tradition where Just War (PPC) and Just War (CD) are in basic agreement. Typically, the just war tradition has held that for an offense to constitute a just cause for war, it must be an actual and not merely a possible or potential offense. An injury must actually have been suffered for one to claim just cause; it is not enough that one simply feel threatened or suspect that an adversary is plotting an unjust attack. Just cause requires that an unjust attack has been suffered, that an injustice has actually occurred.

Having said this, there is a small opening in the tradition for the recognition of the presence of a threat as a just cause for war. Perhaps not unlike the small space it permits for just revolution, the tradition has in recent centuries recognized that in certain circumstances the threat of unjust attack itself may constitute a just cause for war. What are those circumstances?

Here the distinction between what are called preemptive and preventative strikes is important. Insofar as the tradition grants that a just cause for war exists without one actually having been unjustly attacked, it does so by distinguishing between preemptive and preventative strikes and permitting only the former. The distinction hinges on the nature of the threat that one faces. A preemptive strike may be defined as one that responds to a threat that is both *imminent* and *grave*. By *imminent*, the tradition means a threat that is on the verge of being realized, a potential threat that is about to become an actual attack. An example of such an imminent threat might be an enemy amassing troops on one's border in preparation for an unjust invasion. By itself, such an *imminent* threat does not provide just cause for a preemptive strike. Rather, for an imminent threat to justify a preemptive strike it must also be *grave*. A grave threat is one that if carried out would place the survival of the object of that attack at risk. Grotius speaks of this in terms of one's life being put in peril; Walzer speaks of such a threat in the more modern terms of its seriously jeopardizing territorial integrity or political independence; others suggest that it is a matter of crippling military defenses.[22] Not just any attack that is imminent rises to the level of a just cause; the threatened attack must be of such magnitude that if one does not respond preemptively, one may well not be able to respond at all.

In the absence of imminence and gravity, any strike that is launched prior to an actual unjust attack is not properly named a preemptive strike; instead, it is a preventative attack. The tradition uniformly condemns such preventative wars and strikes. Grotius captures well the sentiment of the tradition in this regard when he writes, "I admit, to be sure, that if the assailant seizes weapons in such a way that his intent to kill is manifest [then] the crime can be forestalled. . . . But those who accept fear of any sort as justifying anticipatory slayings are themselves greatly deceived and deceive others."[23] He goes on to argue that when faced with distant threats, to respond with an act of war would itself be a work of injustice. In such cases the proper response would be to seek to forestall the distant threat of violence with other, indirect remedies that are themselves a kind of punishment.[24] The idea that "the possibility of being attacked confers the right to attack is abhorrent to every principle of equity. Human life exists under such conditions that absolute security is never guaranteed to us. For protection against uncertain fears we must rely on Divine Providence, and on a wariness free from reproach, not on force."[25] Reflecting his own sense that the just war discipline finally must be underwritten by the Christian faith, Grotius reminds his readers that war is not meant to guarantee security, nor should it replace faith and trust in divine providence.

Just Policing, Not War?

Under our treatment of the public policy approach to just cause it was noted that there was no clear standard for distinguishing between what kind of attack merited a military response and what kind merited a police or law enforcement response and that in the absence of any clear guidance, the matter was left in the hands of the governing authorities. Does Just War (CD) offer any particular guidance on this issue?

In the years since the horrific events of September 11, 2001, a conversation has begun between pacifists and just warriors regarding the differences between and appropriateness of police and military responses to events such as terrorist attacks. The constructive proposal being advanced is what is called "just policing," and it is presented as an alternative to warfare and military responses to international injustice and violence.[26] On one hand, it is offered as a sort of hoped for "common ground" where persons who are ordinarily at odds in the church—namely, just warriors and pacifists—might be able to join together in a common cause. On the other hand, and more immediately relevant to the issue of just cause, just policing is put forward as an alternative to war. That is to say, according to this proposal war is *never* a legitimate response to injustice and violence; rather, the appropriate response should be a just police response. The reasons given for such a conclusion emphasize the difference between police action and war. Although exactly how those differences are named varies from writer to writer, war is typically distinguished from police action on the grounds that there is no international community or authority to which nations can be held accountable, that in war the judge and executioner are combined in the same agent, that military action (as opposed to police action) is much less capable of discriminating between legitimate targets and civilians, that warfare lends itself to a host of psychological forces and factors—from the adrenaline rush of combat to uncritical patriotism—that render it incapable of being constrained by the rule of law and the common good.

Although these proposals have much to contribute in helping us think through and live out the just war discipline, particularly with regard to the criteria like last resort and those that pertain to how war is waged, on this question of a military versus police response they are not as helpful. Insofar as they rest on a sharp distinction between policing and war, with war being intrinsically incapable of being restrained by the rule of law or the common good, they merely repeat the popular modern claim that war is intrinsically unjust, which was addressed and rejected in chapter 2. Accordingly, for example, when the advocates of just policing argue that warfare is less discriminating than police action, they are generally correct. This, however, is not due to some intrinsic quality of warfare that makes it such; rather, it is because militaries often use different rules of engagement. For example, domestic law enforcement is often taught to use the minimum force necessary, whereas militaries are often trained to use the maximum permitted. But there is nothing inherent in military practice that requires maximum force to be used; indeed, specialized military forces are often trained in more discriminating practices. The same could be said about the adrenaline rush. Not only are police subject to similar pressures but it is also widely recognized that training and proper command significantly reduce risks associated with "going berserk." In other words, several of the features of modern war that render it problematic in the eyes of the advocates of just policing can be addressed by good military doctrine and discipline.[27]

Furthermore, even if the criticisms leveled against the current practice of warfare are accurate—and many of them are—those criticisms do not undermine the propriety of Just War (CD). To the contrary, the criticisms actually reinforce the need for and importance of the church reclaiming the just war discipline and doing so intentionally, as a form of Christian discipleship. For example, many of the criticisms of war hinge on a lack of accountability, either to the common good or in the form of effective institutional oversight. As articulated in Just War (CD), however, legitimate authority does indeed establish that accountability. Moreover, Just War (CD) has never depended on an international authority for its viability; put more accurately, it has never depended on an international authority beyond the legitimate authority God has charged the church with embodying and enacting.

In the end, as just war advocates point out, the differences between just policing and just war are a matter of degree and not kind. No hard and fast line exists between just policing and just war. They exist together—albeit in different places—on a single continuum of the moral use of violence. Both practices are justified and restrained by the same theological and moral logic that we are in the midst of spelling out. Whereas Christians do not defend themselves with lethal force, when called to serve as agents of the governing authorities, they may wield the sword either in domestic law enforcement or in the military, on behalf of their neighbor and for the sake of the common good in accord with the just war discipline (or in the case of policing, with a domestic analogue of the just war discipline). This theological rationale underwrites both just policing and just war.

The question is, if they share the same theological rationale, on what grounds do we distinguish when just policing is an appropriate response to an injustice from when just war is appropriate? What constitutes just cause for war as opposed to a police action? The answer begins with the criterion of just cause but does not end there. It begins with just cause insofar as we know that war is not an appropriate response when the offense in question does not correspond to just cause, as we have spelled it out in terms of the three Rs: repel, recover, and restore. One does not go to war, for example, when the injustice in question is a matter of the clash of two gangs or an individual homicide.

In addition to the three Rs of just cause, several of the other criteria play a role in discerning when to respond with police force and when to respond with military force. Specifically, the criteria of last resort and reasonable chance of success will help determine the proper response to a just cause. These two criteria, in particular, address the matter of the nature and scope of force to be used in responding to injustice. In a sense, they address the threshold on the continuum of force between policing and warfare. At the risk of oversimplifying a bit, we might say that last resort deals with the use of force, such as police force, prior to engaging military force, whereas reasonable chance of success approaches the threshold from the other angle, asking about the effects of using military force to address a given injustice. As we shall see, both of these criteria must be engaged before calling out the troops and tanks instead of the police and investigators. Of course, because it is a matter of a moral continuum of force, there is every reason to believe that there will be situations and contexts (some forms of terrorism, "low-intensity conflict," etc.) where the force that is called for may fluctuate between or necessitate a mix of the scale of force and tactics typical of police action with those typical of military action. And it is precisely here where efforts like those associated with "just peacemaking" and "just policing" may well prove very helpful.

The Challenge for the Church: What Kind of Justice Do We Seek?

The challenges that the criterion of just cause presents for the church stem from how the question, which justice? is answered. To what extent have we embraced "justice for me," that is, the modern conflictual notion of justice that revolves around individuals securing their own interests and rights in a kind of perpetual competition with others? When we think of justice do we think first and foremost of justice for *me*, my rights, my interests, what I am entitled to, or what is due to me and mine?

Consider how we conceive of the church and its mission. Do we conceive of the church as fundamentally a place where we go to have our needs met? Is the first question we ask about worship, "Does it feed me?" When a visitor is in my customary seat in the sanctuary do I take offense because she is in *my* seat?

What does the church preach, teach, and tell the world? Do we proclaim a gospel of *self*-fulfillment and *self*-actualization? Do we reduce the faith essentially to a form of therapy whereby Jesus becomes merely a means to satisfy *my* felt needs and help *me* cope with the stresses of *my* life? A pastor recently shared with me a conversation he had with his congregation. He asked them what their mission was, to which they responded, "Our mission is to be in ministry to ourselves." How many congregations would answer, if not with identical words, with an identical point? Some popular ways of marketing the church today encourage this kind of thinking by suggesting that the fundamental task of the church is to cater to an individual's interests and felt needs.

Although the church ruled that religious differences were not a just cause for war because a sincere confession of faith could not be coerced, that the inducing of confession of the faith is not a just cause for war can help us shed light on how we conceive of justice. How do we react to the dismissal of the use of coercion to enforce Christianity? Reflecting on the heat generated by such things as pledges, public prayers, public displays, and rather generic phrases like "In God We Trust" or "Happy Holidays," it would appear that many Christians want to use more than the Spirit's persuasion through the church's proclamation and witness to instill and enforce confession of the faith.

What do we make of Paul when he exhorts the church in Corinth, "Why not rather be wronged? Why not rather be defrauded?" (1 Cor. 6:7)? Does his exhortation make sense? Do we actually abide by it? Or does that instruction trouble us? Does it strike us as bizarre, alien, and maybe even unethical?

What does all of this have to do with just cause? Simply put, insofar as we are curved in on ourselves and manage to bend the faith, Christ, the church, and even the world until they are all about satisfying our individual interests and felt needs, we show ourselves to be of a character that is perfectly at home in a society where justice is fundamentally "justice for me," where justice is about securing and protecting my interests. Then faith is made into a device for meeting my needs and the church becomes about securing its self-centered interests in the world.

This brings us to the vision of justice that founds Just War (CD). Compare the preceding paragraphs with Martin Luther's famous statement on the freedom of a Christian to be a servant of all, where he argued that in Christ we have everything we need and so our life becomes a kind of surplus to be spent, given to and for the benefit of others.[28] This is but to say that the Christian life is fundamentally about being other-directed, concerned not simply with my rights or my private good but with justice for all—the common good. Accordingly, the challenge for the church is to embody this justice, this passion for the common good. In the previous chapter we highlighted the importance of raising up and encouraging public officials who are devoted to the common good. Of course, the church desires not just for public figures to be devoted to the common good—although by virtue of their public office they do have a particular responsibility in this regard—but for all Christians (indeed, all persons) to be so oriented as well. And forming persons in the virtue of justice so understood is a matter of preaching and teaching on justice and common good to be sure, but it is also a matter of becoming a people who welcome strangers instead of taking offense when they sit in "our" spot. It may also affect how we think about the nature and purpose of worship, how we respond to the increasingly "post-Christian" culture in which we find ourselves, or what we understand the nature and mission of the church to be and how we actually live that out. All such activities and events, no matter how trivial and insignificant they may appear, are opportunities both to reflect on our character as a people who live for others (or, conversely, our failure to be such a people) and to nurture us in our regard for the common good.

If just cause shares with the previous criterion of legitimate authority an orientation toward the common good, just cause provides an opportunity to reflect further on the nature of our devotion to the common good.

Although it is sometimes popular in contemporary society to set the individual and the community against each other, as if the good of individuals will inevitably and necessarily be in conflict with and often sacrificed for the good of the whole, the Christian vision of the common good does not pit the good of individuals against the good of all. Rather, the common good includes the good of individual persons. Thus, Christian devotion to the common good necessarily encompasses the good of Christians, the good of their unjustly attacked neighbors, and the good of their enemy neighbors. Insofar as just cause involves all three aspects or facets of the common good, those three facets provide a helpful way of getting at the challenges that just cause as a part of Just War (CD) presents to the church.

Serving the Enemy Neighbor

First, consider how just cause involves our enemy neighbors. Whereas the modern public policy checklist approach to just war deals with the enemy predominantly as the enemy interferes with my/our rights or interests, Just War (CD) approaches the enemy with an eye toward the common good, which includes the good of the enemy neighbor. Because more will be said about this in the next chapter—under the criterion of "right intent"—here we will focus only on the implications of the fact that just cause entails our being devoted to *the* right and not simply to *my/our* right. As Vitoria reminds us, just cause entails approaching the question of right or justice not as if one were a prosecutor advocating for only one side but as a judge discerning the good of all. In weighing just cause for war one has an obligation to consider the enemy's rationale and intentions in inflicting the injury that gave rise to the specter of war. Just cause, then, entails not only considering *what* the enemy has done but also *why* they have done it. After all, an accidental missile strike is a very different thing from a carefully planned and executed attack. Or, more pointedly, as Grotius says, a nation that has given just cause for war to its enemy cannot turn around and claim just cause when that enemy attacks.[29] In other words, a nation that is guilty of an injustice against its neighbor (or against its own people) that rises to the level of just cause cannot claim to be just in repelling an attack it has in fact provoked by refusing to remedy its injustice. It is this train of thought that prompts Luther to suggest that the first response to an attack should always be to remove the rod from God's hand,[30] by which he means not to blame the victim but to encourage the kind of soul searching that asks, Are we guilty of injustice toward our neighbor and so have provoked a just attack? and prompts, when necessary, the appropriate repentance and reform of life.

To fail to consider the enemy's claims is to be guilty of the sin of pride, to think more highly of oneself than one ought and stubbornly cling to the conviction that one is always in the right and so there is no need to listen to the enemy. Consequently, the challenge for the church is that of displaying and instilling in its members a certain humility that is able to consider the claims of one's adversaries. The challenge for the church is to foster in its own life—and so witness for the wider world—a kind of politics where grievances are aired and engaged instead of dismissed and denied. More will be said about this in the next chapter.

Serving the Unjustly Attacked Neighbor

The second aspect of Christians' concern for the common good involves the good of their unjustly attacked neighbor. The challenge that the commitment to the good of the injured neighbor presents to the church also brings to the fore how Christians attend to their good—or perhaps we should say "how Christians do not attend to their good," since Just War (CD) marginalizes the practice of self-defense. On this point Just War (CD) meshes with what Scripture tells us and the saints show us, namely, that our passion for justice is such that we will surrender our temporal good, including even our lives and the lives of our loved ones, for the sake of our neighbors. Christians will put their lives and the lives of their loved ones at risk in a just war for the sake of their unjustly attacked neighbors. As has been made clear, just cause is not fundamentally self-oriented in Just War (CD) but other-directed.

That this is the case appears at first glance to contradict the claim that the common good does not pit persons against the whole. After all, it appears as if Christians are expected to sacrifice their good for the sake of others in a kind of theological utilitarianism. Certainly it is true that as followers of One who gave himself for others, Christians are asked to do the same, even to the point of sharing death on a cross, something Scripture and worship remind us of regularly. But what makes this sacrifice not a surrender of Christians' good for the sake of the greater good of the whole is the promise of the resurrection. This is how we can make sense of those passages of Scripture that tell us that in giving our life we do not in fact lose it but find it (Matt. 10:39), that though we may die we will not perish (Luke 21:16–19). This also explains Paul's almost mocking dismissal of death in 1 Corinthians 15. Christians can give even their lives in a just war for the sake of the common good of their neighbors because they know that though we and/or our loved ones die, in the end, like Job, we all will be restored and will have lost nothing. Therefore, appearances notwithstanding, just war does not require Christians to surrender their sharing in the common good because just war as discipleship rests on the recognition that in Christ our good and our loves are secured in a manner that cannot be lost in death (Rom. 8:38–39). As will become clearer when we discuss right intent shortly, Just War (CD) is driven by a desire to extend and strengthen the participation of all in the common good.

The challenges for the church that are presented by this aspect of just cause are numerous. Immediately we are confronted with the tradition's qualification of self-defense in general and renunciation of self-defense altogether as a just cause for war. Are we a people who have embraced the cross in the sense that, as Augustine memorably put it, "we would rather be killed than kill"? Do we consciously and intentionally resist the multitude of cultural messages that tell us to put our lives before the lives of others?[31] Do we discuss within the church what constitutes faithful and unfaithful forms of self-defense? And do we communicate clearly to others that they need not kill for the sake of defending us? Although the connection between these "personal" practices and just war may not at first glance be obvious, attending to such matters is one part of forming persons who are able to resist the paralyzing obsession with their own private good and instead turn to others and act on behalf of the common good.

Serving the Common Good

At this point we can expand on the previously stated challenge of fostering a commitment to justice understood as building up the common good and ask if the church is forming people whose devotion to the common good of all extends as far as a willingness to risk their lives and the lives of their loved ones for the sake of others. Is the church a place where we hear a word of justice that invites us beyond ourselves and moves us to act outside of our narrow interests? In the midst of public debates over the propriety of any given war, it is not uncommon to hear someone raise the question, What interest of ours is at stake? or declare, I am against such and such a war because there is no national interest at stake. Could such statements be uttered by members of our churches (or by ourselves?), or are we about nurturing the kind of people willing to serve and sacrifice for others even when there is no direct and immediate benefit to be gained for ourselves?

Along these same lines we can ask about the role models and moral exemplars that the church celebrates and lifts up as persons worthy to be emulated. Do we perpetuate the wider culture's cult of celebrity, power, and wealth, honoring those who have excelled at gathering unto themselves, or do we lift up before one another the lives of the saints who have poured out their lives for others? When we lift up the saints whose lives show us what living (and dying) for others looks like, we are contributing to the formation of the kind of people on whom just war as a form of discipleship depends. Likewise, when we make service to those in need around us (what the tradition calls the works of mercy) a central part of the life of the community of faith, we are forming people in the habits and practices of justice and service of others that are necessary for sustaining the criterion of just cause as part of Christian discipleship. After all, if we are not a people who desire justice for the neighbors we encounter in our everyday life; if we do not care about our immediate neighbors who are unemployed, uninsured, homeless, battered, the victims of crime and the perpetrators of crime, and so on; if we are not in the habit of giving our lives to and for others; then it should come as no surprise when the plight of Croatians, Sudanese, Haitians, or Timorese fails to move us. It should come as no surprise that we are not able to recognize or act on just cause.

If part of the challenge of just cause is acquiring the virtue of justice, which disposes us to give ourselves for the sake of others' participation in the common good, another dimension of the challenge of just cause is that of confronting the obstacles that would prevent us from acting for others. If the first challenge is fostering a desire to aid others, the second challenge is that of acting on that desire. Specifically, the call of justice to give ourselves for others invariably requires us to confront the pervasive sense of fear and inordinate concern for security that threatens to envelop us at the outset of the twenty-first century.[32] Fear abounds, as is attested by our color-coded alerts, militarized airports, latex-gloved mail carriers, electronic eavesdropping, extraordinary renditions and water boarding, and gated and guarded communities. In the face of a hostile world, where bacteria can be used as a bomb and airplanes as missiles, the temptation is to retreat with our duct tape and plastic behind our borders, to try and isolate ourselves. Overwhelmed by this all-pervasive fear, the temptation is to retract, to withdraw from our neighbors and the world because it is just too dangerous, too risky, to reach out to our neighbors.

In the face of this fear, the criterion of just cause speaks to us of the importance of proclaiming the gospel by preaching, teaching, and reminding one another of the good news that Christ has defeated sin and death and that as a result we need not be consumed by fear. In Christ we need not fear those who can only kill the body (Matt. 10:28). After all, as Paul declares, because of Christ's resurrection in which we have the hope of sharing, death has lost its sting (1 Cor. 15:55). As a people who in the waters of baptism began a daily dying to sin, we can join Paul in his fearless exclamation, "I die every day" (1 Cor. 15:31).

The challenge to the church is that of embracing and embodying what we say we believe—that there are worse things than dying and more important things than living. The challenge is to embrace the gift of the perfect love that casts out fear (1 John 4:18), that empowers us to live in holy insecurity, free to risk and even die in service to our neighbor. It takes courage in the face of fear to come to the aid of the neighbor, and it takes courage in the face of the threat of violence to abide by the just war discipline. Beyond preaching, teaching, moral exhortation, and lifting up the saints who exemplify the virtue of courage, there are manifold possibilities for the church to both learn and practice this courage. Whether it is venturing to the homeless shelter downtown to serve, visiting in a prison, standing up for what is right on our jobs or among our friends, traveling overseas to do mission work in conflicted areas, or facing illness and death in our own lives, our everyday life is filled with opportunities to practice courage. These opportunities and others like them are crucial to the formation of a just war people, because a people who lack courage, whether on neighborhood streets, among their peers and coworkers, or in the hospital bed, will be hard pressed when boots are on the ground and fear is thick to resist the temptation either to abandon the neighbor or to discard the just war discipline.

ᴄ᷉

Regarding the matter of just cause, in the end the difference between Just War (PPC) and Just War (CD) is the character of the communities that sustain those respective visions. The public policy checklist approach arises out of and is sustained by a thin modern vision of community. Communities are little more than collections of individuals constantly struggling and competing for the goods necessary to the attainment of their own private interests. Likewise, the community of nations simply mirrors the relations of individuals. (Grotius, the father of international law, was explicit in making this connection.) As a consequence, justice is primarily about securing and preserving the rights of individuals. Just cause in the public policy checklist approach reflects this; it is fundamentally about self-defense.

In contrast, Just War (CD) arises out of and is sustained by the church, which is a community committed to a common good for all. For this reason, the justice that underwrites just cause is other-directed, even to the point of Christians forgoing their immediate temporal good for the sake of their neighbors. And in the end the basic challenge of just cause to the church is simply that of being this community, devoting our lives and livelihood to peace and justice for our neighbors, which brings us to the next criterion to be considered.

At the beginning of the chapter I identified just cause as part of what should guide the deliberations of the legitimate authorities as they contemplate authorizing and waging a war. It bears repeating that just cause is only part of what should guide deliberations. While having a just cause is necessary for waging a just war, it is not by itself sufficient. This bears repeating because one of the prominent ways that the just war tradition has been abused historically has been by treating just cause as if it alone constituted necessary and sufficient grounds for waging war. Yet as the prominent British moralist G. E. M. Anscombe reminded her compatriots in World War II, "men can be made to hate the deeds of their enemies; but a war is not made just by the fact that one's enemies' deeds are hateful."[33] Against the inflation of just cause and dismissal of the other criteria, the just war tradition with all of its teeth holds that just cause is only one factor among several that should guide a just war people's deliberations. It is necessary but not sufficient; it must be supplemented by all of the other criterion. To the criterion of right intent we now turn.

6

Why Fight?

Right Intent

If just cause considers the enemy or potential enemy's behavior, the criterion of right intent focuses on the would-be just warrior's behavior. As was the case with just cause, the difference with regard to right intent between Just War (PPC) and Just War (CD) is significant. Indeed, whereas some have gone so far as to suggest that right intent was the core of the earlier Christian vision of just war, the modern checklist approach all but ignores it.

The Public Policy Checklist Approach to Right Intent

What is right intent according to Just War (PPC) and how did it come to be so lightly regarded? Simply put, Just War (PPC) identifies right intention first with waging war for the sake of peace and second with not waging war for the sake of revenge. We might elaborate on the notion of right intent as the intention of waging war for the sake of peace by juxtaposing that intention with a host of other, illicit intentions—such as waging war for the sake of territorial enlargement, the acquisition of resources, or strategic advantage. As we shall see, however, with regard to Just War (PPC) such a stark opposition would be oversimplified. At least some proponents of Just War (PPC) excuse mixed motives and multiple intentions. According to some, right intention is not necessarily opposed to the intention to extend empire or weaken one's neighbors.

Elaborating on the rejection of revenge, however, is rather straightforward. It is a matter of renouncing the desire to inflict punitive (in the modern sense of the term) destruction and compensatory suffering on the enemy. Unlike the desire for peace, however, no one qualifies the rejection of revenge by permitting mixed motives. Revenge and vengeance are prohibited absolutely, perhaps because vindictive intentions would make restoring peace more difficult and weaken the criteria that address justice in fighting.

In Just War (PPC) little more than this is said about right intent. As long as the legitimate authority publicly proclaims its desire for peace and disavows any desire for revenge, this criterion typically is deemed satisfied. Granted, critics of any given war frequently latch on to right intent and question the motives of the legitimate authority, suggesting ulterior reasons for the war in addition to or besides those publicly acknowledged, as in "it's really about oil" or the "wag the dog" syndrome. This is the issue of mixed motives and pretexts, which will be considered shortly. Nevertheless, right intent is typically identified with a publicly stated desire for peace and an equally public disavowal of revenge. Beyond this the criterion does little or no disciplinary work. Right intent does not serve as the marker for a discipline or way of life that deliberately forms a just war people's character in a particular manner. Instead, it functions as little more than a formality—basically the requirement to publicly state both one's desire for peace and one's disavowal of revenge—that must be checked off on the list of criteria so one can move on.

Minimizing Intent

Although it is perhaps an exaggeration to say that right intent was the heart of the earlier Christian vision, the contemporary minimization of right intent is striking. Whereas the earlier Christian vision consistently held that even if all the other criteria were satisfied, the lack of right intent rendered a war illicit, with the birth of modernity the tradition's rigorous adherence to right intention slowly eroded. Thus, whereas Aquinas could write, "It may happen that the war is declared by the legitimate authority, and for a just cause, and yet be rendered unlawful through a wicked intention,"[1] on the eve of the birth of modernity, Grotius wrote in a decidedly different vein:

> It is necessary to observe that a war may be just in its origin, and yet the intentions of its authors may become unjust in the course of its prosecution. For some other motive, not unlawful in itself, may actuate them more powerfully than the original right. . . . Or he may be influenced by some quite unlawful emotion, such as the pleasure of watching another man's calamity, without regard for the

good. . . . But such motives, though blamable, when even connected with a just war do not render the war itself unjust, nor invalidate its conquests.[2]

More recently Michael Walzer has taken Grotius's logic a step further, and in so doing reflects the effective evisceration of the criterion of any substantial moral force in the modern public policy approach to just war. While acknowledging that right intent is properly a matter of justice, Walzer quickly asserts that it cannot be a matter of pure motives, that we are all about mixed motives, and that what is important is that justice be the *primary* motive.[3]

Mixed Motives

How does such a position diminish the significance of right intention? Beyond the obvious difficulty of not providing any guidance on how one might go about discerning the hierarchy of motives operative at any time, Walzer's invocation of mixed motives weakens the criterion of right intent by inadvertently providing cover for engaging in war with improper motives. His claim that we are always already acting on mixed motives rests on the presupposition that one can simultaneously pursue, say, profiteering or self-aggrandizement *and* justice. He assumes that it is possible to hold and simultaneously act on contradictory motives; it is possible to be simultaneously just and unjust. Yet intentions such as justice and greed are mutually exclusive. My avarice does not simply coexist with my justice; rather, my avarice conflicts with and so diminishes my ability to seek justice. If my pursuit of justice is mixed with avarice then I am not really pursuing justice, but instead only a deficient, corrupt imitation of justice. Likewise, pride and charity cannot coexist; rather, one diminishes the other. Thus, if I am truly just, I will resist and not consent to or act on disordered desires such as greed, pride, or ambition.

Of course, because the intentions of our actions often do not present themselves as clearly and obviously as, say, my name appears on a tag stuck to my shirt, it is understandable that one might think that justice and, for example, imperial greed could coexist. But it is only a temporary illusion that what are actually two divergent modes of behavior may appear to work together. At crucial moments the differences will be manifest, revealing that justice and greed were in fact never walking hand in hand. At some point, it will be evident that what appeared to be an act of justice was actually an act of greed, or what initially appeared to be an act of greed was in fact an act of justice. More will be said about mixed motives shortly.

In the end, affirming mixed motives in this manner reduces the criterion of right intent to a shallow formality. The just war tradition's requirement that the intention of a just war be peace and not vengeance becomes innocuous as a host of other intentions are permitted as well, under the faulty moral assumption that one can simultaneously pursue virtue and vice, the common good and a private good, justice and something less than justice.

Perhaps the clearest example of how the belief in the legitimacy of mixed motives undercuts the moral power of the criterion of right intent is the way in which contemporary wars frequently are accompanied by a veritable laundry list of diverse and often conflicting intentions (often floated, in the language of political spin, as "trial balloons"). That these laundry lists do not prompt any serious reflection on the justice of a given war on the basis of the criterion of right intent says a great deal about the moral role and force of the criterion in Just War (PPC). After all, if right intent means only that the right intentions must appear on the list, preferably in a prominent if not preeminent place, then a war, say, for oil or for the sake of diverting attention from domestic troubles or providing a bump in the opinion polls is not in itself problematic. As long as the war is also for peace and justice, then it is permissible. Yet if right intent means one can wage war for imperial reasons or for the sake of political positioning, then the criterion is no longer functioning in a manner that bears any resemblance to its role in the just war tradition; it has become a hollow formality.

Right Intent, Peace, and the Common Good

That right intent is reduced to little more than a mere formality by Just War (PPC) should be unsurprising given its roots in the modern vision of politics and human community. Modernity understands human community to be a mere amalgamation of individuals who are busy pursuing their individual interests; human communities cannot be bound together by a shared love that is a common good. Indeed, modernity prides itself on giving individuals the "freedom" not to pursue a common good while justice becomes a matter of refereeing the struggle between individuals for their interests and rights—what I called "justice for me."

In this situation, right intent loses much of its moral force as its connection with the common good is severed. Traditionally, right intent has been a matter of intending peace. But what has the tradition meant by peace? Peace was understood to be the fruit of a well-ordered political life. And, as we have already seen, a well-ordered political life was one that was ordered to the common good of all. Thus, the peace that was sought in a just war was linked to the common good; the proper intention in waging a just war was to restore the ordering of political life toward the common good and so bring the benefit of peace to all. Herein lies the problem. The political vision of modernity has replaced the common good as a shared love with a much thinner conception of justice as a kind of truce between necessarily conflicted and competing individuals (and nations). As a result, the political vision of modernity cannot conceive of a genuine peace—one that is the fruit of people sharing a love that is the common good—and right intent is cut loose from its moral anchor.

One of two things happens to right intent when it is set adrift. First, it may become, as we have seen, a mere formality. A warring nation declares its desire for peace and ostensibly disavows revenge and thus the criterion is satisfied. The second possibility is that once disconnected from the common good, the peace to which right intent is ordered might be connected instead to a universal interest. For example, throughout history, great empires have claimed for themselves with some regularity a kind of exceptionalism that prompts them to declare that what is good for them is good for the world, by which they mean that they are the privileged carriers of a universal interest that subsumes and supersedes the interests of all others. Here we might think of ancient Rome or of Napoleon's aspirations for his European campaign. More recently, many equate democratic capitalism or human rights with a universal interest. Others have suggested that the United States, as an indispensable nation whose political power ought to be extended in a kind of benevolent empire, embodies a universal interest. In each case, the peace that is the object of right intent becomes synonymous with the advancement of a particular nation or people's interest, which is now declared to be universal.

The problem with equating right intent with the pursuit of a universal interest is that unlike the common good, universal intent is not reversible. The common good is reversible in the sense that one could say the common good is the good of the person and the good of the person is the common good. In contrast, while one might say, for example, "what is good for the US is good for the world, including France," it is inconceivable that that same person would say "what is good for France is good for the US." Thus, the peace that comes from the advancement of a universal interest might conceivably be more than a mere truce or ceasefire; nevertheless, it remains the fragile or uneasy peace of an occupation rather than the genuine peace that comes from a shared common good.

Just Peace

That the modern political order is unable to sustain a peace ordered to the common good should not mislead one to believe that the early Christian political tradition had no difficulties with envisioning peace. Whether it was the Hebrew prophets denouncing those who claimed "peace, peace" when there was no peace (Jer. 6:14) or the ancient historian Tacitus rebuking the Roman Empire, "They plunder, they slaughter, and they steal. . . . And where they make a wasteland, they call it peace,"[4] peace was every bit as subject to abuse then as it is today. Augustine recognized that the peace intended in war could be something other than participation in a common good. Indeed, he noted, everyone and every war is for peace, albeit peace of a very particular kind:

> Neither is there anyone who does not wish to have peace. For even they who make war desire nothing but victory—desire, that is to say, to attain peace with glory. For what else is victory than the conquest of those who resist us? And when this is done there is peace. It is therefore with the desire for peace that wars are waged, even by those who take pleasure in exercising their warlike nature in command and battle. And hence it is obvious that peace is the end sought by war. . . . Even they who intentionally interrupt the peace in which they are living have no hatred of peace, but only wish to change it into a peace that better suits them.[5]

Every war, Augustine astutely observed, is fought for the sake of peace—for the sake of a peace that better suits the interests of those who initiate war. This prompts Augustine to distinguish the just peace of God from the unjust peace of sinful humanity, which is not worthy of being called peace.[6]

When Just War (CD) identifies right intent with peace, it follows Augustine and further specifies that the peace rightly intended in a just war is a just peace. It is not merely the peace of the strong who are able to impose their will on others, nor is it the unreflective peace of the public policy checklist that is at best a mere formality. Instead it is the peace that is the fruit of solidarity in the common good. It is what Augustine calls civil or earthly peace, whereby citizens live in concord on the basis of well-ordered laws that serve the earthly welfare of all.

Love of Enemy

The church's concern for the common good suggests another dimension of the criterion of right intent as part of Christian discipleship: that the intent of Just War (CD) is not simply the securing of our interests or even those of the unjustly attacked neighbor but extends to the good of the enemy as well points to the underlying power of love. Christ and Scripture are clear. One of the virtues that distinguishes discipleship is charity; one of the hallmarks of the life of the Christian community is love. Christians are called to love their neighbors, including even their enemies (Matt. 5:44).

That Christians may be called to engage in a just war does not excuse them from the call to love. Accordingly, right intent in Just War (CD) is a matter of love. While anger may be permitted, for it is not necessarily opposed to love, hatred is not because it is antithetical to love. As Aquinas says, "to regard your enemy with hatred is against charity."[7] Again, Augustine is instructive when he writes to a civil magistrate about his wielding the sword as part of his civic duties: "You're destroying justice by failing to love the person you are judging. Punishments should be imposed; I don't deny it; I don't forbid it. But this must be done in a spirit of love, in the spirit of concern, in the spirit of reform."[8] Calvin, likewise, appeals to Augustine and exhorts magistrates "to guard particularly against giving vent to their passions even in the slightest degree." He goes on to caution them that if they have to punish they should take care not to "be carried away with headlong anger, or be seized with hatred, or burn with implacable severity."[9]

Earlier we considered two ways of construing just war, either as an act of love or as a lesser evil. Then I argued that faithful discipleship could not be equated with doing evil, even only a lesser evil. Therefore just war, if it was to be a faithful form of discipleship, had to be understood as an act of love. Conceiving of just war as an act of love is both easy and difficult. Just war is easy to appreciate as an act of love when the focus is on the unjustly attacked neighbor. It is not hard to imagine going to war as an act of love when one thinks of defending the innocent from unjust aggression and harm. We respond to aggression because we love the victim of aggression.

What is more difficult to grasp is how just war could be an act of love for the enemy. It is difficult to imagine that one could truly love an enemy whom one confronts with military force, whom one threatens with the destruction of war, and whom one is prepared to kill. The difficulty of reconciling these two apparently contradictory acts—to love and to kill—prompts some to assert that the Christian call to love is preferential.[10] The difficulty of understanding just war as a form of love is resolved by acknowledging that we are called to love everyone but that we are not called to love everyone the same. In other words, there is a hierarchy of love and this hierarchy explains how just war can be a matter of love even as it favors some neighbors over others. Establishing a hierarchy or preferential ordering of love accounts for how we can love our enemies and still wage war against them. We love the innocent more than the guilty, and therefore we will take up arms to defend the innocent and kill the guilty.

Aquinas and the Hierarchy of Love

In support of this argument, appeal is made to Thomas Aquinas.[11] Aquinas argues that we are called to love everyone, including our enemies, but that there is a natural hierarchy of preference to our love. Thus, while we love everyone the same in the sense that we wish all the same good that is eternal happiness, with regard to both intensity of affection and benevolent action we love those who are closest to us more. Our love is preferentially ordered to those who have the greater connection to us; thus, we love our relatives the most, then our friends, then our fellow citizens, then our soldiers, and so forth.

At first glance, this argument is compelling. It certainly would account for how just war could be a form of love—a greater love for the innocent and a lesser love for the unjust aggressor. But the argument fails both because it is a misreading of Aquinas and because it is finally unnecessary. It is a misuse because his hierarchy of love does not necessarily correspond with the innocent and the aggressor in war. He orders love according to nearness of relations, with closer relations holding preference, not simply according to innocence and guilt. After all, in any given war it is possible that the unjust aggressor is actually one who is closer to us than the innocent victim. For example, imagine a situation where a neighboring nation or ally unjustly attacks a distant neighbor with whom we have few if any ties. In this situation, the love that moves us in just war would move us to oppose the nearer neighbor, who is the unjust aggressor, and aid the distant neighbor, who is the injured party. Therefore, simply appealing to Aquinas on the preferential ordering of love does not actually explain how one can attack an enemy and still claim to love them.

Being Prepared to Love All

Aquinas's hierarchy of love is more complicated than the argument above suggests. Consider, for example, how Aquinas distinguishes between affection and the doing of good, which is called beneficence. He observes that the emotions that accompany love are hierarchically ordered such that the most intense affections are elicited by those who are closest to us. With regard to beneficence or the actual doing of good, however, the order of preference is decidedly more complicated. When Aquinas says that love does not require us to do good to all equally he is *not* justifying doing more good for our friends and less good for our enemies. Rather, the reason our beneficence is unequal is that we simply cannot do the same amount of good for everyone. Our beneficence is limited by our resources and opportunities.[12] We are able to do more good for some than for others because of time, place, and circumstance.

Explaining the command to love and do good to all, Aquinas says as much when he writes,

> the precept does not extend to this that we should actually love each and every neighbor in particular or do well by each one in a particular way, because no man is capable of having all men in mind in such a way that he would actually love each one in a particular way, nor is there any one capable of doing good or helping each and every one in a particular way.[13]

Simply put, I am much better situated to aid my next-door neighbor here in Columbia, South Carolina, than I am to aid my neighbor in a barrio of Tegucigalpa or in the rural Chinese countryside that I cannot even imagine, much less name. Granted, the interconnected nature of the globalized world shrinks these distances and can enhance opportunities for connection, but Aquinas's point holds. Our beneficence is unequal because we are circumstantially, providentially situated to aid some more than others.

Aquinas goes on to warn, though, that this inequality of opportunity does not excuse either our ignoring distant or less connected neighbors or our not being prepared to come to their aid should circumstances change. To the contrary, love requires that we be prepared to love everyone. Thus, after naming the order of preference for doing good according to our connection to others, he states an important qualification: "this may vary according to the various requirements of time, place, or matter in hand; because in certain cases one ought, for instance, to succor a stranger, in extreme necessity, rather than one's own father, if he is not in such urgent need."[14] This is to say, while beneficence may normally be preferentially ordered first toward relatives, then friends, and so forth, that ordering does not hold absolutely. The call of God to love in any given circumstance may rearrange that ordering such that the stranger or ordinarily distant neighbor elicits preferential treatment over closer relations.

Lest any suspicion remains that the hierarchy of love sanctions loving enemies less than friends or the righteous, Aquinas goes on to explicitly state that the love we owe our enemies is not simply that of wishing them the blessing of knowing Christ but extends to beneficence. After all, Aquinas argues, while we do not love our enemies as enemies, we do love our enemies as they pertain to God.[15] Our enemy neighbor remains our neighbor whom we are called to love; therefore, Christians love their enemies not just in general but also in particular. No less than our distant or disconnected neighbors, charity requires that we be prepared to love our enemies when time, place, circumstance, or providence place our enemies before us and in need of our beneficence. When circumstance connects us to our enemies, we are to do good to them no less than to others with whom we are connected. Indeed, Aquinas writes, to love one's enemies with the same affection and deeds bestowed on a friend is a more perfect form of love than to love only one's friends: "charity is more perfect through which one is moved, both in loving and in doing good, toward not only neighbors but also foreigners, and beyond this even to enemies, not only in general but in particular."[16] Clearly, when Aquinas says we love preferentially he is not saying we can kill our enemies because we love them less than the innocent.

Not only is this a misreading of Aquinas, but it is also unnecessary to make sense of the claim that Just War (CD) is a form of love both for the innocent neighbor and no less for the enemy neighbor. Just War (CD) is a form of loving one's enemy, in the sense that Augustine argued just war was a kind of benevolent severity or harsh kindness, or in the sense that others have suggested it is an "alien act of charity."[17] It is an *alien* act of love because going to war and being prepared to kill one's neighbor is not ordinarily what we would call love. Yet it is an alien act of *love* for at least three reasons. First, Just War (CD) is an act of love toward the enemy neighbor insofar as it restricts the violence that may be used against them. Because we are called to love even our enemies, because we love them as they belong to God (even if they do not recognize that relation and so do not properly love themselves or others), we will not use any and every violence we can against them. We will not visit any and every kind of harm, destruction, and cruelty on them. Instead, our use of violence is disciplined and restrained. It is confined to the violence that operates in accord with the just war discipline. This restraint is an act of love.

Second, it is a form of love insofar as the duration of violence is limited. As we will see in subsequent chapters, Just War (CD) entails stopping the fight when the enemy yields or redresses the injury and injustice inflicted. Just War (CD) grants to the enemy the opportunity to end the fighting at any moment. Because Christians are called to love even their enemies, even in the midst of war and battle, we will not slay the defeated, refuse to accept surrender ("take no prisoners"), or press a rout for the sake of vengeance or geopolitical advantage.

Third, it is a form of enemy-love to the extent that the goal of a just war is not the death and destruction of the enemy but rather the restoration of the common good, of the order of peace and justice. In other words, the intent of a just war is to bring the benefits of a just peace to the enemy. "Be a peacemaker, therefore, in war," writes Augustine, "so that by conquering them you bring the benefit of peace even to those you defeat."[18] The church's hope and prayer in going to war is that even as war is undertaken, the enemy will repent, turn, and seek justice or reconciliation. This is why Augustine speaks of a *benevolent* severity and a *kind* harshness. The intent in waging a just war is the attainment of the good for *all* involved—the common good, *the* right and not just *our* right.

After all, injustice and aggression are not only bad for the victims of the injustice and aggression; they are bad for the aggressor as well—no matter what temporary, temporal gain they think they are securing. To put this rather baldly and in pointedly theological terms, sin is not just bad for those around the sinner who suffer from the sinner's behavior; sin is bad for the sinner as well. Thus Augustine writes that wars should be waged in a spirit of benevolence, and by this he means among other things that depriving the wicked of the license to pursue their wickedness is a benefit to them.[19]

Because Christians love even their enemies, their desire in waging a just war is *not* to kill them. In distinct contrast with some styles of war, which focus on maximizing the destruction of enemy forces and increasing the "body count," Christians do not desire death and destruction even in the midst of war. "The prince should press his campaign not for the destruction of his opponents," Vitoria argues, "but for the pursuit of the justice for which he fights . . . so that by fighting he may eventually establish peace and security."[20] Along the same lines, Augustine notes that it ought to be necessity and not our will or desire that destroys the enemy.[21] A similar sentiment is expressed by Paul Ramsey: "The objective of combat is the incapacitation of a combatant from doing what he is doing because he is this particular combatant in this particular war; it is *not* the killing of a man."[22]

Hence, in marked contrast with reports of chaplains offering prayers before an operation petitioning God to "help us kill them," the tradition has held that Christians should feel compassion and even regret at every evil that befalls an enemy. For this reason, the tradition admonishes chaplains that, even as they may encourage soldiers in waging wars justly and exhort them to courage, they are not to stir up bloodlust and encourage slaughter during battle. Likewise, Augustine criticizes in particular those persons—not only clergy—who would pray for the deaths of their enemies.[23]

Of course killing does happen in war. But whereas some may rejoice in the fact that war permits one to take off the gloves and eliminate the enemy instead of merely apprehending them, for Christians waging just war as an act of discipleship there can be no such rejoicing. After all, it would be inappropriate to rejoice over the death of one whom Christ loves and whom we are called to love as well. That the enemy has refused to yield, that the enemy has not turned from their injustice, and so the conflict has reached the point where the enemy is attacked with lethal force, should not give rise to a sense of relief, as if one has finally been freed to do what one wanted to do all along. If the enemy is killed, the appropriate posture is not revelry but regret. "Wars and conquests may rejoice unprincipled men, but are a sad necessity in the eyes of men of principle," writes Augustine.[24] Then, reflecting on the necessity of just wars, he reinforces this sentiment, continuing, "Let everyone, therefore, who reflects with pain upon such great evils, upon such horror and cruelty, acknowledge that this is misery. And if anyone either endures them or thinks about them without anguish of soul, his condition is still more miserable: for he thinks himself happy only because he has lost all human feeling."[25] A just warrior is, in a sense, a sad warrior. And the appropriate response to the successful end of a just war is not a celebration of victory—although a just war people will be glad and relieved that the war has ended—but sorrow that war was a necessity in the first place and sorrow for the death and destruction that all involved have suffered.[26]

Complete Justice

Thus far we have unpacked right intent in terms of seeking a just peace and love of enemy. The third and final aspect of right intent as part of Just War (CD) is what might be called "complete justice." In order to best grasp what is meant by complete justice, let us reflect for a moment on what incomplete justice looks like. If we consider all that has been said about the justice that animates Just War (PPC), it begins to look rather thin and incomplete. We might say that its justice is not just enough. It does not seek the common good, "justice for all," but only private or partial interests, "justice for me."

It is incomplete in another sense as well: it is *selective*. Only some injustices merit attention and only some of the time. For example, in a given situation a particular injustice may be denounced and troops mobilized against the offending party, while a host of similar injustices are routinely ignored and other equally just causes pass by unaddressed. The selectivity of justice refers to a partiality that prompts opponents of a war to wonder if the stated just cause and right intent are but a pretext for other less honorable concerns. Selectivity refers to that which gives rise to quips like, "if such and such a country exported pickles instead of petroleum . . ." or "if its citizens were a different color . . . ," then there would be no cries for war, the troops would be in the barracks, and the injustice in question would pass unnoticed.

The selective appeal to justice is not a problem for the public policy checklist approach. If a just cause exists and the legitimate authorities declare that peace is the objective and simultaneously renounce revenge, no questions are asked about the selective nature of the appeal to justice. That those same authorities may routinely ignore similar injustices does not raise any red flags about the rightness of their intent and the sincerity of their commitment to justice. That they may have shown little regard for justice in similar situations in the past does not prompt the question, "Why here and now and not then and there?" Right intent according to the public policy checklist approach only concerns the here and now, this particular instance. All that matters is intention in this particular case. We might say that it is a matter not only of justice for me but also of justice *now*.

The difficulty with this understanding of intention is twofold. The first problem is that it assumes that it is possible to discern intentions by looking solely at the here and now. Yet with a moment's reflection, most of us recognize that our intentions frequently are not so easy to discern. While intentions are not *always* opaque, neither are they always or even ordinarily transparent—particularly when we take into account both our penchant for self-deception and the ubiquity of "spin" and "disinformation" in contemporary politics. Intentions are not as easily ascertained as the public policy checklist approach presumes. One might say that our moral psychology as well as our politics are more complicated than the checklist approach allows for.

The second problem with right intent cast as justice now is that it operates on the faulty assumption that right intentions are fairly easy to employ. It is assumed that anyone can summon and sustain the proper intent in waging war; it is simply a matter of willpower. Simply will yourself to intend justice, peace, and the common good. Insofar as it says nothing about character, the public policy checklist approach assumes that even a vicious person (i.e., one habitually disposed to vice instead of virtue) or a habitually unjust people could bring forth right intention from their sin-calloused hearts at a moment's notice. That one has never given a moment's thought to justice or caring about the plight of the downtrodden, or that one has attained high office precisely by exercising habits of speech and action that work against the common good, is thought to have no effect on one's ability to discern and pursue justice with the single-mindedness that distinguishes right intent.

But the moral life, particularly if that life is to be sustained amidst the trials of warfare, does not work that way. A right intention that is sustainable through the moral challenges of war is not something that can be pulled like a rabbit from a hat. No doubt many of us secretly harbor the hope that even as we are constantly compromising our convictions with regard to little things, when it *really* counts we will suddenly be able to summon the courage of our convictions, stand fast without compromising, and do the right thing.

Unfortunately, as the experience of war shows, such hopes are unfounded. As veterans and those who have attended to the moral stresses of combat remind us, good intentions are not summoned on the spot but must be ingrained, through the preparation of long training and formation. To put this in the starkest of terms, what finally distinguishes the perpetrators of something like the atrocity at My Lai from those who refuse or even resist such actions is not that the latter were able to summon the willpower or intent *ex nihilo*—out of nothing—while the former intended evil. Rather, what matters is character. In an atrocity-producing situation there may well be genuine sociopaths involved, but it is perhaps more likely that there are decent people involved who lacked the character necessary to sustain good intentions in profoundly stressful situations. Just as right intent is not discerned in the moment, neither is it generated on the spot.

In contrast with the public policy checklist approach's selective notion of justice, Just War (CD) understands the criterion of right intention to be a matter of complete justice. In one sense, complete justice hearkens back to the criterion of just cause: not simply justice for me, but justice for all. In another sense—the one that will be the focus here—complete justice refers not only to justice *now*, here in this particular instance, but also to justice in the past and future.

This has the benefit of avoiding the difficulties that afflict intent-narrowly-conceived-as-justice-now with regard both to discerning and to enacting intentions. Consider several common social practices that are regularly involved in discerning intentions. Whether it is confession, counseling, or the judicial system, these practices suggest that intentions are best discerned over time in patterns of behavior that reflect who one fundamentally is. Thus, at its best the practice of confession is not interested in isolated acts but in the underlying orientation of the soul toward the good and away from evil. Likewise, counseling is most illuminating when it is able to position discrete behaviors within the broader narrative direction of a life. And judicial systems consider prior acts as well as character witnesses as an aid to discerning intention. This is not to say that people cannot act out of character or that any given action is not a reflection of character and intention, only that ordinarily intentions are most visible as they are displayed over time in character. Right intent conceived as complete justice recognizes this in a way that the public policy checklist does not.

Attending to intention as it is displayed over time in patterns of behavior that reflect character also addresses the difficulty of enacting intention that troubled intent-understood-as-justice-now. Whereas Just War (PPC) treats intentions as if they were something that could be willed on the spot, complete justice recognizes that intentionality is related to character, which means that fostering right intent depends less on willpower and more on the long-term development and reinforcement of just character. Right intent—the desire for complete justice in war—is the act of a people who habitually, in their day-to-day life, desire justice not selectively or occasionally but always and for everyone. Right intention as the intention for complete justice springs from and is an expression of not the desire of a moment but the orientation of a life.

Justice Looking Forward

One dimension of this intentionality for complete justice is the intention to enact justice in the future. Hence, discerning the intention for complete justice involves considering how one is prepared to implement justice in the future. This can be parsed in two ways. First, it involves the pursuit of justice in the course of actually waging war. One indicator of right intention in going to war, then, is the way that intention is displayed in the commitment to abide by the demands of justice as those demands are articulated in the criteria that discipline how a just war is fought. In other words, declarations of right intention reveal themselves to be true or false by the way they are accompanied (or not) by both preparation for and the actual waging of war justly. If a people goes to war for justice but then shows little regard for distinguishing between legitimate and illegitimate targets, for example, or simply unleashes everything it has against an enemy, then its professions of justice ring hollow. Conversely, an indicator of right intent is the preparation for and execution of war in a manner disciplined by the criteria.

A second dimension of justice looking forward is doing justice after the shooting stops. After all, can claims to right intent really hold if at the conclusion of a war the victorious side simply abandons the defeated? To simply walk away from the defeated would cast serious doubt on one's intention in waging the war to begin with. If one's intent in waging war is indeed just, if one really loves one's enemies and intends to bring the benefits of peace and justice to them, then one will not abandon them when the shooting stops but will be involved in the restoration of a just peace. If one truly desires justice, then one will stay the course and see justice through to completion.

Incidentally, it is not uncommon to hear calls for the addition of a new category to the just war discipline, called justice *post bellum*—justice after the war. But when just war is approached as an expression of the character of a people who consistently seek justice, and the criterion of right intent is understood accordingly, this is unnecessary.

What is entailed in seeing justice through to completion *post bellum* can be approached from two angles.[27] First, there is the question of what the desire for justice requires of the victor in a just war. The answer to this question will vary, depending on the nature of the victory. If the just cause of war was satisfied and the injustice corrected by something short of occupying the enemy country and overturning its government, justice may entail that assistance be given to the governing authorities so that they may indeed govern. Justice may require offering assistance in restoring a just peace and cleaning up after the war, whether that involves exchanging prisoners, rebuilding infrastructure, finding and removing unexploded ordinance, or similar acts.

In other situations, where the unjust party is particularly stubborn or the nature of the injustice that gave rise to the war is of a particular sort—genocide, perhaps—a just victory may find the victor occupying a country and effecting regime change. As Vitoria says, while it is certainly not just to depose a ruler or overthrow a government for any and every injustice—after all, the punishment should fit the crime—there may nevertheless be legitimate grounds for doing so, which Vitoria equates with the extent of the harm inflicted by a ruler or government.[28] In a situation where the injustice in question merited regime change, complete justice would involve a host of matters that today are generally treated under the heading of "exit strategies." To begin with, complete justice would require that one have an exit strategy in going to war. Along these lines, evidence of a just intent in waging war would include a willingness and a preparation to commit the resources necessary to establish the peace and justice that was the stated intention of the war. Such a commitment would include the acts of assistance already mentioned as well as the commitment of sufficient troops and/or police and civil affairs personnel to secure and maintain the peace while the new government is established. It goes without saying that complete justice would entail not replacing one tyrant with another or with one whose chief qualification is that of being more amenable to the victorious nation's interests.

In addition to expectations regarding how one treats the defeated enemy, justice embodied *post bellum* includes obligations toward the victorious power's own citizens and soldiers as well. For example, if the war effort imposed hardships such as rationing, travel restrictions, additional taxes, reordered budgetary priorities, and so forth, the government is obliged with the conclusion of the war to restore civil life as much as possible to the *status quo ante*, to the way civil life was before the war. Furthermore, waging and concluding a war justly entails treating fairly those who actually fight the war, providing appropriate assistance to returning soldiers as they reintegrate with peacetime life and, for some, civilian life. Justice also requires that soldiers be provided appropriate care for the health issues related to their service and appropriate survivor benefits when such service results in death.

The second angle of justice *post bellum* concerns what may justly be required of the defeated enemy. Recalling that just cause includes recovering that which was unjustly seized as well as restoring a just order, right intent in waging war may include seeking reparations. Such reparations include material compensation for the injustice that gave rise to the war as well as costs and damages associated with prosecuting the war itself. Additionally, a certain amount above the costs involved, as a kind of penalty or fine for committing the injustice in the first place, may be included in this compensation. Such a penalty is permitted as part of the restorative character of a just war; it serves the common good as a kind of corrective for the guilty and deterrent for others.

Beyond material reparations, complete justice *post bellum* may also ask of the defeated that they answer for their criminal acts before the bar of justice. In this sense, right intent in waging war does not preclude the possibility of the criminal prosecutions of persons guilty of war crimes. Of course, as an expression of justice, such prosecutions will not properly be a matter of what is sometimes called "victor's justice," where only crimes of the defeated are brought before the bar of justice. Rather, a just people who intend justice in war will expect nothing more from their enemy than they ask of themselves. They will not hold their enemy accountable to a higher standard than they hold themselves.

Having recognized that intending justice *post bellum* does not rule out either reparations or prosecutions, there is one important caveat. Even as it affirms the justice of reparations and prosecution, the tradition is clear that the demand for such ought to be tempered by a certain mercy, lest the enforcement of a rigorous and rigid justice actually undermine the order that it is meant to serve and support. As Suárez says about requiring reparations, reflecting the heart of the tradition, "regard must be had for the future peace."[29] After all, to demand equitable reparations and damages at the conclusion of a just war that left the populace of the defeated nation in dire straits or crippled the defeated government's ability to perform the proper tasks of governing would not actually serve the justice and peace that were the cause and intent of the war in the first place; rather, it would undermine the common good that was the professed end of the war to begin with. Thus justice and right intent *post bellum* entails enduring harm and forgoing claims if doing so promotes reconciliation and the renewal of peace.

Justice Looking Backward

A second dimension of right intent as complete justice involves considering one's past actions in light of the demands of justice. Accordingly, discerning right intent includes looking backward. After all, an unjust past casts doubt on present professions of right intention and makes it more difficult to embody those professed intentions in the present and future.

This means that even as it engages in just war for the sake of holding its neighbor accountable for injustice, the church will shine the light of justice on its own life and on that of the society it would support in waging a just war. Recalling Jesus's exhortation in Matthew 7:5, "First take the log out of your own eye, and then you will see clearly to take the speck out of your neighbor's eye," it will engage in and encourage others to engage in self-examination for the sake of confirming (and where necessary correcting) its own life in accord with the justice to which it would hold others accountable by means of just war. As Luther says, the first response to an injustice suffered should be to "remove the rod from God's hand," which need not mean "blame the victim" but rather examine one's life and where necessary correct it so that one will be better positioned to pursue justice with one's neighbor.

This task of looking backward for justice can be approached in two ways. First, there is the matter of discerning how justice may have been neglected or ignored in the past. This corresponds to what the Christian tradition calls "sins of omission." If its intent is truly just, as the church contemplates sanctioning and engaging in just war, it will take care to ask itself and listen to others regarding past injustices that it may have failed to see or neglected to address. If, for example, its intent is just in going to war against a tyrant who oppresses his people and unjustly threatens his neighbors, then the church will ask itself as well as the governing authorities, "Have we ignored or failed to address similar injustices in the past? Are we doing so even now in the present?" If the church discovers that injustices have been and/or are being ignored or neglected, then it has grounds for being cautious regarding claims of right intent in the present. At the very least, such a revelation should elicit a further set of questions along the lines of, "If here and now, why not also then and there? Why do we seek justice in this situation when we did not (or are not) in that situation?" If present intent is right, then a morally compelling answer to these and similar questions should be forthcoming.

The second way of approaching justice looking backward has a more active focus, akin to what is called "sins of commission." Here discerning right intent entails inquiring about how one has actually perpetrated injustice. A just war people going to war in the name of justice will examine their own life with an eye to how they may have been or are engaged in or complicit with injustice. For example, even as a just war people goes to war against a tyrant who oppresses his own people (perhaps using chemical weapons and torture on them) and threatens his neighbors, if their intent is truly just they will ask themselves if they have in the past supported oppressive regimes (maybe even this regime), perhaps supplying them with weapons and political cover. Once again, if such self-examination uncovers injustice, then one has reason to be cautious in accepting at face value present professions of right intent. At the very least, past injustice should prompt further questions that require satisfactory answers before the right intent of a given war could be recognized. Uncovering past complicity should raise questions along the lines of, what, if anything has changed? What led us to support injustice then and what leads us to reject it now? Is it a change prompted by justice or is it simply a new twist to the same effort to secure private goods and interests, using justice as a mere pretext? Again, if one's intent is right, then morally compelling answers should be forthcoming.

At this point, two objections surface. The first concerns the necessity of justice looking backward. If one is committed to justice in the present and future, what is gained by looking backward? Indeed, might not looking backward undermine the pursuit of justice in the present by sowing doubts? Isn't what is needed in the present not introspection and second-guessing but fortitude and the stubborn determination to stay the course?

The importance of looking backward stems from its contribution to the formation of the character that might sustain just intention in the face of the trials and temptations of war and its aftermath. By looking backward a just war people is able to discern the shape of its intention and take any necessary corrective action for the sake of present and future justice. This is the problem with contemporary calls for a "justice *post bellum*" category. While the desire to sustain justice after the war is praiseworthy, merely adding a future dimension to the public policy checklist approach's narrow focus on justice now is inadequate. Expanding the justice intended in war to the future while ignoring the past leaves the intended justice susceptible to being nothing more than the stubborn determination to persist in injustice.

This is the case because while fortitude and endurance are crucial character traits of a just war people, by themselves they are insufficient to ensure that one is persisting in the pursuit of justice. One could be stubbornly determined to pursue justice and nevertheless wreak havoc because one does not really know what justice entails. Echoing Augustine, we could say that every war is waged for justice. But which justice? Only a willingness to examine one's past behavior can provide an answer to the kind of justice that is likely to be pursued in the present and future. Self-examination is crucial to knowing which justice one is likely to pursue.

Attending to the past is important for another reason. Already we have raised the significance of character for enacting justice. Enacting justice requires more than mere determination or willpower; one must be attuned to what justice is and formed in the habits and practices that render the pursuit of justice second nature. This is what is meant by character. Right intent arises from and is sustained by character. Consider the centrality of drill and repetition, particularly under stressful conditions, to good military training, as well as the importance of being steeped in military tradition and culture. The point is to mold the character of soldiers so that certain dispositions and actions become almost a second nature. The same holds for right intent and the church's desire for justice. If the church does not intend justice in its everyday life, if its members do not habitually desire justice for their neighbors, then the likelihood is greatly diminished that they will intend justice and persevere in that intention under the extraordinary demands that can accompany warfare. The desire for true justice cannot be summoned in an instant out of the blue. It is therefore important that justice look backward and attend to the habits and practices of everyday life, in order that Christians' intentions toward their neighbors might be rightly shaped toward justice. In this way, as right intention becomes central to the character of the church in peacetime, so it is more likely to be sustained in times of war.

Confessing Failures of Intention

This brings us to the second objection to the importance that Just War (CD) gives to looking backward for discerning and enacting right intent. What happens if injustice is uncovered? Does past injustice preclude seeking justice in the present? Does the criterion of right intention require moral purity? Does a people's or ruler's being guilty of wrong strip them of the moral responsibility to pursue right?

A response to this objection is many sided. To begin with, past or even present moral failings do not prohibit one from pursuing what is right and just. Past sin, we might say, is not an excuse for ignoring righteousness in the present. That the history of a nation or people or church is marred by injustice does not absolve them of the responsibility to pursue justice in the present. Past wrongs do not disqualify one from doing right in the present.

It should be noted, however, that acknowledging this fact does not constitute an excuse for ignoring the criterion of right intent and its call for self-examination. The recognition that sin does not disqualify one from pursuing justice could play into the hands of those who would pull the teeth of the just war discipline. For instance, one might argue that violating one or more of the criteria does not prohibit one from pursuing the just cause of confronting evil. Just like past injustice does not preclude pursuing present justice, the good of a war against evil and injustice is not jeopardized by the wrong of violating one or more of the criteria.

Such an argument is flawed because it determines that a given war is right and just apart from the just war criteria. Yet the Christian tradition holds that it is precisely—and only—these criteria that establish a war's goodness. A war, even one waged against a great evil, is not good and just if it ignores any of the criteria.

Moreover, such an argument is not analogous to the claim that past injustice does not preclude present justice. The argument is actually an argument on behalf of an unjust war; as such, it has nothing to do with present justice but with present injustice.

The second side to a response concerns moral purity. Right intent as complete justice does not require that only the morally pure may wage just wars. Neither past nor present sin are necessarily incompatible with the just war discipline and right intent. On one hand, the rejection of mixed motives is not a denial that moral action occurs in the face of conflicted passions. The Christian tradition recognizes that insofar as we are sinners, we remain afflicted by conflicted passions and desires. Alongside the desire for justice may reside a desire for vengeance, greed, or a host of other wicked desires. The presence of these desires, however, does not automatically violate right intention. Right intention does not require the absence of conflicted desires. Rather, what renders intention unjust is not the mere presence of conflicted tempers but consenting to act on them. This is what sets the moral psychology of Just War (CD) apart from Walzer's mixed motives. Whereas Walzer thinks one can, and perhaps even must, simultaneously act on conflicted tempers, the Christian tradition (at its best) holds that one need not consent to vicious tempers and that one cannot act simultaneously on both just and unjust motives. Justice and injustice are mutually exclusive; to consent to an unjust desire corrupts or dilutes the intention for justice. Right intention, then, is not about moral purity; it is about refusing to act on unjust desires.

The third side of a response addresses what is to be done when injustice is discovered. What happens when problems of character and consistency are exposed? Previously it was noted that the discovery of injustice should prompt questions to which there should be morally compelling answers. Among the questions was one that asked what, if anything, has changed between then and now. This brings us to the importance of confession for right intent as complete justice.

Put simply, right intent as complete justice does not preclude sinners waging war so long as would-be just warriors confess their sin and repent of the same. The Greek word for repentance means "to turn," and such turning is precisely the kind of change that backward-looking justice should prompt if it uncovers past injustice. Confessing complicity with and contributing to injustice means naming it, taking responsibility for it, and correcting it—not denying it, excusing it, covering it up, or passing it off on a few lowly scapegoats or "bad apples." And this holds not only for injustice discovered in the past but also for any done during or after a war. In this regard, the just war tradition speaks of reparations being in order even for just warriors. It is not only the side that lacks just cause in a war that owes reparations; even a just war people have a responsibility to make amends for any injustice they perpetrate before, during, or after a just war.

This process of confessing, taking responsibility, and making amends for wrongs constitutes the practice of penance. During the Middle Ages it was not unusual for all warriors who returned from a just war to be required to do penance—not because war was thought to be intrinsically evil but because the difficulty of waging a just war without any sin was recognized.

The point of looking backward as part of discerning and shaping right intent, therefore, is not to check for moral purity and stop those who are not pure from waging a just war. The self-examination that right intent requires is not for the sake of determining *if* a governing authority has a *responsibility* to seek justice for its neighbors. The just war tradition is clear on this point: governing authorities do indeed have a responsibility for justice, a responsibility that is not diminished by the reality of sin and injustice in its exercise of government. Rather, the self-examination that is part of right intent is about the *capability* for justice. Looking backward is necessary not to determine *responsibility* but to help strengthen our *capability* to carry out that responsibility with moral integrity. Governing authorities have a responsibility to preserve peace and justice; right intent is crucial to exercising that responsibility faithfully, and self-examination is a necessary aid in forming that right intent.

Justice on Both Sides?

We are now in a position to consider whether more than one party in a conflict can have a legitimate claim on justice. Although such a question appears to be more suited to the criterion of just cause, its resolution is tied to right intention. Recall that Vitoria addressed this in terms of what has come to be called "simultaneous ostensive justice." More recently, the US Catholic bishops invoked the idea of "comparative justice," by which they meant that just cause was held by the party who had the stronger claim to justice.[30]

Although Vitoria is frequently credited with affirming the possibility that all parties in a conflict could have justice on their side, in fact he rejected the idea. What he said was that all parties might *think* they have justice on their side.[31] This, in itself, is a thoroughly unsurprising claim and not particularly helpful. Few conflicts, after all, begin with one party asserting that they are indeed wrong. Furthermore, Vitoria held that where the parties involved do have just claims against each other, neither may justly go to war against the other. Why is this? Although he does not say so explicitly, the answer is clear: because right intent precludes it. After all, if one has right intent, understood as intending justice for all, then one will address the just claim of one's enemy. In other words, it is a clear sign that one does not have right intent if one goes to war in the name of an injustice *suffered* but is unwilling to address the injustice one has *inflicted*. Such an action appears driven by "my right" and not "*the* right." The same holds for situations of comparative justice. Right intent prompts one to make amends for injustice inflicted and so remove the cause for war against oneself. Thus, there could not be just cause on both sides.

It is worth noting another reason why justice on both sides of a war is unlikely. This involves legitimate authority and the church's practice of intercession and mediation of conflicts. The church has been given legitimate authority to discern and adjudicate conflicts and claims of justice, at least with regard to determining whether Christians should serve in a given war. Thus, when two rulers claim just cause and prepare for war, the church should discern just claims where it is able to, speak the truth in the face of possible pretexts and self-deceptions, point out the imperative to address those just claims as a sign of right intent, and encourage negotiation and mediation. Where negotiation fails and the question of justice remains in doubt, it will not declare a war just on both sides nor will it calculate comparative justice. Instead, acknowledging the lack of clarity, it would remind its members that governing authorities are owed the benefit of a doubt in such situations.

The Challenge for the Church

Fostering a Commitment to the Common Good

The challenges for the church presented by the criterion of right intent begin with right intent as a desire for a just peace that is synonymous with the common good. The primary challenge is fostering a desire not simply for a peace that better suits our interests or a justice that focuses on our rights but for a just peace that is indivisible from the flourishing of the common good.

In this regard, the criterion of right intent cannot be treated apart from both legitimate authority and just cause insofar as they all revolve around fostering a robust commitment to the common good. Right intent puts the same challenge to the church of encouraging an expansive notion of the self that is fundamentally other-regarding. Hence, when the church fosters leaders and governing authorities who seek the common good, or when it is forming its own members through preaching, teaching, and the works of mercy to be attentive to the needs of others, it is shaping a people capable of waging war with right intent.

Learning to Love Our Enemies

A second challenge presented by right intent concerns loving enemies. Because just war does not excuse the church from doing so, we would do well to ask ourselves how seriously we take the gospel's call to love our enemies. For example, do we regularly pray for our enemies in both private and corporate prayer, or do we pray only for our side and our own? We might ask if apart from war we can even name our enemies. Or have we succumbed to a culture of niceness that shies away from doing so because it is considered impolite? If we find it difficult even to acknowledge forthrightly the presence of enemies, we will be hard pressed to love them on those occasions when we cannot avoid facing them. Likewise, recognizing that loving enemies is not something that comes naturally and that we are only likely to sustain those practices and convictions *in* war that we have practiced *before* war, we might ask ourselves if in the midst of a highly charged, ideologically polarized culture the church encourages and models in its own life ways of dealing with conflict that manifest the love of enemies. Or do we simply avoid the difficult task of loving enemies by separating from those with whom we disagree? This is to say, do we model the love that desires to share the benefits of a just peace with our enemies (with the hope thereby of rendering them friends), or do we simply mimic and perpetuate a harsher politics where the winner takes all and the loser is silenced, ignored, or encouraged to leave? Alternatively, do we avoid loving our enemies by repressing conflict altogether or by clinging to a sentimentality that refuses to accept that sometimes love must be tough, benevolence severe, and kindness harsh?

To be more specific, we may recall how waging a just war is an alien act of charity and ask if the church is intentional about forming disciples whose intentions are charitable in waging war. There were three ways that just war was named an alien act of charity. First, just war is an alien act of love insofar as the amount and kind of violence used against the enemy is limited to that which conforms to the just war criteria. The challenge, then, for the church in this regard is of a piece with the challenge of the just war discipline as a whole, namely, to teach the discipline and instill an abiding commitment to live and die by it. Right intent is both shaped and shown by the church's public commitment to the just war discipline with all its teeth.

Second, just war is an alien act of love insofar as it limits the duration of the violence, ceasing to fight when the enemy either corrects the injustice that constituted the just cause for war or surrenders. This may be one of the most difficult challenges for Christians in war. The impulse for vengeance is perhaps strongest in those who have felt the suffering of war the sharpest— be it those who have lost loved ones, the civilian victims of war, or soldiers who have seen their comrades in arms killed. Nevertheless, right intent precludes vengeance and vindictiveness. Hence the challenge for the church is to embody the longsuffering love of its savior, who endures much but does not waver from the path of righteousness and justice. Here the just war discipline may approach a kind of cross bearing, where we are called to suffer injustice without retaliating in kind. In some instances this may mean that Christians are to show more care and compassion for the enemy than the enemy even shows for themselves, much less others. With regard to forming our character such that we would intend this love in war, we might consider who we hold up as role models and exemplars of the life well lived. Do we lift up the saints who displayed this longsuffering love for their enemies? Do we encourage one another to imitate those who do not return evil for evil but forgo wrath and vengeance and patiently pursue what is right? How do we treat those who have wronged us in our daily lives? Do we plot petty revenge and ways of returning tit for tat? How do we deal with criminals? Do we seek and encourage others to seek justice and not vengeance? Do we show them more care and concern than they showed others and perhaps even themselves? A people who do not renounce a vindictive spirit and who do not practice longsuffering love in their daily lives are not likely to be a people capable of sustaining a right intent toward their enemies in war.

The third way just war is an alien act of love is that its purpose is the good of the enemy. The challenges this presents have already been broached. Suffice it here to mention one additional challenge. Recall that a just war people's desire is not to kill or destroy the enemy and that when war results in the death of the enemy it is cause for sadness, not rejoicing. Indeed, just warriors prepare for war hopeful that their enemy will repent of their injustice. A sign of right intent, then, is the presence of hope as well as the appropriate sadness in the face of war and the death that follows from it. The challenge for the church is to foster this disposition of regret coupled with the hope that enemies will turn from their unjust ways prior to suffering death and destruction. In this regard, we might ask ourselves if we are a people who have learned not to rejoice in the troubles that befall those who trouble us. Do we take secret (or not-so-secret) pleasure in the news that a difficult or downright mean coworker or acquaintance has come on rough times? Or do we desire good for even the worst among us? Do we pursue the harsh kindness of justice not with a vindictive glee but with a sense of sad necessity?

Do we refuse to give up on people, always hopeful that they can turn? Do we simply write people off and wash our hands of them, or are we a people of hope? By this hope, of course, I do not mean that Christians are called to be optimistic about the ability of people to change. Rather, Christian hope is rooted in the goodness not of people but of a gracious God who can reach even the chief of sinners, as Paul testified, and make them saints, as the life of the church testifies. Thus, we might ask if our life and worship are ordered by hope, by the expectation that God acts, that the Spirit blows where it will, and so at any given time things can be otherwise. Are we perpetually prepared to be surprised by grace and find the hard heart of our enemy softened?

It is worth noting that addressing these issues in ways that indicate a genuine concern for fostering right intent will require the church to reflect on the nature of military institutions and training. For example, military training and culture should not deaden compassion.[32] Nor should they perpetuate the objectification of women and other cultures, neither of which bodes well for the chances of loving enemies.[33] Likewise, whereas appropriate love for enemies and sadness at their deaths does not necessarily rule out all forms of training that desensitizes soldiers to killing, it will preclude some forms and affect how other forms of that training are done.[34] Just warriors may not be the most effective and efficient killers; but that is not the point of just war.[35]

Seeking Complete Justice

The third challenge presented by the criterion of right intent involves the desire for complete justice. Insofar as complete justice is a matter of acquiring the character capable of sustaining the commitment to a just peace and love of enemies, the challenge it presents is that of being consistently—and not only occasionally or selectively—concerned with justice for all. Accordingly, it intersects with the challenges associated with the criterion of just cause—to be actively engaged in pursuing justice for our neighbors in every aspect of our daily life, be it through prayer, the works of mercy, our daily jobs, and so forth.

Along these lines, complete justice challenges the church to form a people who abide by commitments and convictions even when doing so is costly, when ignoring the plight of others might be easier and cheaper. Such a character trait might be called loyalty, fidelity, or faithfulness. To this end, we might ask, do we in the church find ourselves mimicking the moral logic of a wider culture that acts as if commitments and convictions are infinitely negotiable? Do we act as if every conviction and commitment is only tentative and may finally give way when the cost is deemed too much or too difficult to bear? Or do we teach, model, and lift up as exemplars of discipleship those who do not waver, whatever the cost to themselves or even their loved ones, in their commitment to the good and right?

In addition to the challenge of building character and instilling fidelity to commitments and convictions, right intent as complete justice presents specific challenges related to justice looking forward and backward. In terms of justice looking forward, right intent challenges the church to commit itself to the just war discipline not only prior to war but also in the actual waging of war by faithfully abiding by the criteria of discrimination and proportionality, which will be considered shortly.

Justice looking forward also challenges the church to follow through on the commitment to justice after the shooting stops. This means two things. First it means not abandoning the victims, the defeated enemy, or one's own soldiers at the conclusion of the war. Accordingly, as a just war people Christians will insist that "exit strategies" are developed and that preparations for a just war include anticipating the requirements of the postwar period, which may include a financial commitment, devoting adequate civil affairs and police personal, as well as perhaps coordinating with nongovernmental organizations in the work of reconstruction. Right intent will also take the shape of ensuring that one's own soldiers are cared for in appropriate ways, addressing physical, mental, and emotional needs and assisting in their reintegration into a peacetime society.

Second, it means avoiding enforcing "victor's justice" after the shooting stops. Even as the just war discipline permits requiring reparations and prosecuting war crimes, right intention as complete justice will not ruthlessly exact reparations or selectively enforce justice by confronting only the injustice of the defeated. In this regard, Christians are sometimes known as particularly strong advocates of law and order, and the criterion of right intent (and the criterion of just cause) gives ample support to the importance of a well-ordered civil life. But right intent reminds us that law and order are not ends in themselves but means to serve the spread of the benefits of a just peace. The challenge for the church, therefore, is that of being a people of mercy and compassion as well as justice. Just as its Lord, for the sake of reconciling sinful humanity to God, did not exact a strict accounting of what was due but acted with mercy and compassion, so the church is called to embody that same mercy and compassion even in war, for the sake of renewing the communion of all in the common good. We might say that the challenge for the church is to proclaim the end of the law, which is the upbuilding of human community, and by so doing contribute to the formation of a people whose intent in waging just war will be tempered by mercy and guided by a desire for the restoration of community.

The opportunities for learning compassion in the everyday life of the church are manifold, from how we engage conflict to how we deal with persons who break the law to how we treat those who wrong us in the course of our daily life. Opportunities extend even to such practices as how we care for the sick and dying. Each of these occasions gives us a chance to be formed in the compassion that is crucial to faithfully living right intent in Just War (CD).

In general, forward-looking justice amounts to a call for the patient endurance and courage of the saints. Right intent is a matter of unwavering commitment to justice no matter the cost. The question becomes how the church might be about forming this kind of courage and endurance. We might begin by asking to what extent we honor and actively encourage sacrifice and generous giving for the sake of the good. In the treatment of just cause a similar question was raised regarding forming a people to be other-directed. As I write this, many churches are engaged in their annual "stewardship campaigns." What is striking about several of these is the lengths to which some churches go to put members at ease by emphasizing that in effect giving should be guided by what one feels *comfortable* giving. A vision of discipleship that focuses on meeting people's felt needs and maintaining them in their comfort zone is not likely to shape or sustain a people in the costly discipleship that the criterion of right intent presupposes. On the contrary, it only reinforces the aversion to suffering and sacrifice that encourages attempts to win wars "on the cheap," so to speak, by avoiding responsibilities for the defeated as well as for the victor's own troops. To the end of combating this trend, the church might lift up the disciplines of the Christian life—such as prayer, fasting, and fidelity—that train us in patience and endurance and so prepare us to sustain right intent in war and see justice through to the end, abandoning neither the victims of war and injustice nor the defeated enemy.

Right intent as complete justice also challenges the church with regard to justice looking backward. As suggested above, the church should examine its past to see that its professed concern for justice is not merely a pretext for other less virtuous motives, and if it discovers that its concern for justice has been selective, it should confess and change. This is the challenge of confession, and it calls the church to form a people who are humble enough to name their sin and turn from it even as they name and correct the sins of their neighbors. In a culture and politics that are too often given to rationalizing or excusing moral failure on utilitarian grounds that the good outweighs the bad, that "on the whole we are a force for good in the world," or on the grounds that "dirty hands" cannot be avoided, this is quite a challenge.

Even where the sense remains that sin is both a bad thing and something that should be left behind, many churches have lost sight of the gift of confession, practicing it either infrequently or only in the most vague and abstract manner. Many fail to appreciate how naming sin is a crucial part of being set free from sin. Ignoring our shortcomings will not make them go away, nor will merely wishing to do better in the future make it happen. Rather, confession, repentance, and penance are means of grace God has given the church in God's goodness for the sake of helping it simultaneously unlearn the habits of sin and learn the habits of holiness.[36]

In the context of Just War (CD), naming sin is particularly important. If just war is premised on the intention of justice, and we know that we struggle with conflicted desires, examination and confession become crucial to right intention. Only by naming our conflicts, our failures to pursue justice, and our complicity with injustice can we address them, turn from them, and have confidence that we are indeed about justice for all when we engage in just war. Only by confessing and repenting can we avoid the charge of hypocrisy and injustice in waging a war for justice. Only by naming and unlearning the habits of injustice and learning the habits of justice can we hope to sustain right intent in the midst of the pressures of war and its aftermath. Confession, then, is a gift for the formation of the character of a people capable of engendering and sustaining right intent in war; the challenge is to embrace it as such.

There is an additional dimension to the challenge of confession that needs to be named: the care of soldiers after the shooting stops. As noted previously, right intent challenges the church to care not only for the defeated enemy but for one's own as well. Part of this care includes attending to the spiritual life of soldiers. As both the medieval practice of requiring even just warriors to do penance and contemporary studies of the spiritual and psychological effects of combat on soldiers suggests, the care of returning soldiers requires churches do more than offer accolades and praise.[37] Instead, soldiers need the space and opportunity to make sense of and at times confess, even when they have fought in a just war.[38] This is to say, right intent challenges the church to take seriously the ways even a just war can be spiritually challenging, not to mention an occasion for sin. Hence part of the challenge of confession is that of enabling the church to face the moral and spiritual trauma that soldiers may experience even in a just war instead of excusing it or burying it under yellow ribbons and applause. A church that truly intends justice will be prepared to both make and hear confessions as a means of grace that enables reintegration into the just peace of the common good.[39]

℘

One might argue that in the criterion of right intent the difference between Just War (PPC) and Just War (CD) is most apparent, for here the difference that character makes stands out in sharp relief. Just War (PPC) assumes that anyone can engage in just war simply by summoning the willpower to follow the criteria. Character does not matter. It does not matter if the individuals using the criteria habitually neglect justice. It does not matter if just yesterday they were perpetrating injustice. That their invocation of justice is selective does not raise an eyebrow. So long as they foreswear revenge and proclaim their desire for a generic peace, they can check off the criterion of right intent. So construed, right intent is a mere formality and it is little wonder that it has all but disappeared from the modern discussion and practice of just war.

In contrast, Just War (CD) embraces a much more substantial vision of right intent, one that cannot be enacted and sustained apart from communities that are about the work of forming a people of just character, a people who seek peace and justice for their neighbors in the many facets of its daily life, whether in the midst of war or peace. This vision of right intent depends on the presence of a community that constantly seeks the common good, that is ordinarily disposed to love its enemies and regret the punishments that necessarily befall them, and that is accustomed to confessing, repenting, and changing when it fails to do either.

If the tales soldiers tell are to be trusted, in the crucible of war willpower is unreliable; it is moral character that is tested and tried. Hence right intent is not a matter of what we would like or ought to do but who we are. Only a people of just character, a people for whom justice is the normal tenor of their life, can sustain right intent.

Having considered the "who" and "why" of war, we now turn to the "when," taking up in the next chapter the criteria of last resort and reasonable chance of success.

7

When Fight?

Last Resort and Reasonable Chance of Success

Grotius, after treating the various criteria we have already considered, begins a chapter entitled, "Precautions Against Rashly Engaging in War, Even Upon Just Grounds," with an explanation of why such a chapter is necessary. It is necessary, he writes, "in order to prevent anyone from supposing, that, after establishing the right of war, he is authorized, INSTANTLY or at ALL TIMES, to carry his principles into action."[1] What stands between "the right of war" embodied in the first three criteria and "carrying those principles into action" are the remaining two criteria that address justice in going to war. These two criteria—last resort and reasonable chance of success—together inform the decision of *when* to go to war, of when the legitimate authority ought to act on the just cause with right intent.

As we consider these two criteria, at first glance Just War (PPC) and Just War (CD) appear to offer similar treatments. Unlike the previous criteria, where the differences between the two approaches are rather stark, the differences that distinguish the two with regard to last resort and reasonable chance of success are initially more subtle if finally no less profound.

Consequently, this chapter does not develop as the earlier ones did, first setting forth the criterion according to Just War (PPC) and then considering how Just War (CD) treats it differently. Instead, this chapter begins by considering what is shared by both approaches, then considers how they diverge. I begin with the criterion of last resort before moving to the criterion of reasonable chance of success. I conclude, as has been the pattern in earlier chapters, with the challenges these criteria present to the church.

Last Resort

This criterion holds that the resort to the force of arms is morally justified only after other feasible means of addressing injustice have been attempted and failed. As Suárez writes, a just war is one that responds to a grave injustice "which cannot be avenged or repaired in any other way."[2] A just war is not ordinarily the first response to an injustice that rises to the level of a just cause for war. In this way, last resort is further evidence of the claim made earlier that having a just cause does not by itself give a green light to wage war. Last resort reminds us that just cause is a necessary but not sufficient element of a just war.

The qualifier "ordinarily" above hints at one exception to the requirement that just war be a matter of last resort. The criterion presupposes that ordinarily there is both time and political opportunity to respond to an injustice with means other than war. The tradition assumes that ordinarily the first response and last resort are distinct, although how much space stands between them will vary with circumstances. But there is one circumstance where first response and last resort may coincide—when an unjust attack is underway. The criterion of last resort does not expect a people to refrain from fighting in the face of an unjust attack that is currently underway; in this regard, recall that repelling an attack underway is one of the legitimate causes of a just war. Such a circumstance, however, is not really an exception to the criterion of last resort. Rather, it is an instance of the point of last resort being reached almost immediately.

Means Other Than War

Nevertheless, the tradition expects that usually the first response to a just cause will not be an act of war. Even in the case where one has suffered an unjust attack that has been completed, the just war tradition holds that means of addressing the injustice short of war must first be attempted.

Referring to the fact that princes are bound to avoid war insofar as is possible by upright means, Suárez offers a theological rationale for last resort:

> It is impossible that the Author of nature should have left human affairs . . . in such a critical condition that all controversies between sovereigns and states

should be settled only by war; for such a condition would be contrary to prudence and to the general welfare of the human race; and therefore it would be contrary to justice. Furthermore, if this condition prevailed, those persons would as a rule possess the greater rights who were the more powerful; and thus such rights would have to be measured by arms, which is manifestly a barbarous and absurd supposition.[3]

Suárez's logic is as simple as it is compelling. Without the criterion of last resort, the mighty and powerful would be sorely tempted to resort to their power and might too quickly, even—perhaps especially—when the justness of their cause was in doubt. Last resort serves as a check against this impulse by insisting that time and energy be devoted to settling issues of justice and injustice without the bloodshed and destruction that inevitably follows from war.

Means other than war typically include a host of practices that might be collected under the heading of diplomacy and involve such practices as mediation, negotiation, arbitration, international tribunals, and so forth. Various voices in the tradition even require under certain circumstances—where the justice of a cause is uncertain—that governments submit their claims to binding arbitration. There are, however, several caveats or clarifications that attend the obligation to pursue means other than war first.

The Limits of Last Resort: Four Caveats

The first such caveat concerns the qualifier "reasonable" or "feasible." Last resort does not require that every means that might hold even a 1 percent chance of success must be tried before resorting to the force of arms. A just war people is not obligated to attempt every imaginable means. Rather, the criterion holds that every *reasonable* means must be attempted; every means that has a reasonable chance of succeeding must be tried. This is worth emphasizing because this is sometimes misconstrued by opponents of a given war to mean that every conceivable means that holds out any chance of success, no matter how slim, must be tried. This, however, is not the case. Last resort is not reducible to a mathematical table where all possible means are listed and then systematically crossed off as they are tried. Rather, last resort entails a judgment call regarding what may be successful and what is not feasible.

The second caveat hearkens back to the discussion of legitimate authority, where it was noted that in its current state of development the just war tradition does not require nations to submit their claims to international tribunals. In other words, last resort does not mean that nations are required to obtain UN or Security Council approval before resorting to war. Although the tradition may be moving in this direction, there are at least two reasons it has not done so thus far. First, the UN Charter itself does not unambiguously impose that requirement on its signatories. Second, the mere existence of an international tribunal, such as the International Criminal Court, does not ensure that the rulings of such a body would be either effective (enforceable) or just. In other words, that means other than war must be tried does not mean that particular means—such as international tribunals—must always be tried. Whether a particular means should be attempted depends on a host of variables, not the least of them being both the effectiveness and the character of the means in question, which leads us to the third caveat.

When Suárez articulates the tradition's expectation that a just war be a last resort, he says that princes are obliged to avoid war so far as is possible "by upright means." With this important phrase he gestures toward the third caveat. The expectation that means other than war be pursued does not extend to compromising on justice or appeasing injustice. It is sometimes said that politics is the art of compromise. Whether or not this is true of modern politics, it is not a particularly helpful platitude for addressing the kind of injustice that rises to the level of just cause for war. While last resort may embody the regret regarding war that is part of right intent, it does not embody a reluctance to pursue justice or a willingness to settle for less than justice. In other words, last resort is about creating a space in order to negotiate not *if* justice is to be done but only *how*. Last resort embodies the hope that justice can be renewed and restored without the sad necessity of resorting to war. Last resort provides no justification for appeasing the unjust.

The fourth caveat concerns sanctions. The issue here is whether sanctions constitute a means other than war or are in fact themselves an act of war. In the public imagination sanctions are frequently lifted up as an alternative to war for persuading a recalcitrant government to turn from an unjust course of action. They are popular because they appear more forceful than mere diplomacy, are normally cheaper than waging war, and are thought to be less destructive of both life and property. Yet their popularity notwithstanding, sanctions face significant obstacles to being successfully differentiated from an act of war. Among ethicists, sanctions—especially general economic sanctions—are regularly equated with acts of war. They are often viewed as a kind of modern siege. And like ancient siege warfare at its worst,[4] the effects of general sanctions do not distinguish between soldier and civilian, between legitimate and illegitimate targets, but indiscriminately target a whole society. General economic sanctions cause widespread suffering and harm.[5] What is worse, the brunt of the impact falls on the weakest and least protected in society, while those in positions of power are generally better able to insulate themselves from the effects. Furthermore, beyond nurturing a self-congratulatory sense in those who implement them that sanctions are "doing something forceful" and "sending a message," there is little evidence that sanctions are particularly effective.[6]

For these reasons, general sanctions cannot be embraced as a means that rightly falls under the criterion of last resort. The criterion of last resort *does not* require that sanctions be given a chance to work before direct military force is applied. To the contrary, general sanctions are more appropriately viewed as an act and instrument of war itself and as such are subject to all the criteria of the tradition if their use is to be just.[7]

What might conceivably fall within the purview of last resort are "smart" or targeted sanctions, sanctions that are narrow in scope so as to affect only the political and/or military leadership while largely sparing the civilian population.[8] Here we might think of the seizure of certain assets or the cessation of military aid and so forth. Of course, these narrowly focused smart sanctions will likely lack the public relations appeal of general sanctions while still sharing the limitations and uncertainties regarding effectiveness that haunt general sanctions. Even so, in circumstances where they can be discriminately tailored, they may be an important part of an effort to bring about justice by means other than war.

Whatever the array of means pursued short of war to resolve a just cause, a public declaration of the cause and aim of war must be included among them. Again, I refer to Suárez: "Before a war is begun the [attacking] prince is bound to call to the attention of the opposing state the existence of a just cause of war, and to seek adequate reparation therefore; and if the other state offers such adequate reparations, he is bound to accept it, and to desist from war."[9]

Those familiar with the just war tradition may note that linking the necessity of a declaration of war with last resort is unusual. The tradition commonly associates the need for a declaration of war with the criterion of legitimate authority. This is the case because the legitimate authority properly makes such declarations and because the requirement of a public declaration is one means of seeking to ensure that a war is waged by a genuinely public authority— an authority serving the good of the whole and not undertaking war on the initiative of a small clique driven by narrow interests.[10]

But it is appropriate to treat the requirement of a declaration of war under last resort because of the function or purpose the declaration serves.[11] Simply put, it is part of the effort to address injustice while avoiding war by making it clear to the potential enemy what the injustice is and how it may be resolved without the resort to the force of arms. Beyond this most obvious function, the requirement of a public declaration of war also gives notice to other nations and parties so that they may assess the justice of the cause and conduct themselves accordingly. In this way, a public declaration serves the criterion of last resort by prompting the greater political community to act on behalf of justice, whether that takes the form of clarifying the justice of the cause, bringing pressure to bear on the offending party, or assisting in negotiations.

Divergences

Having traced the common ground, we now turn to the subtle but important differences regarding last resort that distinguish Just War (PPC) and Just War (CD).

Viability of the Criterion. The first difference concerns the viability of the criterion. It would not be far-fetched to say that insofar as Just War (PPC) is concerned, the criterion of last resort is on the verge of a collapse that may leave it as functionally inert as right intent. Last resort has long endured the strain of standing against the trends of a political culture that often equates delay not with patience but with weakness and indecisiveness. Add to this the momentum created by the mobilization and deployment of forces in preparation for war—the sense that troops in theater cannot wait too long and maintain effectiveness—and the space for pursuing means other than war is reduced even further.

What brings the criterion to the edge of irrelevance is that increasingly added to these pressures are the voices of prominent just war thinkers. For example, Michael Walzer has all but dismissed the criterion of last resort, arguing that from the moment just cause exists, the only thing that really matters in deciding when to go to war is whether the costs and benefits of doing so "seem on balance better than those of the available alternatives."[12] In other words, when to go to war is determined solely by calculations of advantage. More recently some just war advocates have argued that the reality of terrorism and "rogue states" renders last resort effectively null and void.[13] It is asserted that in a situation where one is facing a purely evil, irrational, nihilistic enemy that recognizes no other form of power except violence and that is immune from legal, diplomatic, and economic pressures, war becomes the *only* means of response.

What this amounts to is a claim that international terrorism and rogue states render the criterion of last resort obsolete. The argument implies that last resort was a reasonable discipline when nations did not face international terrorism or rogue states, but it is no longer applicable. In the face of such threats, the criterion of last resort goes out the window along with any expectation that means other than war should be attempted prior to engaging in war. Granted, this changed situation does not require that the criterion be completely abandoned; is it reasonable to surmise that it would remain in effect on those occasions when one faces a traditional nonterrorist or nonrogue state enemy.

The difficulty with such an argument, however, is that it cannot help but reduce the criterion of last resort to a mere formality—not unlike the way right intent exists today as little more than a formality. Why is it that once wars against terrorism and rogue states are exempted from the discipline of last resort that the criterion inevitably becomes a mere formality? It is not simply a matter of assessing the likelihood that politicians will resist the temptation to label the prospective enemy—whoever they are—as either terrorist or rogue as a pretext for discarding the criterion, although this is certainly one reason to be concerned about such an exemption. Rather, the problem runs deeper.

To begin with, the argument presumes that one can generalize about entire classes of people, without actually doing the hard work of attempting to engage those people, and can declare with certainty that they are irrational and immune from any and every political, legal, and other form of nonmilitary pressure that might fall under last resort. While not denying that there may indeed be people who are depraved in that manner—we call them sociopaths, and yet even they are not simply executed on the spot without any effort to apprehend them sans bloodshed—the just war tradition is founded on a hope, displayed in both right intent and last resort, that negotiation and other means short of war *might* prevail. In other words, the logic of last resort has been evacuated once permission has been granted to in effect give up on or write off a class of people (those designated international terrorists and leaders of rogue states) prior to any effort to engage them around matters of justice or injustice by means other than military. Thus even where the criterion is retained, its underlying hopeful logic has been eviscerated. As a result, it cannot help but become a formality. It might be dutifully invoked on the eve of a war, but like right intent it does not do any real work.

The second problem with the argument exempting certain wars from the criterion of last resort is that the argument claims to know ahead of time—and without doing any work—what can only be known by doing the hard work embodied in the criterion of last resort. Consider the designation "rogue state." It is said that rogue states are immune to means other than war for settling matters of justice and therefore there is no need to try other means. The problem is that every just war is waged against a rogue entity, since, by definition, to be guilty of an offense that amounts to a just cause for war is in some sense to be rogue. Yet the tradition insists, in the form of the criterion of last resort, that such rogues are to be given the opportunity to make amends and correct the injustice without being subject to the destruction of war.

Moreover, making the claim that such rogues are impervious to legal, diplomatic, and other pressures is something that can only be done after the attempt has been made to engage them in those ways. The tradition permits one to claim that an enemy is impervious to means other than war only after one has tried means other than war. It is the work of last resort that permits one to determine if indeed an enemy is that stubborn. The argument for exempting certain wars from the criterion presumes one can know the outcome of the criterion without actually engaging the criterion. If this were the case, then there would be no need for the criterion. If one could make these kinds of judgments without actually engaging in diplomacy and so forth, the just war tradition would not have developed the criterion of last resort. The other criteria would have been sufficient and, as Walzer suggests, the only issue regarding when to fight would be that of calculating advantage.

So even where the criterion is retained, it loses its moral force. After all, if one can simply know ahead of time that a particular nation or a class of people are impervious to anything but violence, then the work of last resort is not really necessary; it becomes a formality.

In contrast, Just War (CD) upholds the criterion of last resort, even in the face of terrorism and rogue states. But the contrast that Just War (CD) offers with these advocates of the dismissal or reduction of last resort is not a stark one, for there is much in the argument about terrorism that Just War (CD) affirms. For example, it affirms that against some enemies military action may legitimately be the first resort. As previously stated, last resort is compatible with a military first response in some situations, the prime example being that of repelling an attack that is currently underway. Just War (CD) can also affirm that there are indeed peoples and polities that prove themselves not susceptible to means other than war for resolving injustice. In other words, even as Just War (CD) embodies the virtue of hope, that hope is not a cheery human optimism that asserts—against the clear witness of history—that every problem can indeed be talked out and reasoned through. But this affirmation does not properly lead to a dismissal of the discipline of last resort. Rather, it simply reinforces the criterion's recognition that there may indeed by a point of last resort, a terminal point when war is morally legitimate. That point is when all reasonable, feasible means have been tried and found wanting.

It is perhaps worth emphasizing this point. Last resort is not rightly used as a perpetual stalling tactic or the expression of an unfounded optimism in human good will and reason. Just War (CD) is rooted in a divine hope—a proven hope that God is able to soften hard hearts—that also recognizes the divine call to use military force as a form of love against enemies as a last resort. (Incidentally, because last resort is a form of love, even this military action is not a giving up but continues to embody the hope that the enemy will repent and so stop the war at any moment.)

This hope distinguishes advocates of Just War (CD) from those who would weaken or discard the criterion. This hope prevents Just War (CD) from changing the "last" in last resort to "only" and declaring ahead of time, without doing the hard work entailed by the criterion, that some people and polities are impervious to means other than war. In other words, even as Just War (CD) affirms that some people and polities may not be accessible by means other than war, at which point the "last" in last resort is reached, hope in the grace of God prevents Christians from reaching that conclusion prior to or without first attempting means other than war. Against those who think that all disagreements can be resolved without war, Just War (CD) recognizes that some people and polities will not be moved to justice apart from war, but unlike those who dismiss last resort, Just War (CD) holds that it is *only* by passing through the discipline that such a judgment about the intractability of an adversary can be rightly made.

Good-Faith Diplomacy. This theological hope underwrites, as well, the expectation that the negotiations and other efforts short of war will be sincerely engaged in good faith, even if one suspects that one's opponent is not engaged in such efforts in good faith. Here we mark another difference between Just War (PPC) and Just War (CD). Insofar as Just War (PPC) still recognizes the moral force of last resort—and the majority of its proponents still do, even if several prominent voices have challenged it—little or nothing is said about how one is to enter into those means other than war. Indeed, in a manner reminiscent of the way right intent is treated, it appears that as long as the governing authorities assert that they are trying to settle matters without resorting to war, the criterion of last resort is regarded as satisfied. Nothing is said concerning the spirit with which those negotiations or deliberations are to be entered into. No questions are raised regarding reasonable and unreasonable demands, such as making offers and granting reasonable time for the enemy to consider them or, conversely, setting deadlines for troop withdrawals that are logistically impossible to meet. No expectations are spelled out in terms of the necessity of listening to the enemy's case and complaints, the impropriety of engaging in deceit and humiliation and demonization, or the justness of working to undermine negotiated settlements.

While some proponents of Just War (PPC) might suggest that the silence is born of the self-evident nature of these and similar expectations, given the nature of contemporary political discourse such silence cannot be so easily excused. In an age of spin and disinformation, where propaganda is as likely to be directed toward a government's own populace as against its adversaries, treating last resort as though it were satisfied by declarations that other means have been tried and failed, without a serious examination of the kinds of efforts that have been made, is to reduce last resort to little more than an empty formality.

In contrast, Just War (CD) picks up on the longstanding concern within the Christian tradition that a just war people will avoid duplicity in dealing with the enemy. Although the tradition has not simply banned the use of arguably duplicitous tactics like ambushes during war, it has consistently condemned negotiating with the enemy in anything other than an upright and sincere manner. Even as entering a just war does not absolve Christians of the responsibility to love their enemies, neither does it excuse them from dealing forthrightly and sincerely with their adversaries, whether or not their adversaries are loving or forthright in return. This is of a piece with the aforementioned concern that just cause not be a mere pretext for unjust intentions. It is part and parcel of what it means to intend justice in waging war; it is what a just war people will do regardless of the behavior of their adversaries.

Developing Alternatives to War. Distinguishing sincerity from mere pretext and propaganda with regard to last resort brings us to the last divergence to be considered. Again, recalling the previous treatment of right intent, we know that one way of distinguishing pretext from sincerity is by considering character and consistency. And character and consistency are, in turn, discerned by looking at behavior over a period of time. With regard to the criterion of last resort, then, Just War (CD) holds that one measure of the depth of commitment to it is the amount of time, energy, and resources devoted to developing viable means other than war for addressing injustices that amount to a just cause.

Just War (PPC) does not really address this. It does not raise the issue of the kinds of policies, practices, and institutions that make war more likely rather than less. For example, the famous theologian and leader of German Christian resistance to the early Nazi regime, Karl Barth (who was not a pacifist) has argued that the very existence of standing armies works against last resort.[14] Without necessarily endorsing his conclusion that there should be no standing armies, his point is helpful. Last resort entails not simply asking when one may go to war but what one should do before war is even on the horizon to make the resort to war less likely. Just War (PPC)'s silence in this regard implies that last resort is concerned only with whatever means happen to be available in the immediate context of a war.

There is a commonplace saying that "if you have a hammer, everything looks like a nail." Just War (PPC) does not ask why one only has a hammer, nor does it suggest that the just war discipline includes a moral obligation to devote significant resources to developing other tools that might render the need to resort to the hammer less frequent. Instead, last resort according to Just War (PPC) becomes simply a matter of answering the question, when can I use my hammer? even if what one is contemplating whacking is not a nail but a splinter that might have been successfully removed if another instrument had been at hand.

Just War (CD), on the other hand, understands last resort to be a matter not only of determining at what point military action is permissible but also of embodying the hope that war can be averted by developing nonmilitary means of addressing injustice. It not only tries to assess when one may resort to war now but also strives to develop those practices that might make the need for war less likely in the future. According to Just War (CD), in the absence of efforts to develop functioning alternatives, the criterion of last resort is not rightly embodied. Last resort is not properly invoked if on the brink of war one determines that all reasonable means other than war have been tried and failed when in fact one has neglected and/or impeded the development and effectiveness of those other means.

Accordingly, Just War (CD) understands the discipline of last resort to require intentional efforts to develop a range of responses (other than war) to injustice. Certainly international law and organizations that might effectively enforce it are possibilities, if they can be developed and sustained in ways that serve the common good, but international organizations are not the only, or even necessarily the best, way to think about this.

In recent years an initiative called "just peacemaking" has been developed by persons who have increasingly felt that something was lacking in the standard accounts of both pacifism and just war.[15] With regard to just war in particular, they have criticized it for being insufficiently attentive to practices that might make peace possible without the regrettable necessity of resorting to war. In an effort to address this deficiency, the proponents of just peacemaking have begun to identify concrete practices that are intended to reduce the likelihood of injustice arising in the first place or to address injustice when it does arise by means other than war. Among the practices explored are things that one might expect, like developing and strengthening international organizations that protect human rights or supporting efforts at fostering sustainable economic development. But they also name other practices that might not ordinarily come to mind when contemplating ways to resolve injustice short of war: encouraging the efforts of nongovernmental and grassroots organizations that work for peace and justice, civil training in the kinds of nonviolent direct action and conflict resolution skills that have characterized several successful revolutions in recent decades, and reducing the arms trade.

The just peacemaking initiative is a good example of the type of effort that the criterion of last resort calls for as part of the discipline of Just War (CD). Insofar as last resort does not come into play *only* on the eve of a war but rather is rightly lived out in peacetime as well in the form of various efforts, practices, and institutions devoted to preventing and resolving injustice by means other than war, Christians who embrace Just War (CD) will be about just peacemaking.

Military Action or Police Action Revisited. At this point we are in position to revisit an issue that was initially raised under the criterion of just cause. There the question was posed regarding what is rightly deemed a cause for war as opposed to a matter of police action. Just War (PPC) provides little guidance in answering this. Now we can understand why. Because it does not understand last resort to include the responsibility to develop means other than war, it has little or nothing to say about the use of those other means. All it can do is repeat that war should be a matter of last resort.

Just War (CD) suffers no such difficulty because it understands that the discipline of last resort requires the development of a host of practices so that last resort might indeed be the last—instead of the first or only—option. To put this a little differently, Just War (CD) views the governmental use of violence on a continuum, with war at one end of a range of practices that includes policing. Indeed, just war and just policing are not seen as fundamentally different kinds of practices; rather, the difference between them is a matter of degree.[16] One could even say that just war is nothing but just policing writ large.[17] (More will be said about this later.) Accordingly, the question of police versus military action is not an alien one but falls naturally within the scope of the criterion of last resort.

What guidance does Just War (CD) provide for determining the appropriateness of a police or a military response to a just cause? How might it guide legitimate authorities in arriving at a decision on how to respond to an international terrorist organization? For all the heat the question sometimes generates, the answer is surprisingly straightforward. A military response is legitimate when it conforms to the just war discipline—which means when it conforms to all the criteria. And given what has already been said about the criterion of last resort, we know that a military response is justified when attention has been given to developing means other than war and when reasonable efforts have been made to use those means but they have failed. (Reasonable efforts must be made; one cannot simply declare ahead of time that nothing but war will work.) In the particular case of a global terrorist organization, last resort as embodied by Just War (CD) would expect that reasonable efforts at a law enforcement approach be made before turning to military action and that resources would be devoted to the end of making such law enforcement or police actions viable. (Although it tends to be overshadowed by the war in Iraq, the current global campaign against terrorism owes most of the success it has had to police action.) Where such efforts, along with other "just peacemaking" types of practices, are made and fail, military action could rightly be considered a last resort. Where such efforts were not made and military action was initiated as a first or only response, such a war could not rightly be judged a matter of last resort.

But last resort is not the last word on when it is just to fight. The criterion of "reasonable chance of success" also addresses the question of when to fight, and it too sheds some light on this question of police versus military action. To this criterion we now turn.

Reasonable Chance of Success

Reflecting on right intent and in particular how it entails a commitment to the common good and justice for all, we may wonder if Just War (CD) is a recipe for war without end. After all, if right intent means pursuing justice uniformly and universally, does this not imply that we will be constantly at war? The answer is no because having just cause and right intent is not sufficient to wage a just war; the other criteria must be considered as well. And one of the criteria that plays a significant role in the decision regarding when to fight is that of reasonable chance of success.

War Must Be Winnable

Put simply, this criterion holds that the goals of a just war must be reasonably attainable. A just war must be winnable while being fought in accord with the just war discipline. In the popular imagination, and reinforced by more than a few movies, there is an image of soldiers valiantly going off to war or heroically making a last stand when defeat and death are certain, when there is no chance of success. There is an aura of honor around such sacrifice, a sense of righteousness and goodness that is associated with sticking it out until the end and dying for a lost cause. The popularity of such a sentiment notwithstanding, the just war tradition is starkly opposed to it. There is nothing just in engaging the destructiveness of war when there is little or no chance of success, even if the cause and intent are just and right.

The just war tradition is not opposed to standing by one's convictions to the bitter end. On the contrary, as we shall see shortly, the just war discipline at its best requires people who will abide by their convictions and discipline even in the face of great costs and bitter defeat. Rather, just war is opposed to the idea that when confronted with a just cause, one should go to war regardless of the prospects of winning. What is rejected is *not* one's commitment to justice for one's neighbors but rather waging war for justice when such a war has little chance of accomplishing its just purpose.

Benefits Outweigh the Costs

But this is not all. Not only does the tradition insist that a just war be winnable, but it also requires that a prospective war be worth the cost. In the face of the prospect of waging a just war, it must be asked, Will the benefits of this war, should it be successful, outweigh the harm of actually waging war? This is sometimes referred to as a matter of "proportionality," although it should not be confused with the criterion of proportionality, which we will consider in the next chapter. The risks and costs attendant on waging even a just war, including such things as the loss of lives and resources ("theirs" as well as "ours"); the opportunity costs associated with diverting to war resources ordinarily directed toward other important tasks; the risk of increasing local, regional, or global instability and insecurity; and so forth must be weighed against the hoped-for good of correcting an injustice and the benefits of a just peace. To put it rather bluntly, a just war is decidedly not the kind of war that operates according to the logic that says "sometimes to save a village you have to destroy it."

Vitoria, expressing well the sentiment of the tradition in this regard, writes, "Not every or any injury gives sufficient grounds for waging war. . . . Since all the effects of war are cruel and horrible—slaughter, fire, devastation—it is not lawful to persecute those responsible for trivial offenses by waging war upon them."[18] A little later he is more specific: "It is clear that one may have a right to reclaim a city or province, and yet find that right nullified by the danger of provoking greater conflict. As I said, wars should be waged for the common good; if the recovery of one city is bound to involve the commonwealth in greater damage . . . there can be no doubt that the prince should cede his right and abstain from war."[19] This last passage is particularly pointed, in that Vitoria makes it clear that what is at stake in this question of proportionality are not just trivial offenses but even great injustices. And he states that in some circumstances, namely, when war would likely cause disproportionate harm, the right of war that is bestowed by the criterion of just cause is to be relinquished. As Pope Pius XII said several centuries later, "If the injury caused by warfare exceeds the injury suffered by tolerating the injustice done, one may be obliged to suffer that particular injustice."[20]

It is important to note that this expectation that a just war be winnable, although treated primarily as a judgment to be made *before* a war is entered into, remains in effect during the entire course of a war. Thus, a war begun with a reasonable chance of success may be pursued only so long as there continues to be a reasonable chance of it succeeding in its just goal while being fought justly. As mentioned previously, the just war tradition does not embrace valiant last stands, the fatal end of which is clearly foreseen. Granted that in the midst of the ebb and flow of battle this is not always an easy or transparent judgment for the legitimate authorities to make, but in principle it is no different from the judgment regarding the chance of success prior to the initial engagement. That initial judgment is not easy either, and yet it is still possible to make it well.

Limited War for Limited Purpose

In addition to being winnable and proportionate, the criterion of reasonable chance of success entails that a just war is a *limited* war waged for *limited* ends. Of course a just war is limited in the sense that it is not a free-for-all. Beyond this, however, a just war has a very limited goal. Specifically, a just war addresses a particular injustice, namely, the one that constitutes the just cause and that is named in the declaration of war. In other words, a just war is not a war with sweeping or universal goals like wiping out an ideology or achieving absolute security. A war to end all war or to wipe out a particular vision of life (like communism) or even a particular vision of death (like terrorism) is a war that lacks a limited goal. To the contrary, such broad and sweeping goals are by their very nature unlimited, which is why they run afoul of this criterion. Wars with unlimited goals lack a reasonable chance of succeeding.

As a consequence of the expectation that a just war be limited, "mission creep" is ruled out. Just war does not sanction the gradual change or expansion of the war's aims on the fly. It does not permit unlimited war by increments, in other words. Indeed, the continual shifting, expansion, and retraction of a war's aims will give a just war people reason to pause and raise questions about both the stated initial cause as well as the intention in going to war. In other words, a war that is not defined by the declared ends gives reason to wonder if the declared just ends were but a pretext for other, less virtuous ends.

Having said this, the limited nature of a just war does not preclude the possibility that in certain circumstances the aim of a war can change as a new injustice is perpetrated or discovered. Thus, for example, a just war that began as a means of addressing an unjust seizure of land and resources might become something more if in the course of that war the enemy engaged in war crimes or if new atrocities are discovered (for example, genocide or ethnic cleansing). Yet even in such situations, a just war may not become unlimited but rather will continue to be restrained in the sense of being limited to addressing particular acts of injustice. Furthermore, any expansion of a just war's purpose will always be subject to the criteria of the tradition. In other words, such an expansion will not happen either inadvertently by "creeping" or intentionally by subterfuge but will be subject to the same public goods embodied in the tradition, lest what began as a just war becomes unjust as it strays from the discipline in the course of its prosecution.

No Unconditional Surrender

The last thing to be said about just war as limited war concerns the ending of a war. An important implication of the limited nature of just wars is that demanding unconditional surrender is prohibited.[21] As a limited war, a just war seeks only to address the particular just cause for the war; to seek or demand more than that from the enemy is to transgress the limited character of just war. Indeed, to demand unconditional surrender is a punitive act that is more at home in the crusade vision of war than in that of just war. In this regard, Grotius observes that those who surrender are in a real sense completely at the mercy of the victors, who have the power to do as they please. He notes, however, that there is a difference between what is possible and what is just, and the just will exercise charity and moderation for the sake of peace.[22] This comports well with what has been said previously under right intention about seeking a just peace for the enemy tempering the measure of justice in terms of reparations at a war's conclusion.

Because it is a limited war for limited ends, a just war does not seek unconditional surrender but ordinarily strives for something approximating the *status quo ante*. A just war seeks to return to a state of affairs close to what the conditions were prior to the offense that led to war. It seeks a near approximation and not simply a reproduction of the political situation prior to the injustice because, of course, it hopes to establish a more just *status quo*, one where that offense will not simply repeat itself. A just war aims at a more secure, less vulnerable, safer *status quo ante*.[23] Although, as Walzer helpfully reminds us, the key words here are all relative. A just war seeks *less* vulnerability, not invulnerability; *more* safety, not absolute security. A just war is a limited war.

The limited character of the ends sought by a just war and the eschewal of unconditional surrender does not mean, however, that an end as drastic as regime change is unthinkable. As suggested during the discussion of right intent, a just war may under certain circumstances, where the offense that provoked the war merits it, end in the occupation and political reconstruction of another nation. But even in these circumstances a just war people will not demand or expect of the defeated that they submit unconditionally to that occupation and reconstruction. Because a just war people answers to justice, the demands that are made and the terms of surrender set forth should be just, or, in the language of an older military tradition, "honorable."

Divergences

The Moral Imperative of Surrender. Such is the basic contour of the criterion of reasonable chance of success that is generally shared by advocates of just war. There are, however, two significant divergences between Just War (PPC) and Just War (CD). The first concerns those circumstances where a prospective just war does not appear to be winnable, where the criterion of reasonable chance of success is not satisfied. In such a situation, faithfully adhering to the criterion would entail not engaging in war in the first place or—where the war was already underway but the tide has turned against what was previously thought to be a winnable war, such that it is no longer thought to be winnable—the proper thing to do is bring the war to an end either by negotiating a halt or by surrendering.[24]

It is this last possibility that marks a parting of the ways between some adherents of Just War (PPC) and Just War (CD). Some proponents of Just War (PPC) flinch from the full force of the moral imperative of surrender. Instead of recognizing that a just war cannot be fought if it cannot be justly won, they hold that one should abide by the tradition and its criteria only so long as doing so does not jeopardize the reasonable chance of winning. Accordingly, when faced with a situation where following the criteria means likely defeat or surrender, then one need no longer abide by them. In this way, reasonable chance of success effectively is transformed from being a restraint on or discipline of war into a restraint on the just war discipline itself. Instead of shaping judgments on when war is or is not permissible, the criterion is inverted into a kind of judgment on the criteria, deciding whether the criteria should be followed based on their impact on the likelihood of victory. Instead of limiting war, then, it limits the limits on war.

The best known proponent of this kind of stepping back from the full force of the criterion is Michael Walzer.[25] To be fair, he does *not* argue that *any* time one faces defeat or surrender one may discard the criteria. Rather, he restricts overriding the criteria to situations of "supreme emergency." Furthermore, recognizing the possibility that "supreme emergency" could be invoked whenever it seems convenient and advantageous, Walzer restricts what he means by supreme emergency to those occasions when a national community faces a threat that is grave and imminent. This is the same language used in the treatment of just cause, where it marked the difference between an impermissible preventative war and a permissible preemptive strike. Here Walzer uses it in an analogous manner to indicate a situation where a nation's very way of life, the values it cherishes, is on the verge of extinction. A defeat or surrender that was not likely to bring in its wake the destruction of an entire way of life would not rise to the level of a supreme emergency and so would not legitimate dismissing the just war discipline.

Just War (CD) does not attempt to evade or water down the moral force of the criterion of reasonable chance of success in this manner. Rather, it recognizes the moral imperative of surrender as part of the cost of discipleship, of what it means to be a just war people as followers of Christ. This is another and particularly clear example of the earlier claim that living the just war discipline is not easy but difficult and demanding. Being just warriors is not only a matter of living by the discipline but of dying by it as well. It is for this reason that Just War (CD) may be seen as a form of taking up the cross.

One might object, however, that such a claim does not get to the real difficulty. After all, the criterion of reasonable chance of success does not merely ask that Christians take up the cross by either refusing to fight a war that is not likely to be won or surrendering when a war that was begun justly becomes unwinnable; it also asks the unjustly attacked neighbor whom Christians would aid by waging a just war to suffer. In other words, the moral difficulty with reasonable chance of success is not simply that it asks Christians to forgo military defense when that defense is not likely to succeed but that it also withholds the aid of Christians to their neighbors, thereby ensuring that it is those neighbors who will suffer the consequences of injustice and defeat. The appeal to take up the cross, then, misses the point to a degree. The difficulty with reasonable chance of success is that it appears to require that *others* suffer, that others be crucified. Thus, is not the moral imperative of surrender but a pious-sounding form of abandonment of the neighbor to injustice?

Only if the options for action are "fight, even if it is not likely to be successful" or "do nothing." But we know from the treatment of the other criteria, particularly right intent and last resort, that these are not the only options. Because Just War (CD) arises out of a constant and consistent concern for justice and peace for our neighbors, and because war is not the first or only response to injustice but a last resort, the moral imperative of surrender does not mark a capitulation before injustice or a cessation of the struggle for a just peace and the common good. Rather, it is a call for the struggle for justice and against injustice to continue in other ways and other forms. One might say that the criterion of reasonable chance of success marks the threshold not between "doing something" and "doing nothing" but between different forms of action on behalf of justice for our neighbors.

Of course, there is no guarantee that actions other than war will prove more successful. Although there are certainly remarkable instances of successful nonmilitary means of resisting and overturning injustice, it is nevertheless possible that injustice may have to be suffered and endured, at least for the time being. As Grotius notes, "under some circumstances it is impossible successfully to oppose cruelty and oppression, the punishment of which must be left to the eternal judge of [humankind]."[26]

This brings to the fore the essence of the divergence between those proponents of Just War (CD) and those advocates of Just War (PPC) who qualify or dismiss the imperative of surrender. Whereas Just War (PPC) revolves around the nation-state and places its survival as the paramount concern, Just War (CD) is at home in the church and as a consequence faithfulness, not survival, is the principal concern. As the passage from Grotius suggests, Just War (CD)—and the criterion of reasonable chance of success in particular—rests on certain theological convictions that are absent in Just War (PPC). Among them is the conviction that it is not the force of a nation's arms that finally guarantees that justice will prevail, but the Lord, who is able to defeat even death (1 Cor. 15; cf. Ps. 20:7). Thus, even as Christians may wield the sword in a nation's army or support a nation's just wars, they know that nation-states and their armies are not the final line of defense against injustice. Hence Christian just warriors can resist the temptation to step outside the discipline in order to thwart defeat. They can surrender, even in the face of a supreme emergency, because they know that surrender and defeat now does not and cannot mean the end either for Christians or their neighbors. The heavens will not fall because the Just One who rules heaven will not see justice (finally) defeated here on earth.

Admittedly, this is not a fully satisfactory argument for those who are suffering and languishing under the weight of injustice right now. As long as this is the case the Christian just warrior's refusal to discard the discipline and fight will not be able to escape the suspicion that it is really just a form of abandonment. Although continuing the struggle for justice in other forms may dispel some of the cloud of suspicion, until Christ sets all things right, the Christian refusal to fight, when fighting justly is not likely to succeed, will bear the burden of appearing uncaring and perhaps even unjust.

Despite this lingering suspicion, Christians just warriors will abide by the difficult imperative of surrender when a just war is not likely to succeed precisely because their being just warriors is an expression of their faith and hope in Christ. And it is this theological foundation, which undergirds the entire just war discipline but is exposed so clearly in the moral imperative of surrender that is part of the criterion of reasonable chance of success, that sets Just War (CD) apart from Just War (PPC), which requires no faith or hope other than that placed in the nation-state and the force of its arms.

Character and Judgment. That Just War (CD) is anchored in the faith and hope of the church brings to the fore the second divergence in the two approaches' treatment of the criterion of reasonable chance of success. The criterion is sometimes referred to by the name "probability of success." I have deliberately avoided that language because it sounds too mathematical, almost as if one could satisfy this criterion with a calculator: just enter the variables—comparative troop strength, etc.—into a formula and let a computer spit out the probability of success in a manner perhaps not all that different from the BCS college football rankings. Instead, I have consistently used the phrase "reasonable chance of success." This language properly highlights how the criterion is not subject to mathematical certainty but involves human wisdom and judgment. The qualifier "reasonable" was addressed briefly under last resort in terms of the pursuit of all reasonable means other than war. It bears considering again here because it marks a subtle but important difference between the two approaches to just war.

What is meant by *reasonable* is not as obvious as it may first appear. Rather, what is deemed reasonable is intimately related to the character of the persons and communities making such judgments. Thus, for example, Walzer's dismissal of the moral imperative of surrender in the face of a "supreme emergency" makes perfectly good sense, given that his work displays no obvious faith or hope in anything beyond the nation-state and its resources. But for those whose hope and faith is rooted ultimately in another community and Lord, the moral imperative of surrender can be reasonable, insofar as adhering to the moral precepts of the One who sustains and redeems creation is a quite reasonable thing to do.

In other words, even as the two approaches hold in common the criterion of reasonable chance of success, insofar as they presume different kinds of character, formed to different ends, proponents of those two approaches may arrive at divergent judgments regarding reasonable chance of success (and the same holds for last resort as well). Because Just War (CD) is anchored in faith and hope, judgments of reasonable chance of success (and last resort) made by disciples may differ from the judgments of those who do not share that faith and hope.

The Challenge for the Church

As we turn to the challenges that these criteria present to the church, there are several that duplicate or reinforce the challenges presented by the previous criteria, and so we will not devote a great deal of space to them. The first of these concerns the matter of judgment. As we have seen, both last resort and reasonable chance of success involve judgment calls. Insofar as they are matters of judgment, they return us to some of the challenges named previously under legitimate authority. We need not repeat what was said there. Instead let us note that the virtue associated with making sound judgments is that of prudence, and the challenge to the church in this regard is that of fostering and supporting leaders who display such prudence and who surround themselves with wise and prudent advisors. Both criteria also reinforce the challenge to the church to be a place that fosters the virtues of patience, hope, and courage.

Developing Patience

Already we have seen the importance of patience with regard to right intent and the commitment to see justice through the conclusion of a war and its aftermath. The two criteria under consideration here reinforce the importance of patience. Just War (CD) requires people of patience who will take the time and effort to try to resolve injustices without first resorting to war. Patience is required to enter into negotiations in good faith with adversaries who may or may not come to the table in good faith. Likewise, patient endurance is required to abide by the moral imperative to surrender when fighting justly is no longer likely to succeed. Yet in a culture where instant gratification and the avoidance of suffering often appear to be of the utmost importance, patience and endurance are not likely to come easily or naturally. How does the church school disciples in patience? As an Advent people, a people who wait for Christ's return in final victory, patience should be the tempo of our daily life. As a people who have constantly before us the witness of the saints and martyrs, who took up the cross instead of shedding their convictions, patient endurance should not be foreign to us.

Nurturing Hope

Hope is likewise an integral part of embodying these two criteria. Hope is required in order to engage an adversary with means other than war as well as either not entering into war or surrendering one begun because it cannot be won justly. Such acts require hope in the power of God to triumph and set things right, even when the immediate adversary or horizon may provide little ground for hope. As mentioned earlier, this hope is rooted not in an optimism about humanity and human good will but in the power of God that can reach even the chief of sinners. We might say that Just War (CD) rests on an "optimism of grace." And the church is about shaping a hopeful people as it proclaims the good news of redemptive change (the technical theological term is "sanctification") and testifies to the reality of that change in its own life, pointing out to one another as well as to the world ways that God graciously makes us better than we otherwise would be.

This hope, however, is not simply an appeal to miracles but is connected to the various disciplines of the Christian life, from prayer and fasting to accountability groups and the sacraments. In this way, the hope that sustains Just War (CD) is the product of the means of grace in our midst through which God works to change us and others. By attending to them and noting how God can change people, sometimes in spite of themselves and often in unexpected ways and places, we have grounds for hope that even the hardest of hearts can be softened. And we have hope that even where our resources and efforts fail, the Spirit blows where and how it will (John 3:8). Thus, we have hope that even if we lose, all is not lost.

Instilling Courage

Finally, these criteria also challenge the church with regard to the virtue of courage. As was the case with the criterion of just cause, the discipline of last resort demands courage so that it is not distorted into an excuse for either infinite delay or appeasement, both of which are ways of avoiding the responsibility, costs, and risks to seek justice for the unjustly attacked neighbor. The challenge for the church with regard to instilling courage is of a piece with all that has been said thus far. It is a matter of teaching and preaching the virtue, of lifting up as examples the faithful courageous, and of practicing it in our daily lives by, among other things, resisting the manifold ways a contemporary culture of fear works against courage.

Pursuing Means Other Than War

Not only do these criteria reinforce the challenges presented to the church by other criteria but they also offer their own particular challenges. For example, the criterion of last resort challenges the church to develop and promote the development of means other than war for resolving injustice. Insofar as the criterion involves more than a judgment regarding whether or not last resort has been reached, it obliges Christians to be about the hard work of creating conditions (attitudes, institutions, and practices, we might say) that might increase the likelihood that the issues that give rise to just wars be resolved by means other than war. To return to the tool analogy used earlier, the criterion of last resort challenges the church to develop and encourage others to develop toolboxes that contain more than just the latest and greatest hammers. Disciples who are just warriors will devote as much time and energy to establishing and improving means other than war for justly resolving conflict as they do to sharpening the instruments of war.

Hence we might inquire as to how intentional the church is about actively working to foster means other than war for resolving injustices that rise to the level of a just cause. And the force of this query must go beyond asking if the church has a national office devoted to public policy advocacy, for not only is public policy advocacy only a small part of actually forming persons and communities in the virtues and habits necessary to sustain just war, but public policy offices are not particularly effective means of such formation. Instead, the challenge moves beyond national offices and public policy statements to questions of formation at the local level. Here we might do well to recall the kinds of practices and efforts that were associated with "just peacemaking." These include working to establish and strengthen viable international institutions that could mediate and enforce matters of justice, to be sure, but also supporting the work of nongovernmental organizations and fostering local efforts at conflict resolution and training in the habits and skills of civil resistance to injustice, not unlike some churches did during the civil rights struggle in the 1960s. Insofar as all of this is about faithfully following Christ and loving our neighbor, it is all about discipleship.

When we consider the teaching, liturgy, and programming of the church, what do we see? Do we see a community that is about the business of making just war possible by forming a people who are committed to war as a last resort and encouraging the institutions that would support this? Do we see church leaders who appreciate how such tasks and efforts are not secondary to the gospel, something they hand off to a committee or promote if they have time after the "really important" things are done, but are an expression of its very heart, such that their absence suggests a deficiency in their proclaiming and embodying the good news of the One who gives the church a ministry of reconciliation?

Reclaiming the Mediating Role of Church Leadership

In a related vein, insofar as the church has historically been actively involved in mediating conflicts, part of living out the criterion of last resort might entail encouraging and supporting the intercessions of bishops and other leaders of the church in conflict situations. This possibility also returns us to the challenges noted under legitimate authority. What kinds of leaders are raised up in the churches, and what skills and gifts are they expected to exercise? For example, are church leaders formed with the knowledge that one of their roles may well be that of intercessor and mediator in matters of the common good? Are they encouraged to do this at the local level, thereby gaining some of the skills that may one day be called on at the national or international level? Insofar as church leaders are selected on the basis of their ability to function as religious therapists or motivational speakers or administrators, the church may lack the kinds of leaders necessary to truly and faithfully embody Just War (CD).

Of course, these kinds of mediating tasks are not limited to church leadership but may be exercised by laity as well. Thus this criterion challenges the church to identify those in its midst who have the requisite gifts and skills, to assist them in using those gifts and skills for the sake of justice and the common good, and to call on them as necessary to help the church live out the discipline of last resort.

Cultivating Temperance

The final challenge to be lifted up concerns the way in which the criterion of reasonable chance of success insists that just wars are limited wars. The expectation that just wars are limited means that a just war people will not be given to overreaching. They will display a certain humility in their pursuit of the good. They will not demand too much—either seeking to eliminate an ideology or demanding unconditional surrender. As limited wars, just wars require a people whose pursuit of the good is limited, not in the sense that their commitment to the good is only partial, but in the sense that they recognize the limits of their ability to achieve the good through even a just war. They are restrained in their pursuit of the good. The character trait that best captures this is *meekness* and the virtue is *temperance*. So construed, meekness does not mean shy and self-effacing or weak and retiring. On the contrary, just war may well require a kind of courageous assertiveness. Rather, meekness and temperance are opposed to a certain arrogant or self-righteous championing of the good. They represent a mean between a passive capitulation to or appeasement of injustice on one hand and an overzealous, crusading pursuit of the good that ironically ends up perpetrating more injustice on the other.

How might the church ponder the formation of a people whose pursuit of the good is modest, temperate, and limited in the sense that the criterion requires? To the extent that the church lives in the midst of a culture, economy, and politics of immodesty and excess, opportunities abound. From dress to rhetoric to consumption (thought of both in terms of calories and consumer goods) to the way we conceive of ourselves and our nation, any time the church upholds and encourages a disciplined temperance, it is forming a people who may be capable of faithfully waging just war. Likewise, the practice of confession may be central to inhabiting this criterion faithfully inasmuch as it can resist and counter the myth of exceptionalism—the belief that we are better than all others and unquestionably agents of good in the world—in which we too often wrap ourselves and our nation and which feeds an intemperate crusading zeal.[27] Confession reminds us of the shortcomings of our pursuit of the good with regard to our enemy as well as of the persistence of injustice in our own life and thus calls us to a disciplined temperance in the pursuit of that good, both for our own sake and for the sake of our neighbors.

～♱～

At this point we have completed the treatment of the criteria that deal with justice in going to war. We have seen that Just War (PPC) and Just War (CD) share much. For the most part, the basic components of the criteria are the same. Where they differ, however, is in the details—in how those criteria are to be lived out in terms of practices, institutions, and character.

These differences can be traced back to their starting point: the modern nation-state or the church of Jesus Christ? Moreover, these approaches differ in the basic function of the just war discipline. Is it a public policy checklist that anyone can use—one where character does not matter—on the eve of war with little or no preparation? Or is it a set of markers for the whole way of life of a people who habitually seek peace and justice for their neighbors, in times of war and peace?

Finally, these differences are theological as well. As last resort and reasonable chance of success highlighted, it makes all the difference in the world if the people who inhabit the tradition are animated by the faith, hope, and love that is the gift of the blessed Trinity or if they have no faith or hope now beyond that which can be secured by the nation-state's arms.

These similarities and differences will be on further display in the next chapter as we turn to the two criteria that define justice in war.

8

How Fight?

Discrimination and Proportionality

As we turn to the criteria that define justice in waging war, commonly referred to under the heading of *jus in bello*, it is important to note that crossing the threshold from the criteria that pertain to justice before the shooting starts to doing justice while actually waging war is not like passing through a door that slams shut and is barred behind us. Justice in going to war and in waging war are not two separate and distinct disciplines, like, say, building an automobile and driving it.[1] The virtues, practices, and dispositions that are part of justice in going to war are not simply forgotten once the actual fighting begins. On the contrary, the disciplines embodied in proper authority, cause, and intent, for example, remain important components of waging war justly. Likewise, concerns raised under the criterion of reasonable chance of success, including consideration of the costs involved in waging war, continue to play a significant role in what it means to actually fight a war justly. Accordingly, as we turn to the criteria that guide how we wage war justly, they should be thought of as cumulative, as further specifying the shape of the discipline that is just war.

These additional criteria go by the name of *discrimination* and *proportionality*. Together they spell out the parameters of what it means to wage war justly. They define *how* a just war is to be fought. The criterion of discrimination, sometimes also referred to as "noncombatant immunity," concerns primarily who and what is and is not a legitimate target in just war. The criterion of proportionality addresses primarily the amount of force that may be brought to bear against an enemy in the prosecution of a just war.

Discrimination

Historically, this criterion began to take formal shape in the Middle Ages when the church first drew up lists of persons, places, and even times that were off-limits to war.[2] Those lists included persons such as peasants, priests, and women; places such as churches and monasteries; and times such as Sundays and Lent. Alongside these lists, and reinforcing the sense that all is *not* fair in war, was the culture and code of chivalry.[3] Notwithstanding its portrayal in popular media, chivalry, at its best, was integrated into the Christian faith and so became a way of forming just warriors in the virtues of the faith. One significant part of that discipline was discrimination, the recognition that not just anyone could be slain in any way, that in war the ends do not justify the means. Indeed, chivalry instilled in the warrior a positive duty to protect from harm those recognized as noncombatants.

Although the lists drawn up by the church varied both in terms of who and what appeared on them and in the extent to which they were followed, their appearance marks the beginning of the formal recognition by the church that the right to wage a just war is not tantamount to granting a license to do whatever is necessary to win. The lists stand as a testament to the fact that a just warrior has an obligation to exercise care in waging war so that war is directed against combatants and spares noncombatants.

The criterion springs from the recognition that, in the words of Grotius, "it does not suffice that we conceive the enemy, by some fiction, as though they were a single body."[4] In the modern world, where national governments wage war by drawing on all the resources of a nation—its wealth, its natural and human resources, its industrial capacity, and so forth—there is a tendency to see the enemy as a single body, a whole: the enemy nation. Even when the enemy is a guerrilla or terrorist force, there is a tendency to see the civilians amongst whom they hide as part of the enemy and so as legitimate targets. It is this penchant to see nations as wholes, and in the case of the US Civil War to associate civilians with guerrilla fighters, that prompted the emergence in the nineteenth century of "total war," where in effect the entire nation is seen as a legitimate target precisely because the entire nation underwrites the war.

The criterion of discrimination stands in stark opposition to this inclination. The standard here is that a just war is waged only in a manner that distinguishes between combatants and noncombatants whether the enemy is a national army, an irregular guerrilla force, or a terrorist network. Put bluntly and simply, the criterion of discrimination holds that one may not intentionally kill noncombatants. For example, one may not legitimately target cities in the hope of undermining enemy morale and shortening the war, nor may civilians be targeted in order to reduce the number of combatant casualties.

The failure to discriminate between combatants and noncombatants in waging war renders the killing of civilians in war an act of murder. Moreover, it renders those who do such killing little different from terrorists. Although there is no universally accepted definition of a terrorist, all but the most superficial definitions agree that terrorism involves intentionally killing noncombatants for political ends. If the just war discipline is about distinguishing morally legitimate killing from homicide, the criterion of discrimination is where the difference between just war and murder is sharpest. Just warriors who kill are not murderers because they do not target or intentionally kill noncombatants.

Having said this, it is important to be clear that the criterion of discrimination does *not* mean that a just war prohibits *all* civilian or noncombatant deaths. The criterion is sometimes referred to as "noncombatant immunity." I avoid this language, however, because it too easily lends itself to misunderstanding. The criterion does not grant noncombatants immunity from harm or even death. Suggesting that it does makes the criterion too restrictive and is but another way that the tradition is abused. Rather, the criterion insists that noncombatants be protected in the sense that any noncombatant deaths that do occur do so only as the unintended side effect of a just attack on a legitimate military target.

Much needs to be done to unpack what exactly discrimination entails, including addressing such matters as who is and is not rightly considered a combatant; what are legitimate targets, weapons, and tactics; and even where military installations are located. Before engaging these particular issues, however, we consider three more general ways that Just War (PPC) and Just War (CD) diverge.

Military Necessity

The first of these divergences is the way the principle of military necessity is understood. In the previous chapter reference was made to Michael Walzer's argument that in situations of "supreme emergency" the just war criteria could be overridden. As it is invoked by some proponents of Just War (PPC), the principle of military necessity functions in a similar fashion. It is invoked to justify violating the discipline and in particular the criterion of discrimination. Appealing to certain vagaries in international law, some argue that the positive duty to protect noncombatants from harm is binding only when such a duty does not interfere with military advantage or even military convenience.[5] So understood, military necessity reduces the criterion of discrimination to the expectation that the distinction between combatants and noncombatants will be observed only so long as doing so does not interfere with military objectives, be they construed as accomplishing the mission or protecting one's own soldiers from harm.[6] Used in this way, the principle of military necessity stands apart from or above the just war tradition as a kind of trump card that overrules the moral force of the tradition and its criteria.

In contrast, Just War (CD) follows the older Christian tradition of just war reflection that understands military necessity to function in a very different manner. Specifically, it understands military necessity to operate *within* the parameters of the tradition instead of standing *apart* from the tradition, justifying departures *from* the tradition and its criteria. As the likes of Vitoria, Suárez, and Grotius all say, necessity does not mean "advantage."[7] Military necessity, rightly understood, is not synonymous with sanctioning whatever is deemed militarily useful in a given situation. Accordingly, it cannot properly be used to justify whatever means are deemed necessary to complete the mission.

Rather, military necessity means that even when one is justified in going to war and wages war in accord with all the criteria, one is still not permitted to use all the force and wreak all the havoc and destruction one can on the enemy. Rather, one is only justified in using the amount of discriminating force necessary to attain legitimate ends. For example, that just warriors are permitted to kill enemy combatants does not mean they are right to kill as many enemy combatants as they possibly can. Instead, the permission granted to just warriors to kill enemy combatants extends only to killing those combatants and inflicting that destruction that is actually necessary to attaining the just end of the war. (And the criterion of reasonable chance of success reminds us that a *just* end of the war is not the same thing as victory at all costs.)

In other words, military necessity functions not as permission but as restraint. Thus Suárez writes, "it is just to visit upon the enemy all losses which may seem necessary either for obtaining satisfaction or for securing victory, *provided that these losses do not involve an intrinsic injury to innocent persons, which would be in itself an evil.*"[8] As he makes clear, necessity functions within the bounds of the tradition; when the tradition speaks of necessity it presumes the moral force of the other criteria, and the criterion of discrimination in particular.

Granted, Suárez is easily misread. If one lops off the restrictive phrase from the quote above or if one takes out of context his claim that "if the end is permissible, the necessary means to that end are also permissible,"[9] it is understandable that military necessity could be misinterpreted as permission to do whatever it takes to win, without regard for the criteria. In a contemporary culture that is largely utilitarian, it is unsurprising that military necessity would be interpreted as "the ends justify the means." Nevertheless, when understood properly, military necessity is constrained by the criterion of discrimination. One must discriminate between combatants and non-combatants, and once this is done the principle of military necessity then asks, of the legitimate, combatant targets, what is it necessary to attack in order to attain the just end of the war? Military necessity, in other words, is another name for the criterion of proportionality, which we will consider in detail shortly.

Permission versus Responsibility

The second general way in which Just War (PPC) and Just War (CD) diverge concerns whether the criterion of discrimination is properly understood as embodying only a negative force, represented in the basic definition given above of "don't kill noncombatants intentionally," or whether the criterion also entails a positive responsibility to protect noncombatants from harm. The former renders the criterion essentially permissive; it grants just warriors permission to harm noncombatants so long as that harm is unintentional. It renders discrimination a kind of moral minimum, focuses on the least that must be done, and centers on what one can get away with. Construed in this way, the phrase that sums up the criterion is "collateral damage." Discrimination excuses killing noncombatants when that killing is a matter of collateral damage.

Just War (CD) understands the criterion not as setting forth a moral minimum or granting permission to harm noncombatants but rather as an extension of the charity that underwrites the entire discipline of just war. As such, the criterion does not grant permission but rather names a positive responsibility, born of love for the neighbor, to actively strive to protect noncombatants from harm while waging a just war. A phrase that might adequately sum up the criterion from this perspective is "due care." It is not enough that just warriors do not intend the death of noncombatants; they have a responsibility to exercise due care in avoiding noncombatant deaths and protecting them from harm.[10]

The permissive understanding of discrimination is characteristic of Just War (PPC) and it is most clearly captured in the way the criterion of discrimination is explained in terms of what is called "the principle of double effect." With roots going back to Aquinas, the principle of double effect has a long, rich history in Christian moral reflection, and today it is used widely not only in discussions of discrimination in war but also in medical ethics.

The principle is founded on the recognition that actions can have multiple effects, some of which are intended and some of which may not be intended. With regard to discrimination, the principle of double effect is used to argue that the death of noncombatants is permissible if two conditions are met.[11] First, the deaths must be the unintended side effect of an otherwise good action. This is to say, one cannot intend to kill noncombatants either because you want those noncombatants dead or because you want to use those deaths as a means to some other end, like convincing the enemy's political leadership to surrender. Second, the good that results from the action causing the collateral damage must outweigh the harm represented by the collateral damage. In other words, it is not enough that the noncombatant deaths be unintentional (the first condition). The second condition insists that the cost associated with those unintentional deaths must be outweighed by the benefit gained from the action that unintentionally caused those deaths. Thus, if the projected deaths are unintentional but the benefit gained is negligible, they are not permitted.

The permissive character of the criterion when it is construed in terms of the principle of double effect is perhaps easier to grasp when we consider a few examples of what it permits. While one might think that the requirement to discriminate between combatants and noncombatants would prohibit bombing whole cities in order to destroy discrete military installations in those cities, according to some the principle of double effect permits such bombing in situations of "acute urgency," by which is meant a situation where such bombing is the only means of attaining a substantial benefit that outweighs the significant cost.[12] In another instance, it is argued on the grounds of double effect that where the benefit is deemed to outweigh the costs, it would be permissible to use flamethrowers in a cave where fifty enemy combatants are hiding behind several hundred women and children or to shoot through a hostage or human shield in order to kill a combatant.[13] The same author argues that there is nothing intrinsically indiscriminate about using nuclear weapons on cities and that the morality or immorality of doing so depends on the intent (was the object of the attack a legitimate military target in the city?) and on weighing the costs against the benefits (perhaps the target was a meeting of Hitler and his top lieutenants known to be taking place somewhere in the city).

The point is that the logic of double effect is fundamentally permissive. It is not first and foremost about protecting noncombatants. Rather, it is about excusing the failure to protect. It is not about embodying a responsibility to protect noncombatants from harm; rather, it is about the permissibility of harming noncombatants so long as such harm can be construed as collateral damage unfortunately incurred in the pursuit of a greater good.

What is the alternative? If Just War (PPC) renders discrimination too permissive by means of the principle of double effect, how does Just War (CD) enact the criterion of discrimination as a positive responsibility to protect? And, perhaps more importantly, how does it do so in a manner that does not render the criterion too restrictive by prohibiting all noncombatant deaths?

To begin with, Just War (CD) approaches the criterion of discrimination as it does the just war discipline as a whole, namely, as an expression of the character of the Christian community. This is to say, the criterion of discrimination is an outgrowth of the Christian community's positive commitment to love and do good to our neighbors in this life. In this regard, we might recall Augustine's vision of just war as a positive act of love that stands in stark contrast with those who would cast it instead as a kind of necessary lesser evil. Accordingly, as part of a Christian discipline of love in the midst of war, discrimination is not rightly cast permissively. Indeed, such a permissive rendering of the criterion is tantamount to a kind of neglect that could be equated with what is traditionally called a "sin of omission," a failure to do what we ought to do. In this case, the permissive reading of the criterion is a failure to embody the positive responsibility we have to actively seek to avoid noncombatant deaths. In other words, as a people who love and seek the good of our neighbors, be they friend or foe, it is not enough that we do not intend to kill noncombatants when we kill them, or that we only kill them when the benefits are judged to exceed the harm. Rather, we must actively strive to protect noncombatants from harm. We have a responsibility to exercise due care that is not mitigated or constrained by a supreme emergency, military necessity, the success of the mission, or a desire to protect our combatants (a "force protection imperative").

On the face of it, this much more rigorous account of discrimination may appear to preclude any and all noncombatant deaths in war. This is not the case, however. While it is true that it certainly challenges how war is to be waged if it is to be waged justly (see below), it does not prohibit all noncombatant deaths. In fact, the notion of double effect and unintentional, collateral harm remains central to discrimination as positive responsibility. Where it differs from Just War (PPC) is how it unpacks and develops these concepts. Explaining this difference requires briefly considering the origin and development of the notion of double effect.

Already it was noted that the principle of double effect is typically traced back to Thomas Aquinas, although it is widely acknowledged that he did not articulate anything like a formal principle such as is used today. Aquinas broaches the notion of double effect and unintended effects in the midst of a discussion of whether an innocent person may kill an unjust attacker in self-defense. Recalling and respecting Augustine's strong prohibition of self-defense, Aquinas nuances that prohibition by arguing that one may only kill an unjust attacker in self-defense when two conditions are met.[14] First, he is clear that one may only intend to defend oneself; one may not intend to kill the attacker. Second, the act of defense must be proportionate to the end.

Immediately we can recognize the two basic parts of the principle of double effect—unintended effects and the cost/benefit calculation of proportionality. And in the centuries after Aquinas, these rudimentary comments were unpacked and developed into the current principle and linked to the criterion of discrimination. Yet, in the course of this development, these ideas were removed from their original moral context—the Christian community with its positive responsibility to love—and relocated within the modern public policy checklist framework, with the result that they were stripped of their moral force—made permissive—and misconstrued.

We begin by examining how Aquinas's vision of responsibility was watered down and made permissive. Already we have seen how the principle of double effect is permissive; what was not made explicit, however, was how this permissiveness rests in part on allowing harm that is both *foreseen* and *certain* to happen. I *know* that dropping these bombs *will* kill thousands of noncombatants in this city; nevertheless, this is permitted so long as I do not intend to kill them (my intention is to kill several key enemy leaders and destroy military installations) and the benefit of eliminating the targets is judged worth the cost in collateral damage.

In recent decades, the claim that something can be foreseen and still be considered unintended has been criticized; it has been argued that a foreseen effect must be considered an intended effect. Such a claim has been soundly refuted and need not detain us here.[15] What concerns us is how collateral damage that is *foreseen* and *certain* has been linked to double effect and resulted in a permissive understanding of the criterion of discrimination. Aquinas did not hold a permissive but a responsible vision of discrimination. He did not permit collateral harm that was foreseen and certain or even likely, and neither does Just War (CD).

This rejection of unintended harm that is foreseen and certain is a prominent feature of Aquinas's thought, and yet the principle of double effect developed without regard for it. It was able to do this the same way that the principle of military necessity developed, namely, by holding on to the basic idea while jettisoning the moral vision in which it was nestled. The wider vision is the positive duty to love the neighbor that underwrote just war in Christianity from the start. That this positive duty to love involves a responsibility to avoid unintended harm that is foreseeable is evident in several areas of Aquinas's work. I will mention three.

First, there is his repeated reference to the parable of the wheat and the tares (Matt. 13:24–40), which he reads as a clear warning against harming innocent persons, even unintentionally, in the midst of efforts to interdict evil.[16] He writes in the course of a discussion of whether it is ethical to kill sinners that, while it is morally permissible to kill certain sinners under certain circumstances, nevertheless,

> Our Lord commanded them to forbear from uprooting the cockle in order to spare the wheat, i.e., the good. This occurs when the wicked cannot be slain without the good being killed with them either because the wicked lie hidden among the good, or because they have many followers, so that they cannot be killed without danger to the good. . . . Wherefore Our Lord teaches that we should rather allow the wicked to live, and that vengeance is to be delayed until the last judgment, rather than the good be put to death with the wicked.[17]

Thus, the legitimate authority of the governing powers to execute evildoers who threaten the common good is limited by the expectation that it will exercise such authority only when it can do so without at the same time endangering the innocent.

This clear sentiment against even unintentional harm comes through, second, in his treatment of the consequences of actions. Considering the question of whether the consequences of an action increase its goodness or badness, he answers that where the consequences are foreseen, they do indeed matter to the moral evaluation of an act. Furthermore, he argues, even where those effects are *not* foreseen they nevertheless make a moral difference if those unforeseen consequences follow from the nature of the act and *in the majority of cases*.[18] Only when such unforeseen consequences occur accidentally and rarely is the agent of the act morally excused from responsibility for those bad effects.

Third, Aquinas's rejection of unintended effects that are foreseen and/ or frequently follow from an act is clear in a passage from his treatise "On Evil." There he reiterates the point that sometimes an unintended effect is linked only rarely and in very few cases with an intended effect. But he then goes on to note that sometimes an unintended effect always or in most cases accompanies an intended effect. Aquinas concludes, "Therefore, if an evil is in very few cases associated with the good that the will intends, the will can be excused from sin; for example, a falling branch may kill someone when a woodsman is cutting trees in a forest through which people rarely travel. But if evil is always or in most cases associated with the good intrinsically intended, the will is not excused from sin, although the will does not intrinsically intend the evil."[19] The point is not that accidents should now be considered intentional but that according to Aquinas we are clearly responsible for unintentional effects when such effects are foreseen and likely. If I cut down trees in an area where people do not ordinarily walk and yet a tree I cut accidentally kills someone who happened to be walking by, it is no sin. That unintended effect was neither foreseen nor likely. But if I am cutting down trees in the vicinity of a heavily traveled walking path and one accidentally falls on a walker, although that harm was unintended, it was both foreseeable and likely. Hence I am morally responsible.

Accordingly, the criterion of discrimination is not satisfied simply by making sure all noncombatant deaths are unintentional. Rather discrimination as a positive responsibility does not permit just warriors to kill noncombatants unintentionally when such unintentional killing is foreseen and/or likely to occur. It would not permit any of the examples cited earlier—the city bombing, the flamethrower in the cave, and shooting through a human shield. But it would not judge as culpable, for example, the deaths of noncombatants who were unexpectedly present in a troop transport on a battlefield or the death of a noncombatant who stepped in front of a sniper's bullet intended for an officer in an urban command and control center where good intelligence said there was little or no reason to expect noncombatants to be present. In both instances the noncombatant deaths were neither intended nor foreseeable as likely.

But of course proponents of Just War (PPC) who invoke the principle of double effect do not say that all unintentional killing is permissible. Rather, they hold that unintentional noncombatant deaths are permissible when the cost is outweighed by the benefit gained. This brings us to how Just War (PPC) misconstrues what Aquinas says when he says that an unintended double effect is not blameworthy so long as it is not "out of proportion to the end."[20]

As we have seen, Just War (PPC) interprets this to mean that one should measure the anticipated good effects against the anticipated unintended bad effects. In other words, the hoped-for good that killing the combatants or destroying the military installation will accomplish should be weighed against the bad of dead noncombatants that is the foreseen (and perhaps certain) unintended effect. This is the meaning of the second point of the principle of double effect. As popular as it is, however, it is a misunderstanding of Aquinas, and one that renders discrimination improperly permissive. For when Aquinas argues that an act of self-defense should be proportionate to its end, he is *not* comparing the overall good effects with the overall bad effects of an act. Rather, he is arguing that a rightly intended act should not be carried out with more force than is necessary. He is not making a comparison of ends but a judgment of means. If the act is carried out with disproportionate force, then the act is wrong even if it was rightly intended. Put bluntly, Aquinas is argu-ing that while it might be fine to swat the horsefly on your neighbor's head, if you do it with a sledgehammer you are in the wrong, your good intention notwithstanding. (And if we follow his reading of the parable of the wheat and tares, it means that if all we have is a sledgehammer then we will have to let the horsefly live to be swatted another day.) Aquinas is not encouraging us to weigh the morality of collateral damage in a cost-benefit analysis. Rather, he is pointing us to the criterion of proportionality.

In summary, Thomas Aquinas does not endorse a permissive but a respon-sible vision of discrimination. Just warriors have a responsibility to distinguish between combatants and noncombatants not only in the way they are killed (intentionally versus unintentionally) but also by actively seeking to protect noncombatants from unintended harm that is foreseen and/or likely to occur. Just War (CD), rooted in the Christian community's call to actively love the neighbor, shares this responsible vision of discrimination.

Renouncing Responsibility

A third way in which Just War (PPC) and Just War (CD) diverge with regard to the criterion of discrimination concerns how the two approaches deal with situations where the enemy refuses to abide by the criterion of discrimination. How do just warriors respond when the enemy does not respect the distinction between combatants and noncombatants? There are a number of situations where this issue typically arises. For example, the enemy abuses the white flag or other traditional signs of surrender—which ordinarily are an indication that one has renounced one's status as a combatant—to launch an attack under subterfuge. Or the enemy uses noncombatant "human shields" in the hope of protecting their combatants and military installations from attack. Or unarmed, unknowing, and maybe even unwilling women and children are used to retrieve weapons and other items in a battle zone. Perhaps the most com-mon way this arises is in connection with the use of what are called irregular or guerrilla forces that operate in the midst of civilian populations.

It is not unusual for proponents of Just War (PPC) to argue that just warriors need abide by the criterion of discrimination only so long as their opponents do. If the enemy hides behind or among civilians, then the enemy alone is responsible for any noncombatant deaths. In other words, Just War (PPC) excuses just warriors from responsibility for noncombatant deaths when the enemy violates the criterion. For the most part it is not that the criterion is simply discarded but that responsibility for violations are shifted to the enemy alone. In its more mild or hesitant form, this shifting begins by speaking of a "shared responsibility" for noncombatant deaths when just warriors launch indiscriminate attacks but quickly shifts "major responsibility" to the enemy before declaring finally that in such situations the enemy left the just warriors with "no alternative" to the destruction of towns, villages, and so forth. The effect is to absolve just warriors of any responsibility.[21]

A more forthright renunciation of responsibility for discrimination is offered by Paul Ramsey, who, in the course of addressing the use of guerrillas by the enemy, writes, "The insurgents themselves have enlarged the target area [and] it is legitimate for counter-insurgents to attack, so far as the principle of discrimination is concerned."[22] He continues by asserting that in such a counter-guerrilla situation, the moral principle in play is proportionality and not discrimination, since the guerrillas themselves have already violated discrimination.[23] In other words, once the enemy has violated discrimination, just warriors cannot be condemned for the noncombatant deaths that result from their response, so long as that response is proportionate. The responsibility for the noncombatant deaths lies with the enemy alone. The logic of this kind of argument clearly echoes in the instruction regarding rules of engagement given to military officers that "when the enemy used human shields or put legitimate targets next to mosques or hospitals, he, not we, endangered those innocents."[24]

Finally, an even more extreme version of this renunciation of responsibility does not merely shift responsibility to the enemy but goes even farther by arguing that civilians who "allow" themselves to be used as shields become legitimate military targets.[25]

Just War (CD) rejects this renunciation of responsibility in all of its forms. It holds that assigning blame in this manner is not the same thing as positively living out and embodying the criterion of discrimination. Rather, such a renunciation is understood as but another way the just war tradition becomes permissive instead of encouraging the positive responsibility to protect noncombatants. Moreover, such a passing of the buck strikes an oddly discordant note within the whole tenor of the Christian life. In what other situation do Christians legitimately assert that because their neighbors are not living the moral life they are thereby excused from doing so? Since when does living faithfully as disciples depend on whether or not our enemies are doing likewise? The enemy's failure to adhere to proper moral restraint in the waging of war does not absolve the just warrior from doing so.[26]

This does not mean that Just War (CD) denies that the enemy bears any responsibility for the risk and attendant harm that falls on noncombatants when the enemy maliciously abuses white flags, uses noncombatants as shields or gophers, engages in guerrilla warfare, locates military installations in the midst of civilian populations, and so on. Quite to the contrary, Just War (CD) recognizes that failing to discriminate and exercise due care to protect noncombatants is wrong and that those who do not discriminate, who fail to protect, and who abuse noncombatants in the aforementioned ways are guilty of war crimes and so are subject to just judgment after the war.

What Just War (CD) asserts is that two wrongs do not make a right. The enemy who is guilty of abusing noncombatants and violating the criterion of discrimination does indeed share responsibility for any harm that befalls noncombatants. They may even shoulder the majority of the guilt. But be that as it may, that does not justify, excuse, or permit just warriors to ignore the criterion of discrimination in favor of proportionality alone. Likewise, it does not permit creating a kind of moral "free fire zone" where the shoeshine boy or the woman with a gun to her head are simply declared combatants because they are in the wrong place at the wrong time.

What then is a proper response to such violations? How does Just War (CD) engage situations where the enemy is abusing noncombatants? What does the positive responsibility that discrimination rightly understood embodies look like? Put bluntly, when weighing an attack against an enemy who is using noncombatants as shields, the proper response is not to assign blame and then do what has to be done. Rather, the proper, just response is to be more discriminate. Instead of using air power, one might have to send in ground forces. Instead of using a tank or artillery, one might have to use infantry. Instead of using an M-16 or hand grenade, one might have to use a sniper. And, indeed, in some situations, it may be that no available weapon or tactic can be used without foreseen and almost certain noncombatant deaths, and so destruction of that particular military target may have to be forgone, at least for the time being. As Aquinas reminds us, when one cannot get at the chaff without also harming the wheat, one is obligated to exercise patient endurance and forgo destroying the chaff.

Such an understanding of discrimination will undoubtedly strike many as too rigorous. In the words of Paul Ramsey, it seems like "granting the enemy immunity from attack because he had the shrewdness to locate his missile bases in the heart of his cities."[27] This is obviously an overstatement insofar as Just War (CD) does *not* grant the enemy immunity from attack even when installations are surrounded by noncombatants; rather, in obedience to their Lord, Christian just warriors refrain from making *indiscriminate* attacks. The enemy is granted no immunity from discriminate attacks. For example, if enemy troops hide in civilian housing, whereas discrimination would rule out using bombs and artillery or Ramsey's flamethrower, it might not rule out the use of snipers and door-to-door searches. The unfortunate reality of the abuse of noncombatants by unjust combatants means only that just warriors will need to work that much harder to develop more discriminating weapons and tactics, not to mention nonmilitary means of addressing injustice.

Targets, Weapons, Tactics, and Installations

Having considered the criterion of discrimination in general terms, we now take up specific details with regard to what constitutes legitimate targets, tactics, weapons, and military installation locations.

Targets. With regard to targets, already the basic distinction between combatants and noncombatants has been spelled out. But who and what constitute a legitimate combatant or military target? As war has developed in the modern world and more of society's resources have been drawn on to support military efforts, it has become increasingly difficult to distinguish between combatants and noncombatants. While international regulations like those that insist lawful combatants have a chain of command, wear uniforms or identifying emblems, and bear arms openly are intended to aid in distinguishing between combatants and noncombatants, those regulations are not sufficient. What is the status of a soldier who is off duty or home on leave? A soldier who has been captured as a prisoner of war? Moreover, many militaries receive their orders from civilian political leadership and heads of state. Are such political figures legitimate targets? What about employees of the private companies that supply armies in war, such as workers in tank factories or the laborers sewing uniforms or packing field rations? And what about plants that produce trucks or other items, only some of which may be used in the prosecution of the war while others are put to strictly civilian uses?

While there is no simple consensus on answers to all these questions, the distinction between who or what constitutes a legitimate target and who or what does not is generally recognized as a functional one. It turns on what and how the person or object in question contributes to the war effort. Sometimes this is cast in terms of the difference between subjectively supporting the war with displays of patriotism or propaganda, or even rationing versus active material participation in the war effort. At other times this difference is construed in terms of the difference between soldiers who pose a lethal threat, as well as civilians who serve the fighting needs of those soldiers, and those whose do not pose a lethal threat or who serve the human needs of soldiers by providing medical or religious care, food, and so forth.[28] Oliver O'Donovan captures both the clarity and ambiguity that attends the criterion of discrimination with regard to identifying legitimate targets when he writes:

> Material co-operation . . . is not confined to armed forces. The politicians who dictate the policy, the information technologists who handle communications, the mechanics who service the hardware, the administrative staff on whom logistics depend, all these co-operate directly and materially. . . . A well-aimed missile might knock out a mechanic, a politician, a computer operator and driver, all technically "civilians," without causing one truly non-combatant death. On the other hand, a doctor, a chef, a lawyer and a plumber may all be in uniform, and yet effectively non-combatants. Drawing the line can be a nice matter: provisioning an army on campaign is obviously an act of material co-operation, while selling food to the army or preparing for consumption is doing no more than would be done in peacetime. Yet while we puzzle over the twilight cases, we cannot overlook the difference between day and night: a soldier in his tank is a combatant, his wife and children in an air-raid shelter are non-combatants.[29]

In summary, soldiers actively prosecuting a war are legitimate targets because they embody a threat, whereas soldiers who do not embody that threat are not legitimate targets. Thus, reservists who have not been called up are not legitimate targets; neither are soldiers who have been incapacitated or taken prisoner. Likewise, soldiers who are medics or chaplains are not properly combatants, unless they bear arms. On the other hand, some civilians are regarded as legitimate targets. Politicians involved in prosecuting a war as well as civilian contractors who work alongside soldiers in the prosecution of a war are generally regarded as combatants, as are civilians who directly and materially enable the lethal threat by manufacturing and supplying that lethal force.

In making these judgments there is no bright line distinguishing Just War (PPC) from Just War (CD). The shape of the distinction between combatants and noncombatants is the same in both. Where they differ concerns how the distinction is handled, either permissively or in terms of a positive responsibility to protect.

The issue of discriminate targeting, however, extends beyond persons to encompass places, structures, and institutions as well. Not only must just warriors distinguish between combatants and noncombatants, they must also distinguish between civilian and military installations and so forth. For example, the just war tradition has long declared that certain places, such as churches and hospitals, are not legitimate military targets. In recent times such immunity has been extended beyond religious sites to include important cultural sites as well. Likewise, civilian infrastructure, such as farmland, electrical grids, and water purification plants, are normally protected from attack on the reasoning that they are essential to the survival of noncombatants, even if that same infrastructure services the human needs of soldiers.

The protection afforded religious and cultural sites and civilian infrastructure, however, is not absolute; they are not simply immune from attack. Rather, they are off-limits to attack unless and until they are used by combatants to launch an attack. Thus, for example, a church or water purification plant may not be attacked unless the enemy is using them as concealment in the course of attacking or to store materials used in battle.

Here a subtle distinction between the Just War (PPC) and Just War (CD) approaches emerges. While both recognize that the protection afforded such places and structures is not absolute, they embody different standards for evaluating when such places and structures lose their immunity. This difference might be cast in the language of *primary* use versus *dual* use. Just War (CD), in accord with its positive responsibility to preserve and protect noncombatants and in keeping with Aquinas's warning against harming the wheat to get at the tares, gives the benefit of the doubt to civilians. Thus, if an electrical grid, warehouse, or bridge is *primarily* used by civilians, it cannot be considered a legitimate target unless it is being used by the enemy to launch an attack. In other words, one cannot destroy a civilian bridge in the middle of a city just because the military might use it. It may only be attacked if the military *is* using it. And when it is being used, just warriors may strike it only insofar as they do so in a discriminate manner. This is to say, the strike must be directed at the enemy and not merely use the enemy's presence as a pretext for destroying the bridge in the hope of increasing the suffering of civilians and undermining the enemy's war-fighting resolve. Just War (PPC), on the other hand, insofar as it is more permissive, tends to give the benefit of a doubt to the military. If something has a *dual* use capability then that is sufficient to justify its being targeted. According to this logic, much if not most of the civilian infrastructure is subject to preemptive attack and destruction simply because it may be used by the military.[30]

Weapons and Tactics. The criterion of discrimination also affects the choice of weapons and tactics used in war. Since at least the Middle Ages, the just war tradition has included prohibitions on the use of certain kinds of weapons, although the exact rationale for the various bans on things like crossbows or gunpowder is debated. Nevertheless, some weapons may be regarded as intrinsically indiscriminate. For example, cluster bombs and land mines, even when their use might be carefully circumscribed to battlefields, are inherently indiscriminate unless they are designed to disarm themselves after the fighting stops. Likewise, chemical, biological, and nuclear weapons may be judged intrinsically indiscriminate insofar as their immediate and/or long-term effects cannot be restricted to the space and time of the battlefield. The wind may shift and carry a nerve gas into a civilian area, or the fallout from a nuclear weapon may poison the environment for generations. Some weapons may not be intrinsically indiscriminate but rather are so in particular contexts. Thus a gravity bomb used against a battleship on the high seas far from any non-combatants might be discriminate, but that same bomb dropped on a military target in the midst of a densely populated city might not be. Likewise, using a fighter jet to attack soldiers on a battlefield might be discriminate whereas using that same jet to attack enemy combatants holed up in a room in a high rise apartment complex might not be.

Along these same lines, some tactics may be intrinsically indiscriminate. Declaring whole areas "free fire zones" where discrimination no longer applies or preemptively declaring that anyone spotted in a certain area is automatically to be considered "hostile" and shot are examples of intrinsically indiscriminate and therefore unjust tactics. So are "counter population" or "counter city" targeting as well as the obliterating bombing of cities. Other tactics may be regarded as indiscriminate when used in particular settings but not in others. Thus, carpet bombing enemy forces in a remote area in preparation for a ground attack is far different from carpet bombing a city with the intention of softening enemy forces prior to an attack.

On this matter of weapons and tactics, the difference between Just War (PPC) and Just War (CD) is a matter of the distinction already drawn between reading the criterion permissively or reading it responsibly. Just War (PPC) is more permissive in the sense that it renders discrimination with regard to weapons and tactics *relative*. It effectively says, "use the most discriminating weapon you have or can spare." For example, suppose the target is a combatant in the middle of a crowded marketplace. Just War (PPC) would permit the attack as long as the most discriminating weapon one could spare was used. In this case, it might be a hand grenade instead of a gravity bomb, unless, say, you only had one hand grenade and it would be militarily advantageous to save it for a later action. In which case, using a gravity bomb in a crowded marketplace would be permissible because it was the most discriminating weapon you could spare and the noncombatant deaths that followed from its use were unintended, as per the principle of double effect.

In this way, Just War (PPC) renders discrimination relative. It is relative to what is available and compatible with military necessity or advantage. By way of contrast, Just War (CD) is not permissive but responsible. The responsibility to avoid intentional noncombatant deaths and even foreseen unintentional noncombatant deaths does not permit discrimination to become a kind of sliding scale, relative to what one has available or what military necessity dictates. Rather, if a weapon or tactic cannot be employed in a manner that avoids foreseen and likely (although unintentional) deaths, then it cannot be used even if this means not attacking at this time and place. Thus, in the case of the soldier in the marketplace, discrimination would not permit the use of either a hand grenade or a gravity bomb. Instead, it would call for a more discriminate approach, perhaps using a sniper. And if circumstances were such that the only options were to either use a hand grenade or drop a bomb, then the criterion of discrimination would entail that a just warrior forgo that attack on that target at that time. There is no permissive relativizing of the criterion.

Military Installations. The final aspect of discrimination that bears mentioning is its implication regarding the location of military installations. Implicit in all that has been said thus far is the duty to respect noncombatant populations even when they are in the vicinity of legitimate military targets. But the criterion entails more than this when it comes to the location of military installations. It entails asking why noncombatants are in the vicinity of legitimate targets in the first place. Said differently, abiding by the criterion means that not only will one seek to avoid noncombatant deaths but one will also avoid placing noncombatants at risk by avoiding locating military installations in their midst. A just war people will embody the criterion of discrimination not only in the way they attack the enemy but also in how they locate their own military installations and other legitimate targets, being sure to place them apart from civilian populations. Although this does not receive much attention in Just War (PPC), it is implicit in the condemnation of the abuse of noncombatants. Just War (CD) takes what is implicit and makes it explicit. Faithfully living out the just war discipline with regard to the positive responsibility to discriminate means that one will be intentional is seeing to it that those things that might ordinarily be deemed legitimate targets are not placed in the midst of one's civilian population.

Such are the basic contours of the criterion of discrimination. We now turn to the second criterion concerning how a just war is fought, namely, the criterion of proportionality.

Proportionality

A Relatively Neglected Criterion

The criterion of proportionality does not receive much attention in contemporary treatments of just war. More often than not, it is overshadowed by the criterion of discrimination. There are at least two reasons for this relative neglect, and they provide a nice entry point into what the criterion means and how it is understood differently by proponents of Just War (PPC) and Just War (CD).

To begin with, the criterion of proportionality does not receive much attention in Just War (PPC) because it is thought that proportionality has already been adequately explained in the course of treating the other criteria: under reasonable chance of success, where the costs and benefits of a prospective war are considered, or under discrimination, where the benefits of an attack are weighed against the unintended harm done to noncombatants.[31]

Some advocates of Just War (PPC) suggest the criterion of proportionality should be recognized as a distinct criterion with its own function apart from the criterion of discrimination. Specifically, they suggest the criterion of proportionality is a *second* cost/benefit calculus that involves combatants instead of noncombatants.[32] It weighs the good to be accomplished by an attack against the value of the combatants who will likely be harmed in the attack.

Whether proportionality is collapsed into discrimination or is recognized as a separate cost/benefit analysis pertaining to combatants, the result is the same: the criterion does not garner much attention because its basic substance has been dealt with under the prior criteria.

A second reason that this criterion does not receive much attention involves the perception that it is rather straightforward and simple. This is most apparent among those advocates of Just War (PPC) who suggest the criterion of proportionality is about the *purpose* for which force is used. Understood in this way, proportionality ensures that force is only used to advance the just purpose of the war. This is another example of how just war is limited war: a just war uses military force only for the sake of the just cause that gave rise to the war. This is to say, the criterion of proportionality requires that the force used in war be *directed* to the just cause and not stray outside the just ends and intentions of a war. In other words, proportionality means that just force is not gratuitous; it is not force that is exercised merely because one can. Neither is just force vindictive, that is, exceeding the just cause and right intent in order to inflict retributive suffering and harm. Nor is it force used under the cover of "justice" to pursue more narrow interests, such as enrichment or territorial expansion or the extension of geopolitical influence.

This is the sense of proportionality alluded to previously in the discussion of military necessity. Whereas military necessity is frequently invoked as a rationale for violating the just war discipline, rightly understood it serves as a further specification of that discipline. In particular, military necessity is another name for the criterion of proportionality; it is another name for the discipline that insists just wars only employ force necessary for the attainment of the just cause.

As such, the criterion of proportionality is deemed to be rather simple and straightforward and, unlike its neighbor discrimination, to merit no extended treatment.

Economy of Force: Minimum Necessary or Maximum Allowed?

Just War (CD) shares with some advocates of Just War (PPC) this understanding of proportionality as a discipline that directs just force only to the just ends and purpose of a war. Just War (CD), however, carries the discipline of proportionality a step further, including what might be called "economy of force."

Economy of force is a military term that typically refers to the idea that force is best used when it is directed at the main objective and not diluted by being directed at secondary objectives. This could be characterized as an expectation that the use of force be efficient. Force should not be wasted in directions that do not advance the main objective. So understood, it meshes well with the sense of proportionality as the imperative to direct force only toward the just objectives of a war and not toward objectives that contradict or exceed the just cause and right intent of the war.

When employed by Just War (CD), however, economy of force takes on an additional meaning. As part of a Christian discipline, it refers not only to the *directed* use of force but also to the amount or quantity of force that is used. We might say that the criterion of proportionality encompasses the *measured* use of force.

According to Just War (CD), the criterion of proportionality means not only that just force is directed at the just end of a war but also that it is measured force, in the sense that it is limited to the *amount* of just force necessary to attain that just end. Having the right to go to war does not mean that one may unleash all possible force and destruction on the enemy. The criterion of proportionality rules out the application of *maximum* force and the sentiments that underwrite such disproportionate force, such as "the crueler war is, the sooner it is over." Proportionality as a distinctly Christian discipline calls for the use of the *minimum* force necessary instead of the maximum allowable. As Aquinas says, in an oft-misunderstood passage, an act is disproportionate when it employs more force than is necessary.[33] One may justly use only the discriminating force that is militarily necessary to address the just cause and achieve the right intent of the war. Thus, a just war, we might say, does not permit *overkill*. In this regard, the criterion of proportionality is akin to the kind of discipline exemplified in many domestic law enforcement agencies and police departments with regard to the use of force. It is at odds with modern military trends toward the use of maximum or overwhelming force.[34]

Another way to explain this is to compare the criterion of proportionality with proportionality as a dimension of reasonable chance of success. Prior to the start of a war, proportionality as part of reasonable chance of success calls for a determination (which continues during the war) of whether one can muster *enough* just force to win. The criterion of proportionality in waging war functions as a kind of complementary determination. It entails exercising care that *too much* force is not used, that just force is directed and measured. Proportionate force is no more just force than is necessary to attain the just ends of the war.

All of which is to say that the criterion of proportionality is not satisfied with a cost/benefit analysis; rather, the criterion encompasses a responsibility to reduce harm by minimizing the use of force. So understood, the criterion further exemplifies how Just War (CD) is not permissive but responsible. Just as the criterion of discrimination expresses a positive responsibility toward noncombatants, the criterion of proportionality names a positive responsibility toward combatants. As an extension of the way of discipleship even into battle, just war is not a license to kill any and all combatants by bringing to bear whatever force one can. The expectation that a just war people will employ the minimum force necessary is an expression of the positive commitment of Christian just warriors to love their enemies and to intend, even in the midst of war, not their death and destruction but their turning and sharing in the benefits of a just peace.

Furthermore, the expectation that force be proportionate or measured applies to every aspect of war, from the weapons used to the decision to engage in a particular battle to the larger strategic vision that plans the path to victory. Thus, for example, while proportionality permits using hand grenades on legitimate combatants, it does not permit using hand grenades packed with glass, which is invisible to x-ray (and therefore much harder for medics to remove) and thus inflicts harm well beyond that necessary to render the enemy incapable of obstructing justice. Likewise, while proportionality permits engaging the enemy who obstructs justice, it recognizes that the destruction of every enemy combatant or military facility may not be necessary in order to attain a just victory. In particular, the criterion does not permit vindictive harm or the destruction of a routed or defeated enemy, unless the enemy is only fleeing in order to regroup and continue the fight. In the same way, even as proportionality sanctions killing combatants when it is militarily necessary, it does not permit the destruction of combatants for ends or purposes that exceed the just cause and intent of the war, such as weakening the enemy to the extent that after the war they are all but required to become a client state subservient to the will and interests of the victor.

The Challenge for the Church

The Invisibility of Moral Responsibility

As we turn to consider the challenges presented here, the first issue that needs to be addressed concerns *who* is challenged by these criteria. It is not uncommon for the responsibilities associated with the just war discipline to be divided up neatly between civilians and soldiers. The civilian leadership is said to be responsible for considerations of justice in going to war, while the military leadership is thought responsible for overseeing and implementing justice in the waging of war. This latter responsibility is sometimes even further parsed so that only officers, and high ranking ones at that, are thought responsible for the moral decisions involved in waging war. This division of moral labor has the effect of absolving civilians of being overly concerned with justice in war, and it may also exacerbate the pressure that civilians often put on the military to ignore such practices as discrimination and proportionality. It also excuses soldiers from wrestling with the questions of justice that should surround any decision to go to war.

According to this arrangement, because the church is situated on the civilian side of the divide, even as its members participate in governments and militaries, the challenges presented to it by the criteria concerning how war is to be waged are minimal. The church might educate its members who join the armed forces about justice in war and encourage the military to take the criteria seriously, but beyond this it would have little to do or say.

From the perspective of Just War (CD), such education and exhortation would be important, as the treatment of the other criteria have suggested. But the challenges run much deeper because this division of moral responsibility does not hold, for, as we have argued from the outset, Just War (CD) is part of a whole way of life. It arises out of—as an extension of—everyday Christian discipleship, and it is sustained by the character of the Christian community, whose life is ordinarily marked by virtues such as charity, justice, prudence, and courage. Character and the attendant virtues simply cannot be divided up in the way the typical allocation of responsibility suggests. To be a people of character means being a people who are consistently virtuous across a spectrum of activities and roles, whose life is not fragmented into morally distinct compartments and whose moral behavior does not change dramatically from one role or place to the next.

In other words, the commonplace division of responsibilities falsely assumes that soldiers could embody justice in war while simultaneously relinquishing or renouncing concern with justice in going to war. Yet, as suggested earlier, one cannot simply summon forth justice in an instant, apart from the daily, ongoing engagement and formation in what justice is and does. Civilians cannot accurately claim to be concerned about justice in going to war if that concern is not seen through to completion, both during and after the war is waged. Although the people involved in a just war will vary in their particular gifts and skills as civilians and soldiers or officers, nevertheless they will be the same kind of people—a people of a certain kind of character. The kind of people needed to live out justice in war are the kind of people who will be concerned about justice before, during, and after war. The kind of people who are only concerned with one part or the other of the just war discipline are not the kind of people capable of living out that discipline as a faithful form of Christian discipleship. Just war as a manifestation of character simply cannot be parsed in that manner.

Thus, according to Just War (CD), while civilians and civilian institutions might play a preeminent role in matters of justice prior to war and the military may well take the lead on matters of justice in waging war, the church cannot surrender its moral responsibility to reflect on and pursue justice in all aspects and phases of war. After all, Christians in the military do not cease to be members of the church, and as members of the church they continue to have a responsibility to participate in the church's discernment regarding the justice of a prospective war. Indeed, given their particular vocation and skills, soldiers may have an especially important and unique contribution to make to that process of discernment. Likewise, although civilian Christians are not likely to participate in the waging of war in the manner that soldiers do, they do not cease to be concerned with the just waging of war, both because they are concerned about and committed to supporting their Christian sisters and brothers who are directly involved in waging war and because they are concerned about their enemies, whom they desire to see treated justly even in the midst of war. For these reasons, the criteria that guide the just waging of war are of deep concern to the church, even if much of the church would be classified as civilian and so not directly involved in waging a war.

Hence the first challenge to the church presented by these criteria is that of bringing its members—civilians and soldiers—together so that they can engage in mutual, corporate deliberation and counsel on matters concerning these and all the criteria. Moreover, this mutual engagement would be something other than sending care packages and wearing memorial or solidarity ribbons. Even as churches do these things, many soldiers do not feel as if their stories concerning war are welcomed, whether those stories are stories of pain and guilt or wisdom and insight that might correct civilian misperceptions. Conversely, many soldiers, for all their experience in military matters, do not evidence a working grasp of the church's moral vision of war. In this situation of mutual need, practicing corporate deliberation and support not only would enhance the church's fidelity to its call before, during, and after a war but it might also strengthen its exercise of legitimate authority.

The moral incoherence of the commonplace division of responsibility is further displayed in the way the criteria of discrimination and proportionality reiterate the challenges presented to the church by the other criteria. Put simply, these criteria challenge the church to form persons—civilians and soldiers— whose character is marked by the virtues that are necessary for faithfully living out the other criteria. Faithfully enacting justice in war requires the kind of people who faithfully enact justice prior to the start of a war.

Inhabiting the Virtues

Thus the second challenge presented by the criteria of discrimination and proportionality would be the ongoing one of forming persons in the virtues of charity, patience, fidelity, courage, temperance, and so forth. For example, discrimination requires of the church an extraordinary patience. Patient endurance is needed in the face of the realization that indiscriminate acts might bring a war to a victorious conclusion more rapidly than a war that is waged justly by distinguishing between combatants and noncombatants. Patience is a particular challenge for civilians who recognize that being faithful to the criterion of discrimination means that their loved ones in the military may face more risk and may face it longer. It is a particular challenge for soldiers who in the midst of battle feel the anguish and anger that tempts one to strike out at enemy civilians in retaliation or reprisal for harm and loss. It is a challenge for the whole church insofar as adhering to discrimination may mean that the unjust and wicked, by hiding like weeds among the wheat, may be spared for a time and so continue to perpetrate their injustice and wickedness. Likewise, both discrimination and proportionality require the virtue of charity. After all, they are both concrete forms of loving the enemy. Discrimination is a form of loving enemy civilians by sparing their lives, and proportionality is a form of loving enemy combatants by tempering the force used against them to only what is justly necessary. Temperance and prudence are also required insofar as both criteria embody a kind of judgment about when and where to use measured force. In the same way, courage and fidelity are needed to stay the course and abide by our convictions and commitments when ignoring these criteria would appear to spare us suffering and perhaps hasten victory.

Developing Discriminating Force

Because the need for these and other virtues was raised in earlier chapters, they need not be revisited now. Instead, let us briefly consider some of the specific, concrete challenges that these criteria put to the church as it strives to live out Just War (CD).

First, both of these criteria challenge the church to encourage and support the development and deployment of weapons that are capable of being used in a discriminating and measured way. Reinforcing a point first made under the criterion of last resort, these criteria call for the development of weapons that span the spectrum of force. Just warriors cannot be concerned solely with developing ever-more devastating or overwhelming forms of force. To the contrary, justice in war calls for precision and even nonlethal applications of force.[35] The church may even need to consider recovering the medieval Christian practice of banning certain weapons, either outright or in particular circumstances, if the church discerns that such weapons cannot currently be used in ways consonant with its commitment to discrimination and proportionality.

This last point is worth stressing. What matters with weapons is not simply the weapon itself but the weapon's use. And a great deal of the morality of a weapon's use hinges on the character of the one employing the weapon. In other words, the issue with regard to weapons is not one of technology. As the history of warfare suggests, advances in weapons technology can lead either to more discriminate and proportionate fighting or to less. For example, when the machine gun was first invented, its adoption was resisted by military leaders who recognized a deep threat to the virtues and character that sustained the moral parameters of war in the technology that enabled killing to be industrialized.[36] Likewise, the introduction of air forces in the early twentieth century is widely recognized as a setback to discrimination in war. But while a particular technology may encourage or threaten fighting that is discriminate and proportionate, whether or not it does so finally depends on the character of the persons using that technology. After all, even the most precise missile can kill noncombatants when the users of that technology are negligent in their intelligence gathering, imprudent in their decisions, or unjust in their intent.

Using Force

As a consequence, a second challenge that discrimination and proportionality put to the church is that of taking a deep interest in the development and deployment of weapons, as well as forming persons who will develop and deploy weapon systems in ways that encourage the practice of discrimination and proportionality. This is but another way of saying that discrimination and proportionality challenge the church to take an interest in the training and tactics of soldiers. In particular they suggest that the church will question tactics and training that elevate the protection of combatants—what is often referred to as the force protection imperative—above the responsibility to protect noncombatants or to use measured force. Already I suggested that proportionality may require that just warriors be trained more like civil law enforcement to evaluate and use the minimum force necessary instead of the maximum permissible. While there are no doubt circumstances where the minimum necessary force would be the maximum force, in a world where warfare increasingly looks like humanitarian intervention or a fight against a guerrilla or terrorist organization embedded in urban settings and civilian populations, training along the lines of a police or law enforcement model will be more important and increasingly necessary. Whether such training is appropriate to all military forces or just to some—such as Special Forces or military police—I will leave to others to contemplate.

Locating Installations

The third concrete challenge presented by these criteria, especially by the criterion of discrimination, concerns the location of military installations and other facilities that would be regarded as legitimate targets in a war. Insofar as the church is committed to discrimination, it will work to see that military installations will not be located around civilians. Perhaps this means that the church will work on behalf of zoning laws that would require a buffer between military-related industries and civilian populations and infrastructure. Certainly it means that Christians on both sides of the civilian/soldier divide will work, regardless of zoning laws, to see that noncombatants are not put at risk by the location of the military infrastructure.

Reparations

The fourth concrete challenge presented to the church by these criteria is the challenge of reparations. While justice in waging war does not prohibit the killing of either noncombatants when such killing is collateral damage or combatants when such killing is proportional, killing nevertheless carries with it a responsibility to make amends. That responsibility is not born of moral *guilt*. After all, Just War (CD) is not intrinsically sinful (recall chap. 2) and so the just killing in such a just war bears no burden of moral guilt. Rather, the responsibility is born of love, of the intent to bring a just peace to the enemy in waging a just war. It is an expression of the sadness and regret that characterizes a just war people. It is part of the effort to see a just war achieve its stated end—the renewal of communion in the common good. The challenge, then, is to work both for the reconstruction of communities after the shooting stops and for the compensation of particular victims and particular losses. This may take the form of governmental action but it may also engage the church in various aid and assistance efforts, including housing refugees, procuring medical care for the injured, and sending resources and people to aid in rebuilding and recovery.

At the outset, it was suggested that the just war discipline, when lived as a form of Christian discipleship, is not easy. I argued that it was a demanding discipline, one that was not likely to be popular and that might even be said to be a form of bearing the cross. In the criteria of discrimination and proportionality we come face to face with the stark reality of how demanding the discipline is and how it may entail just warriors taking great risks and enduring great loss for the sake of loving and seeking justice for their neighbor, even their enemy neighbor. For in the end, these criteria boil down to the questions: How much are we willing to risk in order to follow Christ in loving our enemies? Are we willing to risk our lives and the lives of our loved ones for the sake of sparing noncombatants? Are we willing to bear risk for the sake of making measured response to our enemies?

I suspect that a truthful answer to this challenge would be that, left to our own devices and relying on our own willpower, we would risk very little. But, as I have argued from the start, we are not alone. Just War (CD) is the work not of individuals but of a community called the church. We now turn to consider the spirituality of this community that would embrace the just war discipline as a form of Christian discipleship.

Conclusion

Spirituality and Just War

Just war lived intentionally as Christian discipleship, as a way of faithfully following Christ in times of war, is a difficult, demanding discipline. As the preceding chapters suggest, it asks a great deal of those who would submit to its discipline. Certainly it asks more than Just War (PPC), an approach that is much more permissive and can be used by anyone at any time, with little preparation.

Just War (CD) is a costly form of discipleship, one that might well be characterized as a form of taking up the cross.[1] It asks that extraordinary risks be taken and burdens borne in the name of loving and seeking a just peace for our neighbors, including even neighbors whose injustice makes them our enemies.

The Difficulty of the Discipline

This is not something that comes easily to us. Honesty compels us to admit what the critics of this effort will surely say. Just War (CD) asks too much of us. It is too hard, too demanding. Granted, when it comes to the authority to kill other human beings, those whom Christ calls us to love, one would expect the standards to be high. But Just War (CD), it may be argued, sets the moral bar too high.

First, it asks us not to lash out in righteous rage, not to succumb to the impulse to do *something*, anything, in the face of great evil and injustice.[2]

Instead, it asks us to respond to injustice temperately, charitably. It asks us to respond in a manner measured by *all* the criteria of just war. It asks us not to pursue justice selectively but to seek a just peace for all, including our enemies. It asks us to develop and attempt in good faith means other than war. And when war is a last resort, Just War (CD) calls us to resort to it only when it is likely to succeed in attaining a just peace and only to continue the fight when it can be justly won. It expects that we will not knowingly kill noncombatants or attempt to annihilate the enemy with maximum or overwhelming force, and it expects that when we do kill, we do so with heavy hearts.

Second, Just War (CD) asks too much of us in that it may lead to more wars instead of fewer. If the rigor of the discipline prompts some to think that it reduces the number of occasions when a military response to injustice is fitting, the way in which Just War (CD) is fundamentally other-directed may lead others to wonder if this is not a blueprint for war without end. If Just War (CD) is rigorous, it is also more aggressive, legitimating intervention and military force beyond mere self-defense.

Whether or not living this discipline would increase or decrease the number of wars in which Christians were engaged is something I doubt can be determined in the abstract. What is indisputably true is that Just War (CD) calls us out of self-absorption, apathy, fear, and indifference in order to risk much—indeed, everything—in service to others for the sake of the common good.

Reflecting on the whole of the discipline and all that it asks, who is not tempted to respond in a manner similar to the disciples who, when confronted with another seemingly impossible task on the way of discipleship, uttered in despair, "Then who can be saved?" (Matt. 19:25)? Just War (CD) asks a great deal—too much, in fact, for any single, solitary individual.

A Communal Discipline

But this is not a crippling critique, for Just War (CD), no less than any other aspect of the Christian life, is not a matter of persons simply mustering the willpower to just do the right thing. Living the discipline—following Christ, bearing the cross—exceeds the ability of individuals. This has been one of the principal claims of the argument.

Accordingly, a major characteristic of Just War (CD) is the centrality of community. Living just war faithfully as a form of Christian discipleship requires the support and accountability of a community, the community called church. Living Just War (CD) is dependent on the care, counsel, and correction of our sisters and brothers in the faith to make us better than we otherwise would be. We simply cannot be this good, apart from a community that instructs, sustains, supports, corrects, and forgives.

But the presence of community is about more than ensuring that individuals have adequate moral support. The point of the emphasis on community is that individuals *cannot* be just warriors in the robust sense of Just War (CD). The point is that Just War (CD) is the practice of a community or it is not practiced at all—just as one cannot play softball by oneself. This can be seen in several ways.

To begin with, I have argued that under the extraordinary stresses of war, the call of justice as expressed in Just War (CD) simply exceeds any individual's willpower. As wise warriors can testify, in battle—as in any morally challenging situation, frankly—it is character that makes the difference. Willpower cannot be relied on to sustain convictions under the duress of war. Fidelity to conviction is a matter of character.

And how is character formed? Not suddenly, on the eve of a war, by memorizing a checklist of criteria and willing oneself to be just, whatever that might mean. Not by sitting through a few hours of ethics instruction by a Sunday school teacher or chaplain. We cannot learn the virtues that constitute our character from reading a book or browsing a Web site in the privacy of our own homes. Rather, character is formed over time and in a community of character whose daily life, whether in times of war and peace, is distinguished by virtues like patience, courage, justice, and temperance. We become people of character only as we are surrounded by people of character. In imitating them, we become like them. To be loving, patient, courageous, and wise, as the just war discipline demands, requires that one spend a lifetime in the company of those who are wise, courageous, patient, and charitable, doing the things that wise, courageous, patient, and charitable people do—tending to one another and neighbors, including enemies, in countless, ongoing ways.

Beyond the requirements for the formation of character, however, Just War (CD) is necessarily a communal practice because it depends on a particular ordering of communal life. Just War (CD) depends not just on persons of character but on a host of institutions as well—military, political, civic, cultural, and ecclesial (church). At various points in the treatment of the criteria this has been acknowledged. The nature and character of a people's political institutions are central to the ability to faithfully inhabit the just war discipline. Some political forms and practices may make exercising legitimate authority or waging war as a last resort more difficult than others. The same holds for church institutions. What is preached and taught; how the church worships, prays, and conceives of its mission; the kinds of leaders it calls; and the way decisions are made all play an important part in making Just War (CD) a viable discipline. Likewise, a culture of service will have a very different impact on the possibilities for faithfully embodying just war than will a self-absorbed and suffering-averse culture. For example, appeals to the common good or the call to serve and risk even when my self-interest or national interest is not at stake will gain more traction in some cultures than in others. Obviously, too, the way a military is organized and how it trains soldiers has a tremendous impact on the prospects for just war. Whether it is a matter of the kind of motivation instilled in soldiers, the risks taken for the sake of avoiding civilian casualties, the approach to the economy of force, the accommodation of SCO, or the status and authority of chaplains, a military formed around the just war discipline will look very different than one that is not.

The emphasis on community and character, as well as the recognition of the importance that institutions hold in embodying Just War (CD), may go some distance toward mitigating the sense that the discipline asks too much, but it does not alleviate the concern entirely. Even anchoring Just War (CD) in character and community does not finally convince that this is indeed a viable, practicable way of life.

A Just War Spirituality

And this is as it should be, because Just War (CD) is more than just another moral vision that is virtue-focused, tradition-dependent, or community-based. The lingering sense that it asks too much of humans is exactly right. It does ask too much of humans, even humans immersed in communities of character. After all, as the Christian tradition has long recognized, we are fallen—we are sinners. We are just not that good, even—maybe especially—when we gather in communities and groups.

This is why Just War (CD) must be rooted in not simply community and character but also spirituality. We could say that Just War (CD) is a religious war, in the particular sense discussed in chapter 5. It is a discipline undergirded by certain claims about God. Actually, it is not so much driven by certain ideas about God as it rests on the truthfulness of particular convictions regarding what God is doing in the world here and now, as well as in the future.

Just War (CD) is intrinsically connected to the virtues of faith and hope, which are quite fitting companions for the love that has been central to this account of just war. Put a little differently, the previous chapter concluded with the challenge, "how far are we willing to go, what will we risk in loving our neighbors, including our enemy neighbors?" As Jesus reminds us, loving those who love us is not such a challenge. Even loving the innocent, unjustly attacked neighbor is not beyond the scope of the imagination. But loving our enemies in the concrete ways expected by the just war discipline is something else altogether. Especially when those enemies murder thousands of our friends and neighbors, when they systematically terrorize, torture, rape, and show little inclination to stop anytime soon. No wonder Jesus associated loving enemies with being perfect (Matt. 5:43–48). It is a super-human love, or better yet, a supernatural love.

Yet, as Augustine argued, this is the love that is the foundation of the Christian practice of just war. So we see how Just War (CD) from start to finish rests on faith and hope in God. The Christian faith rests on the claim that God gave the gift of love to the church (not only to the church but also to the world)[3] in Jesus Christ. Just war, as part of the practice of that faith, rests on the trust that God continues to make that love available to those who follow Christ so that they are able to love as he loved—loving even their enemies—as they bear the cross in the form of the just war discipline. Just War (CD) is an act of faith that God in Christ, through the means of grace available to the church, can and does make us better than we would be if we were left to our own feeble resources. It is an act of faith that God sanctifies, and it is an act of faith that God in Christ does this, not simply at some undisclosed point in the future but even here and now.

Of course, being sanctified, as wonderful as it is, is not a guarantee of victory in war. Faithful just warriors can die and just wars can be lost. As we have seen, faithful just warriors may be morally obligated in certain circumstances not to fight in the first place or to surrender once the fighting is underway. So we see how Just War (CD) rests on hope as well. It rests on the hope that in giving to and risking for others, we receive; in losing life, we will find it; and though we and our loved ones may lose or die for following the discipline, we shall not perish. Just War (CD) rests on hope in Christ's resurrection as the ultimate victory over sin, injustice, and death. No less than the best theological accounts of Christian pacifism,[4] Just War (CD) is an act of faith in God.

Like Gideon, who was required to reduce the size of his army so that it was obvious that victory was ultimately God's, Christians can wage war justly, following the discipline with all of its teeth even when that discipline entails more risk, cost, and suffering for us and for those we love. But we can wage just war only as an act of trust and hope in the final victory of God. As the great Christian thinkers of just war have long reminded us, we do not wage war because the force of our arms and the strength of our legions are all that stand between us (or our neighbors) and chaotic oblivion. Rather, we wage war in this very disciplined way as an act of obedience to God and so as a pointer to God. We wage war in this way, and only this way, in the hope that others will note our justice, restraint, long-suffering love, mercy, and care for the common good and will join us in this common good, this communion, that rests finally in God.

Just War as Witness

Just War (CD) is ultimately a form of witness. It is a way of pointing to the One who desires all to share in the common good, to receive the blessings of a just peace, and who will one day break the bow, shatter the spear, and beat the sword into a plowshare. Just War (CD) rests on the truth of the claim that Jesus is Lord of history even now and not just in the future. Just War (CD) stands or falls on the truth of the claim that we are not alone, even now. God is with us. For this reason and this reason alone Christians can shoulder the burdens of Just War (CD). Because God in Christ is active here and now, Christians are able to love and take risks for their neighbors, even their enemy neighbors, in accord with the discipline of Just War (CD).

This is what makes just war discipline a form of discipleship and not a lesser evil, not a concession to the supposed "fact" that in this complex modern world where many of us feel the weight of earthly responsibility we cannot really follow Jesus, or at least follow him too closely, and certainly not all the way to the cross, defeat, death, and destruction.

This is the heart of the matter. This is the difference that makes all of the difference. This is what the difference between Just War (PPC) and Just War (CD) boils down to. Just War (PPC) does not require God to make sense. Granted, many adherents of Just War (PPC) are Christians and believe in God. That is not the point. Rather, the point is that the God of Jesus Christ makes no real, material difference here and now in how war is waged according to Just War (PPC). Anyone can use the public policy checklist; Jesus and the sanctifying grace that is offered by him through the Spirit in the church are not required.

Just War (PPC) is so often construed as a lesser evil precisely because it is thought that God is *not present* now, making us capable of the good. Just War (PPC) serves the kinds of polities and politics who do not know the power of God or the gift of resurrection, faith, and hope. It suits the kind of people and polities that believe there is nothing but the force of their arms, the numbers of their chariots, and the speed of their horses that stand between them and oblivion, the dustbin of history.

As a result, Just War (PPC) has to pull teeth or water down the criteria so that they are manageable within merely human resources and means. It is permissive because it does not recognize or rely on God. It attempts to articulate the best we can do when we are left alone—without God's sanctifying grace and even without communities of character. The result is mixed motives, supreme emergency, double effect, universal interest instead of common good, selective justice, maximum force, and so on. We are alone; God is not sanctifying us now. We cannot love our enemies. We cannot surrender. We cannot avoid collateral damage. We cannot take that much risk. Because God is not active now, because God has left us alone at least for the time being, we cannot afford to shoulder the responsibility embodied in Just War (CD). Instead, we must settle for something more permissive, less demanding.

Just War (PPC) also embodies a spirituality. But it is not a spirituality of witness; it is a spirituality of survival. Its goal is finally not the good. (It is a lesser evil, after all.) Its point is not to direct us to the good that is God and the communion of all in that just peace, but survival. It is a spirituality of life lived in God's absence. It is a vision of war waged without God, by merely human means, and with merely human ends. And it makes perfectly good sense if God is not active in history now, sanctifying us such that we can indeed love our neighbors, even our enemies, in war.

In the Gospels Jesus encourages his disciples that when they hear of wars and rumors of wars, they should not be alarmed (Matt. 24:6; Mark 13:7; Luke 21:9). In a world up in arms, disciples can count on Christ's presence. That presence is what makes discipleship possible.

Just War (CD) counts on that presence; Christians who enter just war as a form of discipleship do so in response to that presence, in the hope of witnessing to that presence through their love for their neighbors, both innocent and unjust, in a way that is made possible by that presence.

Hence, the conclusion of the last chapter notwithstanding, the question on which Just War (CD) rests is not that of what *we* are willing to risk and endure for others, but what Christ risks for us. Is Christ present here and now, forming a people who will bear the responsibility and risk of waging wars justly? *This* is the challenge that Just War (CD) puts to the church. It is a challenge that cannot be answered with words and treatises. It can only be answered by its life.

Appendix

Two Just War Traditions

	Just War as Christian Discipleship	Just War as Public Policy
General	Augustine—Aquinas—Vitoria	Modern—International Law
	• reflection of the character of Christian community	• public policy checklist for nation states
	• emerges from consistent concern for justice and neighbor	• anyone can use: character is irrelevant
	• JW with teeth: all criteria must be honored	• tendency to pull teeth

	Justice in Going to War	*Jus ad bellum*
1. Legitimate Authority		
Who wages?	• God → state (104)*	• state (102)
Who decides?	• prince with wise advisors, soldiers, church (108)	• state → international bodies (107)
2. Just Cause	• other-directed (repel, recover, restore) (133, 136) • actual offense vs. preemptive strike (imminent and grave) vs. preventative war (140)	• self-defense (intervention is a problem) (127, 132)
3. Right Intent	• just peace (157) • love, not hatred or revenge (158) • character: the consistency and completion of justice (164)	• unreflective peace (153) • no revenge

Continued

*Numbers in parentheses correspond to the page numbers in the text where the topic is discussed.

	Justice in Going to War	Jus ad bellum
4. Last Resort	• good-faith diplomacy (184, 191) • develop alternatives (192)	• diplomacy (184) • little attention to alternatives (192)
5. Reasonable Chance of Success	• attainable, limited ends (195, 197) • proportionality: cost vs. benefit (196)	

	Justice in Waging War	Jus in bello
1. Discrimination	• responsibility to protect non-combatants: avoid unintended *and* foreseen or likely casualties (213) • targets: legitimate if primary use is military (222) • weapons (224) • location of installations (226)	• permissive: noncombatant deaths permitted if unintended and worth the cost (213) • targets: legitimate if used by military (222) • weapons: relativity (use most discriminating) (224) • installations: (shifting responsibility) (226)
2. Proportionality	• economy of force: directed and measured (228) • military necessity rightly understood: minimum force needed (211, 228)	• maximum force necessary (228)

Notes

Introduction: Living Faithfully in a Time of War

1. Drawn from Bentley 1984 and Schmidt 1959.
2. Drawn from Zahn 1986.
3. Yoder 1983, 82.
4. Ramsey 1968, 35, 42–69.
5. Walters 1973.

Chapter 1 Love and Evil in the Christian Life: The Emergence of Just War

1. Tertullian 1994, 19.3.
2. For more on this debate, see Hunter 1992 and 1994; Kreider 2003; Swift 1983; Cadoux 1982; Harnack 1981; and Driver 1988.
3. Hunter 1994, 170; Kreider 2003, 424–25.
4. What follows is drawn from Russell 1975, 3–8.
5. Aristotle 1981, 79; Russell 1975, 3.
6. Christopher 1999, 10–11.
7. Keegan 1993, 389–90.
8. As noted in Russell 1975, 6–7.
9. Tacitus is quoted in Barnes 1982, 783.
10. Russell 1975, 7–8.
11. Ambrose 1994, III.4.27.
12. Quoted in Fitzgerald 1999, 875. See also Augustine 1950, 19.7.
13. Augustine 1994b, 22.75.
14. Augustine 2001, 32, 34, 184–85; Augustine 1994b, 22.76–77.
15. Augustine 1994b, 22.77.
16. Augustine 2001, 188.
17. Augustine 1994b, 22.74; Augustine 2001, 38–39.
18. See Augustine 1994b, 22.76, 79; Augustine 2001, 37.
19. Augustine 2001, 38.
20. Augustine 1950, 1.21.
21. Augustine 1994b, 22.73, 78; Augustine 1950, 1.21.
22. Augustine 1994b, 22.70.
23. Augustine 1994a, 293.

24. Augustine 2001, 135–36.

25. Ibid., 30–42.

26. Ibid., 135.

27. On the miseries of even just war, see Augustine 1950, 19.7.

28. Augustine 2001, 125.

29. Ibid., 38

30. Ibid.

31. Ibid., 217.

32. Ibid.

33. Augustine 1994b, 22.74.

34. Ibid., 22.79. See also Augustine 2001, 135.

35. The paradigmatic exemplar of this ethic of a "lesser evil" is, of course, Reinhold Niebuhr.

36. Augustine 2001, 217.

37. Ramsey 1988, 73, 83, 129.

38. Ibid., 113. The distinction between disciples and admirers belongs to Clarence Jordan. See McClendon 1990, 103.

Chapter 2 Can War Be Just? A Brief History of Just War

1. This is part of the reason why there is so much training. It is also the rationale for certain aspects of military training, typically associated with "boot camp," that can appear as unnecessarily harsh or merely sadistic to an outside observer. Learning to adapt and function in the midst of chaos and under great stress is crucial to good soldiering.

2. See Janda 1995; Weigley 1973, 128–52.

3. Ramsey 1961, 145.

4. What follows relies heavily on Russell 1975, 57–85.

5. Russell 1975, 69–70. Augustine is often misunderstood on this point owing to a mistranslation of a key passage. See Swift 1973, 369–83.

6. Johnson 1981, 153–54.

7. See Verkamp 1988 and 1993; Cole 2002b.

8. See Verkamp 1993 for consideration of the various reasons. The exception in this regard may be the Eastern Orthodox tradition, which from very early on may well have approached war as a necessary lesser evil. But, as Allyne Smith argues, the Eastern Orthodox tradition is not finally a just war tradition but something else; hence, it is not treated here. See Smith 2004.

9. Contamine 1984, 270–74.

10. Thomas Aquinas 1981, II–II 64.2.

11. Thomas Aquinas 1981, II–II 64.7.

12. Johnson 1981, 175.

13. Vitoria 1991, 306.

14. Ibid., 235.

15. Ibid., 309

16. Ibid., 311–12.

17. Ibid., 308; Vitoria 2000, 119.

18. Vitoria 1991, 302–3.

19. Vitoria unpacks this in some detail in "On the American Indians." See ibid., 231–92.

20. Ibid., 333.

21. Ibid., 313. See also 278–84.

22. Thomas Aquinas 1981, II–II 42.2.

23. Vitoria 1991, 304, 315–16.

24. Ibid., 314.

25. Vitoria 2000, 127; Grotius (1995, 3.1.2) cites Vitoria on this point as well.

26. Vitoria 2000, 124.

27. Vitoria 1991, 320.

28. Ibid., 314.

29. Cajetan first made this move. Mangan 1949, 52; Ramsey 1961, 47.

30. Vitoria 2000, 122.

31. Vitoria 1991, 325–26.

32. Ibid., 321.

33. Grotius 1995, 20.

34. See Cavanaugh 1995.

35. See Dunn 1979. Dunn's work reinforces Cavanaugh's point, although it is clear that Dunn does not always recognize the force of his own argument in this regard.

36. Grotius 1995, II.22.10.1.

37. Ibid., II.1.2.

38. Ibid., II.1.5.

39. Ibid., II.22.5.

40. Ibid., II.1.17.

41. Ibid., II.22.17.

42. See Glover 1982.

43. Clausewitz 1976, 78, 87, 90.

44. See Johnson 1981, 239–67, 284–91; Janda 1995; Weigley 1973; Harsh 1974.

45. Quoted in Johnson 1981, 301.

46. Quoted in ibid.

47. Wells 1992, 51.

48. See Roberts and Guelff 2002, 6, 271–72.

49. O'Brien 1991, 165.

50. National Conference of Catholic Bishops 1983.

51. See Walzer 2004, 3–22.

52. Contamine 1984, 256.

53. See, e.g., James Turner Johnson's (1984, 48–52) comments on the Falklands war of 1982.

54. John Courtney Murray, SJ, makes a similar point. Murray 1988, 265.

Chapter 3 Just War as Christian Discipleship: Presuppositions and Presumptions

1. Walzer 1977.

2. Christianity is occasionally accused of making a negative difference regarding how just war is understood. The typical examples in this regard are the Crusades and the so-called Wars of Religion, which we discussed in the previous chapter.

3. For more on this, see Ricks 1997b.

4. See the argument of Osiel 1999.

5. See Fick 2005.

6. Caputo 1996, xx; Shay 1994.

7. For an interesting study of these issues in the context of the Vietnam War, see Baritz 1985; Caputo 1996.

8. Ricks 1997a.

9. There are many virtues and kinds of character. The character that a given military forms may or may not be compatible with the character and virtues necessary to sustain Just War (CD). For a brief overview of a variety of "warrior values," written by an instructor at a US military academy, see French 2003.

10. A great many trees have been killed in this debate. Among the more succinct statements of the issues are Johnson 1996, Griffiths and Weigel 2005, and Winright 1996.

11. Although the latter terms—war, violence, force—are not synonymous, they tend to be lumped together in this debate.

12. National Conference of Catholic Bishops 1983, ¶80, 81, 83, 93, 120.

13. It may be worth noting that Christian pacifism (at least in its most recognizable form) does not hold a presumption against war or violence that is shared with just war; rather, pacifism embodies an absolute prohibition of war and violence.

14. The dental analogy was suggested by Yoder 2001, 63.

15. Cited in Barnes 1982, 783.

16. Walzer 1977, 251–68; Walzer 2004, 33–50.

17. See, for example, Maguire 2007, who is up front about his intention to use just war in this way.

18. Weigley 1973.

19. Suárez n.d., 7.21.

20. Grotius 1995, II.22.17.

21. Johnson 2005, 20.

22. Weigel 2003, 23.

23. See O'Brien 1981, 78–79, 83–84, 98.

24. Ramsey 1968, 143–44.

25. Thomas Aquinas 1981, I–II 18.4.

Chapter 4 Who's in Charge? Legitimate Authority

1. See Johnson (1997, 260–62) on the interpretation of this agreement.

2. Max Weber offered the classic definition of the modern nation-state when he wrote, "a state is a human community that (successfully) claims the monopoly of the legitimate use of physical force within a given territory" (1946, 78; see also Giddens 1987).

3. See the 1977 Geneva Protocols I and II in Roberts and Guelff 2002, 419–512.

4. Augustine 1950, 1.21.

5. For a succinct overview of the tradition on revolution, see Shinn 1978.

6. Thomas Aquinas 1981, II–II 42.

7. Aquinas refers to the office of ruler in Thomas Aquinas 1978, ¶49.

8. For an insightful reflection on what this would entail with regard to legitimate authority, see O'Donovan 2003, 27, 65–66, 73.

9. Calvin 1960, IV.20.30–31.

10. Paul VI 1976, ¶31.

11. Johnson 1981, 170, 304.

12. Thomas Aquinas 1978, ¶68.

13. Ibid., ¶42.

14. See Luther 1962, 115.

15. Vitoria 1991, 306–7.

16. Ibid., 308.

17. Grotius 1995, II.23.4.

18. Suárez n.d., 4.7.

19. Vitoria 1991, 235.

20. Note that a mistranslation of Augustine is responsible for the widespread belief that he did not permit Christian soldiers to deliberate on the justice of a given war. See Swift 1973.

21. This is to say that the option not to participate does not extend to refraining from supporting a war financially by means of taxes.

22. Suárez n.d., 6.7.

23. Vitoria 1991, 307.

24. Ibid., 308.

25. Ibid., 311.

26. It is worth noting that Vitoria condemns closing one's eyes to the whole question of justice on the grounds that one cannot know. See Vitoria 2000, 1.8.

27. See Augustine's correspondence with magistrates and other secular authorities in Augustine 2001.

28. For a sample list, see Appendices I and II in Eppstein 1935.

29. Figgis 1960, 5.

30. Thomas Aquinas 1981, II–II 40.2.

31. Vitoria 1991, 262.

32. Suárez n.d., 2.7.

33. See Cavanaugh 2005.

34. John Paul II's Address to the Vatican Diplomatic Corps on January 13, 2003, was widely received as a condemnation of the war in Iraq. For instance, then–Cardinal Ratzinger and now–Pope Benedict XVI interpreted that address as a condemnation of the war in an interview with Zenit on May 2, 2003. John Paul II's address is available at http://www.vatican.va. The interview with Cardinal Ratzinger is available at http://zenit.org/article-7161?l=english.

35. For a good treatment of this, see Potter 1968.

36. See Hutter 1999; Szura 1984; Paul Griffith's contribution to Griffiths and Weigel 2002; Dodaro 1991; and Davis 1992, 111–36.

37. Szura 1984, 126. On the presentation of war, see Fussell 1975; Marvin and Ingle 1999; Frantzen 2004; Hedges 2002.

38. Hutter 1999, 75.

39. Griffiths and Weigel 2002, 32.

40. This section is informed by Bergen 2004.

41. See Thomas Aquinas 1981, II–II 40.2; Vitoria 2000, art. 2; Suárez n.d., art. 3.

42. See Mahedy 2004; Lifton 2005.

Chapter 5 Why Fight? Just Cause

1. The Charter of the United Nations, article 2, principle 4 states: "All Members shall refrain in their international relations from the threat or use of force against the territorial integrity or political independence of any state, or in any other manner inconsistent with the Purposes of the United Nations." http://www.un.org/aboutun/charter/chapter1.htm (accessed November 3, 2007). For a succinct treatment of the interpretive issues, see Johnson 1973, 464–75.

2. The Charter of the United Nations. http://www.un.org/aboutun/charter/chapter7.htm (accessed November 3, 2007).

3. Typically, such assertions amount to little more than declarations of the deficiencies of existing international organizations and institutions. What is uniformly overlooked are the possibilities for international cooperation in policing and law enforcement that do not depend on the United Nations, possibilities that are in fact already actualities. Consider, for example, recent high profile international manhunts or the manifold ways that the current effort against terrorism is actually conducted as a law enforcement/police action. Granted, the omnipresence of the Iraq war in the US public imagination distorts the public perception of the struggle against terrorism, inclining many to view successful police actions around the world as military successes.

4. Walzer 2004, 40, 43.

5. See Cook 2001; Cook 2004, 115.

6. O'Donovan 2003, 25.

7. Vitoria 1991, 326–27.

8. Burtchaell 1989, 226.

9. Thomas Aquinas 1981, II–II 64.7.

10. Augustine 2001, 30–42.

11. Augustine 1950, 19.17.

12. See King 1964, 77.

13. Vitoria 2000, 117–18. See also Davis 2002, 67–71; Davis 1997.

14. National Conference of Catholic Bishops 1993, 5, 15.

15. Grotius 1995, 2.20.4; see also Thomas Aquinas 1981, II–II 108.1 on vengeance.

16. Johnson 2003, 11.

17. Vitoria 1991, 302–3.

18. Thomas Aquinas 1981, II–II 10.1.

19. See Tyerman 2006.

20. Thomas Aquinas 1981, II–II 10.1.

21. See Vitoria 1991, 231–92.

22. Grotius 1995, 2.1.5; Walzer 1977, 85.

23. Grotius 1995, 2.1.5.

24. Ibid., 3.16.

25. Ibid., 2.1.17.

26. See Kauffman 2004; Schlabach 2007. See also Stassen 1992 and 1998.

27. See Fick 2005 for an account of the invasion of Iraq that shows both sides of this—the effect of both good and bad command and discipline.

28. Luther 1957, 364–68. The most immediately relevant passage is, "we should devote all our works to the welfare of others, since each has such abundant riches in his faith that all his other works and his whole life are a surplus with which [the Christian] can . . . serve and do good to his neighbor" (365–66).

29. Grotius 1995, 2.1.18.

30. Luther 1967, 170–71.

31. This is in no way an encouragement to simply endure domestic violence. For more on this see Bell 2009.

32. See Bader-Saye 2007.

33. Anscombe 1981, 72.

Chapter 6 Why Fight? Right Intent

1. Thomas Aquinas 1981, II–II 40.2; see also II–II 64.7.

2. Grotius 1995, 2.22.17. For a more recent statement of this sentiment see Childress 1982, 78.

3. Walzer 2004, 94.

4. Tacitus is quoted in Barnes 1982, 783.

5. Augustine 1950, 19.12. Clausewitz (1976, 370) makes a similar observation.

6. Augustine 1950, 19.12.

7. Thomas Aquinas 1984, 69.

8. Augustine 2001, 125.

9. Calvin 1960, VI.20.12.

10. Cole 1999, 65; Ramsey 1961, 305; Ramsey 1968, 143.

11. Thomas Aquinas 1981, II–II, 25.8; 26; 27.7; 31; Thomas Aquinas 1984, 66–80.

12. The one exception that Aquinas notes is praying; we can do good for all in the sense that we can pray for all.

13. Thomas Aquinas 1984, 69–70.

14. Thomas Aquinas 1981, II–II 31.3.

15. Thomas Aquinas 1984, 71.

16. Ibid., 70–71, 73.

17. Ramsey 1988, 73, 83, 129.

18. Augustine 2001, 217.

19. Ibid., 38.

20. Vitoria 1991, 326–27.

21. Augustine 2001, 217.

22. Ramsey 1968, 397.

23. See Augustine 1993, ¶6.

24. Augustine 1950, 4.15.

25. Augustine 1998, 19.7.

26. See Iasiello 2004.

27. For a thoughtful and more detailed account of the elements of justice after the war, see Iasiello 2004; Allman and Winright 2007. See also Schuck 1994.

28. Vitoria 1991, 325–26. See also Johnson 2003, 17–18.

29. Suárez n.d., 7.7.

30. National Conference of Catholic Bishops 1983, ¶92–93.

31. Vitoria 1991, 312–13.

32. Philip Caputo notes how his training for the Vietnam War diminished his compassion (1996, 21).

33. See Morris 2000; Butler 2000.

34. On the psychology of killing, see Grossman 1996. See also Nadelson 2005.

35. And, it might be noted, it has not always been the point of being a warrior either. See Neff 1952 and Contamine 1984 for fascinating histories in this regard. See also Keegan 1989; Ellis 1975.

36. For an accessible treatment of the gift of confession and forgiveness, see Jones 1995.

37. Mahedy 2004; Marin 1980, 1981; Lifton 2005; Shay 1994, 2002; Iasiello, 2004.

38. See Gray 1959 for a profound reflection on what war does to warriors.

39. An example of a liturgy for this purpose can be found in the appendix of Mahedy 2004.

Chapter 7 When Fight? Last Resort and Reasonable Chance of Success

1. Grotius 1901, 2.24.1.

2. Suárez n.d., 4.1.

3. Suárez n.d., 6.5.

4. At its best, the practice of siege warfare included provisions for sparing noncombatants. Grotius (1995, 3.11.14) mentions this favorably. It could even represent an alternative to bloodshed insofar as protocols existed for ending a siege prior to protracted suffering and bloodshed. In 1705, for example, French regulations permitted surrendering with honor a besieged fort after only a small breach had been made in the fortifications (Neff 1952, 156, 191).

5. See Gordon 1999a, 1999b, 1999c, 2002.

6. For an overview of the issues, including several case studies, see Weiss, Cortright, Lopez, and Minear 1997.

7. For a thoughtful effort to articulate conditions whereby general sanctions might be distinguished from war and so morally licit, see Christiansen and Powers 1995. For a helpful treatment of sanctions that distinguishes them from acts like selectively refusing trade or severing aid, see O'Donovan 2003, 95–108.

8. For one effort to articulate "just sanctions," see Pentland 2002.

9. Suárez n.d., 7.3.

10. Potter 1969b, 219.

11. Grotius 1995, 3.3.11; Potter 1969b, 219.

12. Walzer 1977, xv; Walzer 1992, 6.

13. Weigel 2003, 26.

14. Barth 1961, 460.

15. See Stassen 1992 and 1998.

16. Potter 1969a, 49–50, 61.

17. See Schlabach 2007 and Kauffman 2004.

18. Vitoria 1991, 304.

19. Ibid., 314.

20. Pius XII 1954, 4.

21. Ramsey 1961, 136, 142; Murray 1988, 265.

22. Grotius 1995, 3.20.49–50; 3.15.

23. Walzer 1977, 121–22.

24. Ramsey 1961, 151; Yoder 1986.

25. Walzer 1977, 251–68; Walzer 2004, 33–50.

26. Grotius 1901, 2.25.7.

27. See Baritz 1985, 19–54.

Chapter 8 How Fight? Discrimination and Proportionality

1. The tradition holds that an unjustly begun war should still be fought justly, lest the crime of starting an unjust war be made even worse. While it may be possible to imagine such a scenario under Just War (PPC), under Just War (CD) such a scenario is difficult to imagine simply because those who lack the disciplines and dispositions to start a just war are not likely to be capable of waging a war justly. Furthermore, and certainly not difficult to imagine, the tradition recognizes that a war begun justly can nevertheless become unjust in the course of its prosecution.

2. Note that these efforts were not limited to restraining war. Indeed, many of them began as efforts to rein in unemployed warriors who roamed the countryside.

3. Johnson 1975, 64–75; Strickland 1996; Kaeuper 1999.

4. Grotius 1995, 3.11.16.

5. See Christopher 1999, 158–59.

6. Pfaff 2000 and 2002; Cook 2004, 92.

7. Grotius 1995, 2.22.5; Vitoria 2000, 2.6; Suárez n.d., 7.6; 7.17.

8. Suárez n.d., 7.6. Italics added.

9. Ibid., 7.6; 7.17. See also Thomas Aquinas 1975, 1.83.5; Sepúlveda 1984, 66; Vitoria 1991, 304; Vitoria 2000, 1.15; Grotius 1995, 3.1.2.

10. To be fair, some advocates of Just War (PPC) speak of a duty to care. But its moral force is circumscribed by a particular way of using the principle of double effect, which will be discussed shortly.

11. This is a simplification of what is typically summarized in four points. For a fine introduction to the principle of double effect, see Cavanaugh 2006. For an excellent summary of the debate over how to interpret the principle, see Berkman 1997.

12. O'Donovan 2003, 44.

13. Ramsey 1968, 474–75.

14. Thomas Aquinas 1981, II–II 64.7.

15. See Cavanaugh 2006, 73–117.

16. Walters (1971, 160–62) notes at least six times Aquinas uses this parable in arguing against harming the innocent in the course of pursuing the guilty.

17. Thomas Aquinas 1981, II–II 64.2.

18. Ibid., I–II 20.5. See also Anscombe 2001, 64–65.

19. Thomas Aquinas 2003, 1.3.15.

20. Thomas Aquinas 1981, II–II 64.7.

21. O'Brien 1981, 100.

22. Ramsey 1968, 435. Italics omitted from original.

23. Ibid., 436; cf. 508.

24. Fick 2005, 182.

25. Peters 2002. It is worth noting the author is a retired military officer. Ramsey (1968, 436) suggests something similar.

26. James Turner Johnson (1984, 59–60, 135) makes this point.

27. Ramsey 1968, 437.

28. Campbell 1990, 116.

29. O'Donovan 2003, 38.

30. See Gutman and Rieff (1999, 226–28) for a concise list of what is permitted under international law.

31. Cole 2002a, 101; Ramsey 1968, 153; Phillips 1990, 182; O'Brien 1981, 339; Gutman and Rieff 1999, 294; Regan 1996, 95–98.

32. O'Donovan 2003, 43–47. See also Walzer 1977, 127–37.

33. Thomas Aquinas 1981, II–II 64.7. See Renick 1994, 447ff.; Anscombe 2001, 65.

34. See, for example, Kleinig 1996, 96–122, esp. 101; Pfaff 2000 and 2002.

35. For a sense of some of the challenges pertaining to the development and deployment of nonlethal force, see Stanton 1996 and Lorenz 1996.

36. See Ellis 1975.

Conclusion: Spirituality and Just War

1. Just war was conceived in precisely this manner during the Middle Ages. See Frantzen 2004, 13–28.

2. For a compelling reflection on this impulse, see Williams 2002, 29–48.

3. Insofar as this book is about Christianity and just war, I refrain from addressing the question of how non-Christians might relate to this discipline. Suffice it to say that the Christian tradition has long recognized the moral capacity of non-Christians, sometimes addressed in terms of natural law, sometimes in terms of a kind of "civic righteousness." At the very least, such notions hint at interesting theological possibilities for discerning convergences, overlaps, and mutual edification with non-Christians. For one example of a non-Christian virtue/character-based approach to just war, see Davis 1992.

4. See the work of John Howard Yoder and Stanley Hauerwas.

Reference List

Allman, Mark J., and Tobias L. Winright. 2007. *Jus Post Bellum* Extending the Just War Theory. In *Faith in Public Life*, ed. William J. Collinge, 241–64. Maryknoll, NY: Orbis.

Ambrose. 1994. On the Duties of the Clergy. In *Nicene and Post-Nicene Fathers*, 2nd ser., vol. 10, ed. Philip Schaff and Henry Wace, 1–89. Peabody, MA: Hendrickson.

Anscombe, G. E. M. 1981. The Justice of the Present War Examined. In *The Collected Philosophical Papers of G. E. M. Anscombe*, vol. 3, 72–81. Minneapolis: University of Minnesota Press.

———. 2001. Medalist's Address: Action, Intention, and "Double Effect." In *The Doctrine of Double Effect*, ed. P. A. Woodward, 50–66. Notre Dame, IN: University of Notre Dame Press.

Aristotle. 1981. *Politics*. Translated by Trevor J. Saunders. New York: Penguin.

Augustine. 1950. *The City of God*. New York: Random House.

———. 1993. Sermon 211. In Sermons III/6 (184–229Z) on the Liturgical Seasons. Edited by John E. Rotelle, OSA, translated by Edmund Hill, OP. New Rochelle, NY: New City Press.

———. 1994a. Letter 47. In *Nicene and Post-Nicene Fathers*, 1st ser., vol. 1, ed. Philip Schaff, 292–94. Peabody, MA: Hendrickson.

———. 1994b. Reply to Faustus the Manichaean. In *Nicene and Post-Nicene Fathers*, 1st ser., vol. 4., ed. Philip Schaff, 155–345. Peabody, MA: Hendrickson.

———. 1998. *City of God*. Edited by R. W. Dyson. Cambridge, UK: Cambridge University Press.

———. 2001. *Augustine: Political Writings*. Edited by E. M. Atkins and R. J. Dodaro. New York: Cambridge University Press.

Bader-Saye, Scott. 2007. *Following Jesus in a Culture of Fear*. Grand Rapids: Brazos.

Baritz, Loren. 1985. *Backfire: A History of How American Culture Led Us into Vietnam and Made Us Fight the Way We Did*. Baltimore: Johns Hopkins University Press.

Barnes, Jonathan. 1982. The Just War. In *The Cambridge History of Later Medieval Philosophy*, ed. Norman Kretzmann, Anthony Kenny, and Jan Pinborg, 771–84. Cambridge, UK: Cambridge University Press.

Barth, Karl. 1961. *Church Dogmatics III.4: The Doctrine of Creation*. Edited by G. W. Bromiley and T. F. Torrance. Edinburgh: T&T Clark.

Bell, Daniel M., Jr. 2009. God Does Not Demand Blood: Beyond Redemptive Violence. In *God Does Not . . .* , ed. Brent Laytham, 39–61. Grand Rapids: Brazos.

Bentley, James. 1984. *Martin Niemöller*. New York: Free Press.

Bergen, Doris L., ed. 2004. *The Sword of the Lord: Military Chaplains from the First to the Twenty-First Century*. Notre Dame, IN: University of Notre Dame Press.

Berkman, John. 1997. How Important Is the Doctrine of Double Effect for Moral Theology? Contextualizing the Controversy. *Christian Bioethics* 3 (2): 89–114.

Burtchaell, James T. 1989. *The Giving and Taking of Life*. Notre Dame, IN: University of Notre Dame Press.

Butler, Jennifer. 2000. Militarized Prostitution: The Untold Story (U.S.A.). In *War's Dirty Secret*, ed. Anne L. Barstow, 204–32. Cleveland: Pilgrim.

Cadoux, C. John. 1982. *The Early Christian Attitude to War*. New York: Seabury, 1982.

Calvin, John. 1960. *Institutes of the Christian Religion*, 2 vols. Edited by John T. McNeill. Philadelphia: Westminster.

Campbell, Courtney S. 1990. Moral Responsibility and Irregular War. In *Cross, Crescent, and Sword*, ed. James Turner Johnson and John Kelsay, 103–28. New York: Greenwood.

Caputo, Philip. 1996. *A Rumor of War*. New York: Henry Holt.

Cavanaugh, T. A. 2006. *Double-Effect Reasoning: Doing Good and Avoiding Evil*. New York: Oxford University Press.

Cavanaugh, William T. 1995. A Fire Strong Enough to Consume the House: The Wars of Religion and the Rise of the State. *Modern Theology* 11 (October): 397–420.

———. 2005. To Whom Should We Go? Legitimate Authority and Just Wars. In *Neo-Conned*, ed. D. L. O'Huallachain and J. Forrest Sharpe, 269–90. Vienna, VA: Light in the Darkness.

Childress, James F. 1982. *Moral Responsibility in Conflicts*. Baton Rouge: Louisiana State University Press.

Christiansen, Drew, and Gerald F. Powers. 1995. Economic Sanctions and the Just-War Doctrine. In *Economic Sanctions: Panacea or Peacebuilding in a Post-Cold War World?* ed. David C. Cortright and George A. Lopez, 97–117. Boulder, CO: Westview.

Christopher, Paul. 1999. *The Ethics of War and Peace*. 2nd ed. Upper Saddle River, NJ: Prentice Hall.

Clausewitz, Carl von. 1976. *On War*. Edited by Michael Howard and Peter Paret. Princeton, NJ: Princeton University Press.

Cole, Darrell. 1999. Thomas Aquinas on Virtuous Warfare. *Journal of Religious Ethics* 27 (Spring): 57–80.

———. 2002a. *When God Says War Is Right*. Colorado Springs: Waterbrook.

———. 2002b. Just War, Penance, and the Church. *Pro Ecclesia* 11 (Summer): 313–28.

Contamine, Philippe. 1984. *War in the Middle Ages*. Oxford, UK: Basil Blackwell.

Cook, Martin. 2001. Soldiering. *Christian Century* 118 (22): 22–25.

———. 2004. *The Moral Warrior*. Albany, NY: SUNY.

Davis, Grady Scott. 1992. *Warcraft and the Fragility of Virtue*. Moscow: University of Idaho Press.

———. 1997. Conscience and Conquest: Francisco de Vitoria on Justice in the New World. *Modern Theology* 13 (October): 475–500.

———. 2002. Humanitarian Intervention and Just War Criteria. *The Journal of Peace and Justice Studies* 12 (1): 63–94.

Dodaro, Robert. 1991. Pirates or Superpowers: Reading Augustine in a Hall of Mirrors. *New Blackfriars* 72 (January): 9–18.

Driver, John. 1988. *How Christians Made Peace with War*. Scottdale, PA: Herald.

Dunn, Richard S. 1979. *The Age of Religious Wars, 1559–1715*. 2nd ed. New York: Norton.

Ellis, John. 1975. *A Social History of the Machine Gun*. Baltimore: Johns Hopkins University Press.

Eppstein, John. 1935. *The Catholic Tradition of the Law of Nations*. London: Burns, Oates, and Washbourne.

Fick, Nathaniel. 2005. *One Bullet Away: The Making of a Marine Officer*. New York: Houghton Mifflin.

Figgis, J. N. 1960. *Political Thought From Gerson to Grotius: 1414–1625*. New York: Harper & Brothers.

Fitzgerald, Allan D., ed. 1999. *Augustine through the Ages: An Encyclopedia*. Grand Rapids: Eerdmans.

Frantzen, Allen J. 2004. *Bloody Good: Chivalry, Sacrifice, and the Great War*. Chicago: University of Chicago Press.

French, Shannon E. 2003. *The Code of the Warrior*. Lanham, MD: Rowman & Littlefield.

Fussell, Paul. 1975. *The Great War and Modern Memory*. New York: Oxford University Press.

Giddens, Anthony. 1987. *The Nation-State and Violence*. Berkeley: University of California Press.

Glover, Michael. 1982. *The Velvet Glove: The Decline and Fall of Moderation in War*. London: Hodder and Stoughton.

Gordon, Joy. 1999a. *Using a Pick-Ax for Brain Surgery: The Ethics of Economic Sanctions and Their Predictable Consequences*. Occasional Paper No. 15. Notre Dame, IN: Joan B. Kroc Institute.

———. 1999b. Economic Sanctions, Just War Doctrine, and the "Fearful Spectacle of the Civilian Dead." *Cross Currents* 49 (Fall): 387–400.

———. 1999c. A Peaceful, Silent, Deadly Remedy: The Ethics of Economic Sanctions. *Ethics and International Affairs* 13: 123–42.

———. 2002. Cool War: Economic Sanctions As a Weapon of Mass Destruction. *Harper's* 305 (November): 43–49.

Gray, J. Glenn. 1959. *The Warriors: Reflections on Men in Battle*. New York: Harper & Row.

Griffiths, Paul, and George Weigel. 2002. Just War: An Exchange. *First Things* 122 (April): 31–36.

———. 2005. Who Wants War? An Exchange. *First Things* 152 (April): 10–12.

Grossman, Dave. 1996. *On Killing*. Boston: Little, Brown.

Grotius, Hugo. 1901. *The Rights of War and Peace*. Translated by A. C. Campbell. London: Dunne.

———. 1995. *De Jure Belli ac Pacis Libri Tres*, vol. 2. Translated by Francis W. Kelsey. Buffalo: Hein.

Gutman, Roy, and David Rieff, eds. 1999. *Crimes of War*. New York: Norton.

Harnack, Adolf. 1981. *Militia Christi: The Christian Religion and the Military in the First Three Centuries*. Philadelphia: Fortress.

Harsh, Joseph L. 1974. Battlesword and Rapier: Clausewitz, Jomni, and the American Civil War. *Military Affairs: Journal of the American Military Institute* 38 (December): 133–38.

Hedges, Chris. 2002. *War Is a Force that Gives Us Meaning*. New York: Public Affairs.

Hunter, David. 1992. A Decade of Research on Early Christians and Military Service. *Religious Studies Review* 18 (April): 87–94.

———. 1994. The Christian Church and the Roman Army in the First Three Centuries. In *The Church's Peace Witness*, ed. Marlin E. Miller and Barbara Nelson Gingerich, 161–81. Grand Rapids: Eerdmans.

Hutter, Reinhard. 1999. Be Honest in Just War Thinking! Lutherans, the Just War Tradition, and Selective Conscientious Objection. In *The Wisdom of the Cross*, ed. Stanley Hauerwas, Chris Huebner, Harry Huebner, and Mark Nation, 69–83. Grand Rapids: Eerdmans.

Iasiello, Louis. 2004. *Jus Post Bellum*: The Moral Responsibilities of Victors in War. *Navy War College Review* 57 (Summer/Autumn): 33–52.

Janda, Lance. 1995. Shutting the Gates of Mercy: The American Origins of Total War, 1860–1880. *The Journal of Military History* 59 (January): 7–26.

Johnson, James Turner. 1973. Toward Reconstructing the *Jus Ad Bellum*. *The Monist* 57 (October): 461–88.

———. 1975. *Ideology, Reason and the Limitation of War: Religious and Secular Concepts, 1200–1740*. Princeton, NJ: Princeton University Press.

———. 1981. *Just War Tradition and the Restraint of War*. Princeton, NJ: Princeton University Press.

———. 1984. *Can Modern War Be Just?* New Haven: Yale University Press.

———. 1996. The Broken Tradition. *The Public Interest* 45 (Fall): 27–36.

———. 1997. *The Quest for Peace*. Princeton, NJ: Princeton University Press.

———. 2003. Aquinas and Luther on War and Peace. *Journal of Religious Ethics* 31 (Spring): 3–20.

———. 2005. Just War, As It Was and Is. *First Things* 149 (January): 14–24.

Jones, L. Gregory. 1995. *Embodying Forgiveness*. Grand Rapids: Eerdmans.

Kaeuper, Richard W. 1999. *Chivalry and Violence in Medieval Europe*. New York: Oxford University Press.

Kauffman, Ivan., ed. 2004. *Just Policing*. Kitchener, Ont.: Pandora.

Keegan, John. 1989. *The Illustrated Face of Battle*. New York: Viking.

———. 1993. *A History of Warfare*. New York: Knopf.

King, Martin Luther, Jr. 1964. *Why We Can't Wait*. New York: Signet.

Kleinig, John. 1996. *The Ethics of Policing*. Cambridge, UK: Cambridge University Press.

Kreider, Alan. 2003. Military Service in the Church Orders. *Journal of Religious Ethics* 31: 415–42.

Lifton, Robert Jay. 2005. *Home from the War: Learning from Vietnam Veterans*. New York: Other.

Lorenz, F. M. 1996. Non-Lethal Force: The Slippery Slope to War? *Parameters* 26 (Autumn): 52–62.

Luther, Martin. 1957. The Freedom of a Christian. In *Luther's Works*, vol. 31, ed. Harold J. Grimm, 327–78. Philadelphia: Muhlenberg.

———. 1962. Temporal Authority: To What Extent It Should Be Obeyed. In *Luther's Works*, vol. 45, ed. Walther I. Brandt, 75–130. Philadelphia: Fortress.

———. 1967. On War Against the Turk. In *Luther's Works*, vol. 46, ed. Robert C. Schultz, 155–206. Philadelphia: Fortress.

Maguire, Daniel C. 2007. *The Horrors We Bless: Rethinking the Just-War Legacy*. Minneapolis: Fortress.

Mahedy, William P. 2004. *Out of the Night: The Spiritual Journey of Vietnam Vets*. Knoxville: Radix.

Mangan, Joseph T. 1949. An Historical Analysis of the Principle of Double Effect. *Theological Studies* 10: 41–61.

Marin, Peter. 1980. Coming to Terms with Vietnam. *Harpers* 261 (December): 41–56.

———. 1981. Living in Moral Pain. *Psychology Today* 15 (November): 68–80.

Marvin, Carolyn, and David W. Ingle. 1999. *Blood Sacrifice and the Nation*. Cambridge, UK: Cambridge University Press.

McClendon, James William, Jr. 1990. *Biography As Theology*. Philadelphia: Trinity.

Morris, Madeline. 2000. In War and Peace: Rape, War and Military Culture. In *War's Dirty Secret*, ed. Anne L. Barstow, 167–203. Cleveland: Pilgrim.

Murray, John Courtney. 1988. *We Hold These Truths*. Kansas City, MO: Sheed & Ward.

Nadelson, Theodore. 2005. *Trained to Kill: Soldiers at War*. Baltimore: Johns Hopkins University Press.

National Conference of Catholic Bishops. 1983. *The Challenge of Peace*. Washington, DC: USCC.

———. 1993. *The Harvest of Justice Is Sown in Peace*. Washington, DC: USCC.

Neff, John U. 1952. *War and Human Progress*. Cambridge, MA: Harvard University Press.

O'Brien, William V. 1981. *The Conduct of Just and Limited War*. New York: Praeger.

———. 1991. The International Law of War as Related to the Western Just War Tradition. In *Just War and Jihad*, ed. John Kelsay and James Turner Johnson, 163–94. New York: Greenwood.

O'Donovan, Oliver. 2003. *Just War Revisited*. Cambridge, UK: Cambridge University Press.

Osiel, Mark J. 1999. *Obeying Orders: Atrocity, Military Discipline, and the Law of War*. New Brunswick, NJ: New Transaction.

Paul VI. 1976. *Populorum progressio*. In *The Gospel of Peace and Justice*, ed. Joseph Gremillion, 387–416. Maryknoll, NY: Orbis.

Pentland, Ray. 2002. Just War—Just Sanctions. *Political Theology* 3: 178–95.

Peters, Ralph. 2002. Civilian Casualties: No Apology Needed. *The Wall Street Journal*, July 25, A10.

Pfaff, Tony. 2000. *Peacekeeping and the Just War Tradition*. Strategic Studies Institute. http://www.strategicstudiesinstitute.army.mil/pdffiles/PUB302.pdf (accessed June 24, 2008).

———. 2002. Noncombatant Immunity and the War on Terrorism. Paper presented at the Inter-University Seminar on Armed Forces and Society, Kingston, Ont., October 25–27. www.rmc.ca/academic/conference/iuscanada/papers/EWTERR.doc (accessed June 24, 2008).

Phillips, Robert L. 1990. Combatancy, Noncombatancy, and Noncombatant Immunity in Just War Tradition. In *Cross, Crescent, and Sword*, ed. James Turner Johnson and John Kelsay, 179–96. New York: Greenwood.

Pius XII. 1954. Discourse to the Delegates Attending the Sixteenth Session of the International Office of Military Medical Documentation. In *Catholic Documents #15* (September): 1–9.

Potter, Ralph. 1968. Conscientious Objection to Particular Wars. In *Religion and the Public Order #4*, ed. Donald A. Giannella, 44–99. Ithaca, NY: Cornell University Press.

———. 1969a. *War and Moral Discourse*. Richmond: John Knox.

———. 1969b. The Moral Logic of War. *McCormick Quarterly* 23 (November): 203–33.

Ramsey, Paul. 1961. *War and the Christian Conscience*. Durham, NC: Duke University Press.

———. 1968. *The Just War*. New York: Scribner's Sons.

———. 1988. *Speak Up for Just War or Pacifism*. University Park: Pennsylvania State University Press.

Regan, Richard J. 1996. *Just War: Principles and Cases*. Washington, DC: Catholic University of America Press.

Renick, Timothy. 1994. Charity Lost: The Secularization of the Principle of Double Effect in the Just-War Tradition. *The Thomist* 58 (July): 441–62.

Ricks, Thomas E. 1997a. *Making the Corps*. New York: Touchstone.

———. 1997b. The Widening Gap Between the Military and Society. *The Atlantic Monthly* (July): 66–78.

Roberts, Adam, and Richard Guelff, eds. 2002. *Documents on the Laws of War*. 3rd ed. Oxford, UK: Oxford University Press.

Russell, Frederick H. 1975. *The Just War in the Middle Ages*. New York: Cambridge University Press.

Schlabach, Gerald, ed. 2007. *Just Policing, Not War*. Collegeville, MN: Liturgical Press.

Schmidt, Dietmar. 1959. *Pastor Niemöller*. Garden City, NY: Doubleday.

Schuck, Michael J. 1994. When the Shooting Stops: Missing Elements in Just War Theory. *The Christian Century* 111 (30): 982–84.

Sepúlveda, Juan Ginés de. 1984. *Demócrates Segunda o de las justas causas de la guerra contra los indios*. Translated by Angel Losada. Madrid: CSIC.

Shay, Jonathan. 1994. *Achilles in Vietnam: Combat Trauma and the Undoing of Character*. New York: Touchstone.

———. 2002. *Odysseus in America: Combat Trauma and the Trials of Homecoming*. New York: Scribner.

Shinn, Roger L. 1978. Liberation, Reconciliation, and "Just Revolution." *The Ecumenical Review* 30: 319–32.

Smith, Allyne. 2004. Can War Ever Be Just? Light from the Christian East. Unpublished essay.

Stanton, Martin. 1996. What Price Sticky Foam? *Parameters* 26 (Autumn): 63–68.

Stassen, Glen. 1992. *Just Peacemaking: Ten Practices for Abolishing War*. Louisville: Westminster John Knox.

———, ed. 1998. *Just Peacemaking: Transforming Initiatives for Justice and Peace*. 2nd ed. Cleveland: Pilgrim.

Strickland, Matthew. 1996. *War and Chivalry*. Cambridge, UK: Cambridge University Press.

Suárez, Francisco. n.d. *A Work on the Three Theological Virtues Faith, Hope and Charity: On Charity, Disputation XIII*. Vol. 2. Translated by G. L. Williams, A. Brown, and J. Waldron. Oxford, UK: Oxford University Press.

Swift, Louis J. 1973. Augustine on War and Killing. *Harvard Theological Review* 66: 369–83.

———. 1983. *The Early Fathers on War and Military Service*. Wilmington, DE: Glazier.

Szura, John Paul. 1984. Vatican II Foundations of the U.S. Peace Pastoral: Source of Strength, Source of Weakness. In *Biblical and Theological Reflections on 'The Challenge of Peace,'* ed. John T. Pawlikowski and Donald Senior, 123–34. Wilmington, DE: Glazier.

Tertullian. 1994. *On Idolatry*. In *Ante-Nicene Fathers* 3, ed. Alexander Roberts and James Donaldson, 61–78. Peabody, MA: Hendrickson.

Thomas Aquinas. 1975. *Summa Contra Gentiles*. Translated by Anton C. Pegis. Notre Dame, IN: University of Notre Dame Press.

———. 1978. *On Kingship*. Translated by Gerald B. Phelan. Toronto: Pontifical Institute of Mediaeval Studies.

———. 1981. *Summa Theologica*, 5 vols. Translated by Fathers of the English Dominican Province. Westminster, MD: Christian Classics.

———. 1984. *On Charity*. Milwaukee: Marquette University Press.

———. 2003. *On Evil*. Edited by Brian Davies, translated by Richard Regan. New York: Oxford University Press.

Tyerman, Christopher. 2006. *God's War: A New History of the Crusades*. Cambridge, MA: Harvard University Press.

Verkamp, Bernard J. 1988. Moral Treatment of Returning Warriors in the Early Middle Ages. *The Journal of Religious Ethics* 16 (Fall): 223–45.

———. 1993. *The Moral Treatment of Returning Warriors in Early Medieval and Modern Times*. Scranton, PA: University of Scranton Press.

Vitoria, Francisco de. 1991. *Vitoria: Political Writings*. Edited by Anthony Pagden and Jeremy Lawrance. Cambridge, UK: Cambridge University Press.

———. 2000. On War. In James Brown Scott, *The Spanish Origin of International Law*, 115–31. Union, NJ: Lawbook Exchange.

Walters, LeRoy, Jr. 1971. *Five Classic Just-War Theories: A Study in the Thought of Thomas Aquinas, Vitoria, Suarez, Gentili and Grotius.* Ann Arbor, MI: UMI.

———. 1973. The Just War and the Crusade: Antitheses or Analogies? *The Monist* 57 (October): 584–94.

Walzer, Michael. 1977. *Just and Unjust Wars.* 2nd ed. New York: Basic Books.

———. 1992. Justice and Injustice in the Gulf War. In *But Was It Just? Reflections on the Morality of the Persian Gulf War,* ed. David E. DeCosse, 1–17. New York: Doubleday.

———. 2004. *Arguing about War.* New Haven: Yale University Press.

Weber, Max. 1946. *From Max Weber.* Edited by H. Gerth and C. Mills. New York: Oxford University Press.

Weigel, George. 2003. Moral Clarity in a Time of War. *First Things* 129 (January): 20–27.

Weigley, Russell F. 1973. *The American Way of War.* Bloomington: Indiana University Press.

Weiss, Thomas, David Cortright, George A. Lopez, and Larry Minear, eds. 1997. *Political Gain and Civilian Pain: Humanitarian Impacts of Economic Sanctions.* New York: Rowman & Littlefield.

Wells, Donald A. 1992. *The Laws of Land Warfare: A Guide to the U.S. Army Manuals.* Westport, CT: Greenwood.

Williams, Rowan. 2002. *Writing in the Dust.* Grand Rapids: Eerdmans.

Williams, Rowan, and George Weigel. 2004. War and Statecraft: An Exchange. *First Things* 141 (March): 14–21.

Winright, Tobias. 1996. The Complementarity of Just War Theory and Pacifism. In *Religion, War and Peace: Proceedings of a Conference Sponsored by the Wisconsin Institute for Peace and Conflict Studies,* ed. Deborah Buffton, 216–20. Ripon, WI: Ripon College.

Yoder, John H. 1983. *Christian Attitudes to War, Peace, and Revolution.* Elkhart, IN: Co-op Bookstore.

———. 1986. Surrender: A Moral Imperative. *Review of Politics* 48 (Fall): 576–95.

———. 2001. *When War Is Unjust.* 2nd ed. Eugene, OR: Wipf and Stock.

Zahn, Gordon. 1986. *In Solitary Witness.* Springfield, IL: Templegate.

Index